THOTH
JESUS OF EGYPT

By

LOUISE TOTH

Order this book online at www.trafford.com
or email orders@trafford.com

Most Trafford titles are also available at major online book retailers.

Art
Cover &
Illustrations by:
Louise Diane Toth
Melody Spring Owens
Kendall Cameron Petersen
Visual Effects Artist Jason Toth
My Talented Pyramid Professionals

Printed in the United States of America.

ISBN: 978-1-4669-3648-5 (sc)
ISBN: 978-1-4669-3649-2 (hc)
ISBN: 978-1-4669-3647-8 (e)

Library of Congress Control Number: 2012908934

Trafford rev. 01/23/2013

 www.trafford.com

North America & international
toll-free: 1 888 232 4444 (USA & Canada)
phone: 250 383 6864 ♦ fax: 812 355 4082

CONTENTS

THOTH

The Ancient Egyptians considered the God Thoth to be the 'Mind Behind the Cosmic Order.' Before their knowledge of the Biblical Genesis 1:1, Thoth was their God of Wisdom. Could the Egyptian God be a Jesus like messenger between man and the true Great Universal God? When Jesus was in Egypt, did He instruct the son of Cleopatra?

This novel is my story. I tell how my famous name, knowledge and personality invited Egypt to lay out gifts beyond my wildest imagination; opening doors for me in the mystical land, blessing me with a three hour ceremony in the Great Giza Pyramid, under the wisdom of Lakota elder, Chief Wallace Black Elk.

Is there a secret prophecy code inside Pharaoh Khufu's Pyramid? Many of us at the educational conference in Cairo have questions to ask. Our Professor Doctor Zahi Hawass of the Supreme Council of Antiquities knows many of the answers.

Join our team, and pack your dreams for an captivating magic carpet ride winding through the pharaoh's playground. Intrigue, history and mystery in the shadows of the pyramids waits for you. Be entertained by the beautiful illustrations as they draw you in and transport you to the romantic lush Nile Valley.

For those who love to read, life will always be an inspiring adventure.

CREATIVE GENIUS

I thank my inspiring, creative genius friends for their uplifting love and support.

Ben Vereen, singer
Boaz Rauchwerger, speaker
Gail and Peter Ochs
Gerrie and Dennis Weaver
Ginger Pottin, designer
James Bradley Toth
Jason Toth, Sokul designs
Judy Smith, Health Wavez
Lillian Blouin, artist
Mary Blouin, writer
Meagan Marriott, publicist
Melody Spring Owens, artist
Michael Moses Quartez, World Gemological
Nick Matyas, Web Royalty
Pat Parsons, psychologist
Stephen Christensen, Concordia University
Steve Sakane, concept creator, Batmobile
Zhayra Escobar, designer, Sacia O Hats

CAST LIST

Louise, Seeker of Wisdom

Chief Black Elk, Lakota Chief and Lecturer
Doctor Amir, Professor
Doctor Amon, Professor
Doctor Elizabeth, professor
Doctor Christopher, Professor
Doctor Zahi Hawass, Chief Inspector of the Giza Pyramid Plateau

Young Jesus, Son of Creator

Alexandria, Amir's mother
Ali, Concert singer
David, Amir's driver
Moon Bear, Lakota companion
Sharon, Seeker of Mysteries
Todd, Seeker of Knowledge

Amun Ra, Great Sun God
Pharaoh Khufu, Builder of the Giza Pyramid
Thoth, God of Wisdom

Friends at the conference

Anastasia
Daniel
Ginger
James
Jason
Jheri
Meagan
Michael
Sacia
Yasuko

Many names have been changed for privacy.

FOREWORD

The ingredients of adventure are mystery, history, romance and intrigue. Please join Louise and her magic carpet ride adventures; the meeting of the famous Doctor Zahi Hawass, the Chief Inspector of the Giza Pyramid Plateau, the renown Indian Shamans, Chief Black Elk and Moon Bear. You will want to walk like an Egyptian in Professor Amon's party in front of the Sphinx, spend your afternoon inside the Giza Pyramid, travel through the Turkish Bazaar, and meditate inside the sacred tomb of King Tutankhamun. Was Jesus at the pyramids? Can you be in Cairo and not go to the Giza Pyramid? What does the wisdom of the God Thoth reveal?

Egypt is the land of creative art, carved and painted on the walls of palaces and tombs, the sacred hieroglyphics symbols were used on papyrus papers, and in holy temples. Picture the talented gold smiths who created, forged and inlaid lapis onto the golden mask of the Pharaoh Tutankhamun.

My name is Ben Vereen. As a singer, actor, dancer and some say legend, I have graced the screens more times than I care recount. Yet, I always say, "I am at my most creative when I am live on stage." When I can feel your energy, the energy of my audience. It is your enthusiasm that warms my heart. It is your appreciation for my creative talents that make me want to take my art to a higher level.

The stage is my playground full of sumptuous dreams and imagination. We teach the youth how to use art as a life form. In fact, using art, dance, theater, painting, designing, singing, etc, opens the channels of the brain for clearer expression. I want to be part of empowering tomorrow's leaders, giving young people the tools to be creative, empowered beings.

I feel blessed when as I look forward to doing more workshops for performers. I want give back as much as I can! It is a blessing if you have the opportunity in the expression of who you are through the creative process that the truth of who you are is seen by all.

I am involved in a program called, "Pathway to Excellence Through the Arts." It is all about empowering the youth to look to a greater field of excellence. I want them to move past their circumstances, to look beyond their social and economic limitations. I want them to know that dreams can become a reality. The youth need to "keep their eye on the prize," to define what their prize may be. Youth have power. They must choose actions that empower them, not actions that hold them back or block their greatness.

I have been inducted into two Hall of Fames. One for Theater and one for Dance. Yet, I am best known for my iconic role as Chicken George in the television miniseries, "Roots." My 'Roots' are African and Egypt is located in North Eastern Africa.

Many people admire the silver ankh I wear around my neck. In Egypt it is known as a handled cross, the symbol of life. It was carried by most of their gods and kings. Young Pharaoh Tutankhamun carried the ankh in the second syllable of his name.

Tut Ankh Amun

This is how I came to know Louise Toth and her inspirational work in Egypt. Creativity not only involves open channels of the brain; but also an open heart to the world of possibilities. Her interest in Egyptian antiquities gives us a view of a past civilization that revered the creative spirit and held open the door to the heart of peace, love and joy. As you read the words written here, remind yourself of what it was like to be a child; unencumbered by stress and worry. Take time to reflect, rest and just create. The Ancient Egyptians were part of the cultural fabric dedicated to artistic excellence! Enjoy the journey...

Thoth

Enoch

Jesus

Welcome to Cairo

Choose for yourself this day whom you will serve. As for me and my house, we will serve the Lord. Joshua 24:45

When we are creating we are closest to God. He is our Creator and we are made in His image. Thus, prayer and creating are the highest form of the soul's expression. I learned early in my life, the important things are always about serving others, it is not about me, it is about the pleasure of watching the children's minds open to the possibilities God has available.

One day, I was invited to a wisdom conference in Cairo. My name is Louise Toth. The Ancient Egyptians believed the God Thoth was the "Mind Behind Cosmic Order." They believed his version of the Ancient Bible of Egypt', written over 5,000 years ago, was the truth.

'Bereshit bara Elohim et hashamayim ve'et ha'arets.' These are the words from the first phase of the ancient Hebrew Torah of Moses. When translated into Greek, 2,255 years ago, Bereshit became Genesis. In English, it means 'In the beginning.' Genesis 1:1 'In the beginning God created the heavens and the earth.'

Is it possible for us to open our imaginations? Could we explore the thought process from the earliest Egyptian culture who had not yet heard of Genesis? This was a culture who believed the universe was so spectacular many gods were required. Put yourself in their shoes. Please enjoy my journey.....

Picture this!

The spot light is on You. Come, join us in your daytime dreams. Make yourself a cup of Turkish sweet tea, sit on your magic carpet and take a ride with me in the mystical land of Egypt.

Sharon and I are in the foreground with our luggage, the back drop, Cairo, Egypt, the capital and largest city on the entire continent of Africa. We booked suites in the historic Mena House Oberoi, the hotel of kings, prime ministers, and world leaders. This exclusive grand hotel is set on forty lush perfumed acres of jasmine scented gardens. Formerly, the hotel was a royal lodge of King Khedive Ismail the Magnificent built in 1869. It was named after the first of the 76 kings listed on the famous Tablet of Abydos, fitting history and intrigue upon the grounds of the old hunting lodge. Only a king could build between the Great Pyramid and the Sphinx, the location is the best in all the country, perfectly private for a Royal King and Queen!

Imagine a unique neighborhood of cultural landmarks, the Great Leo Sphinx, the Great Giza Pyramid of Pharoah Khufu, the pyramid of his son Khafre and of his son Menkaure, plus the oasis of this luxury hotel. Really, three pyramids and a sphinx, no wonder the world leaders want to stay here in a home of a former King. Location, location, location.

We are quite fashionably dressed as we enter the hotel, I am wearing a 'Sacia O' couture hat with a few elegantly placed feathers, it is called a millinery fascinator with rare and beautiful Egyptian Peacock feathers. As we walk into the lobby, we are aware of the regality of the exclusive ambiance, and the nobility of the guests. Cairo has the oldest and largest film and music industries in the Arab World, the Cairo International Film Festival has just completed its event. We smile as we walk through the lobby past Omar Sharif.

The hotel is everything we expect, glamour and excitement with an intriguing international flavor.

The bellman escort us to our suites, as I open my door I gasp, "I have the pyramid off my patio. When does this ever happen? Not just any pyramid, Thee Great Giza Pyramid! Talk about a room with a view."

To have the mighty pyramid view from my bed, to experience the awesome inspiring 'wonder of the ancient world' appearing before my eyes. Imagine the workers coming from all parts of Africa at the Pharaoh's call to build a spiritual connection between man and heaven under a blazing orange sky.

Think about the powerful people that stayed here; Dr. Henry Kissinger, President Roosevelt, Nixon, and Carter, King Mohammed, King Gustav, King Farouk, and King Juan Carlos, they all rested their heads upon the pillows of this grand hotel.

With adventure in the my blood I fantasize about the romances of Winston Churchill, Hollywood's Cecil B. DeMille, Charlie Chaplin, and Frank Sinatra.

Can you imagine the stories written in the exotic hotel? The cast of Agatha Christie's "Death on the Nile" stayed at this very lodge and spoke of murder, and clandestine love affairs stimulated by the multi national cultures in this mystical land.

The feeling of aristocratic energy. The efficiency of great hotels is always the same, respect the guests and their privacy. It all seems so fitting, I feel right at home, staying with prime ministers and kings, I am completely comfortable with that high level of energy, it is nurturing. 'People are being so kind to me. Their eyes looking directly at mine, I know people only do this when they want something. What is it that they want?'

I have a few minutes to lie down on the rich garnet colored bedspread, admiring the carved furniture, the interesting fruit baskets, the unique chocolates, and succulent flowers in the shimmering crystal vase. I know the trip will be complicated, a private luxurious room is a true delight at the end of the day. I have a furniture business, the value of comfortable hard and soft goods is important, which translates to a yummy bed and fluffy quilts. I begin to imagine a hammock on my private patio, lying under the stars, gazing at the glory of the magnificent structure, and picturing myself basking under the moonlight of the majestic pyramid. Walking onto the patio I have a perfect view of my romantic dream, the Great Giza Pyramid, across the grass through the palm trees of the hotel, to the desert sands, the pyramid stands. Living here makes me feel like Queen Toth. A queen could not have it better, I can have someone massage me, bring my dinner and desserts, any pleasure I desire.

I wrap the sari around me over a black body suit out of respect for the diverse religions. The turquoise silk is beautiful, romantic blonds can never go wrong with turquoise in any country, it is one of the refreshing and alluring colors, now I will be the exotic one. Walking to Sharon's room I catch myself in the mirror and smile. She is ready, we are opposite looks, her eyes and hair are as dark as mine are light. We walk through the lobby toward the dining room when Sharon notices a very handsome man on the other side of the room watching me.

"Look at the man by the concierge." She whispers. "Smile."

He slowly walks to our area to welcome us.

"Hello, my name is Amir. What a color on you to match your eyes, it is my favorite color in all the world. I was watching as you entered the lobby, you in turquoise silk takes my breath away, yet I want to be polite and hold my distance. May I please ask your name?"

"My name is Louise."

"Hello, my first name is Sharon." She put herself in between us for protection. "We are thinking of having dinner, which restaurant would you suggest?"

"I will tell you if you allow me the pleasure of treating both of you lovely ladies to a cocktail?"

"You are on," Sharon chuckles.

"May I?" He smiles graciously.

"Yes," I beam looking up at those dark brown eyes."

"Are you here for the educational conference?"

"Yes, we arrived earlier today. It is so wonderful, this hotel, the Sphinx, the pyramids. I have a pyramid off my patio," I say with delight.

"You picked a grand hotel, the best of the best. I am helping at the conference, I believe you girls have a light day tomorrow, don't you?"

"Yes. It is an easy day tomorrow, we have an orientation in the morning, and a class after lunch. Doctor Christopher will be teaching about Christian questions in a Muslim Country. I have a question, do you believe Jesus was at the pyramids when he was a young man?"

"Of course, if you ask the old timers and Bedouins, the Arabian ethnic groups, you will hear amazing stories. If people take down the 'Do Not Enter' sign and open up their minds to the possibilities everyone will learn from the masters. The old timers talk of the time Cleopratra's son came to speak with Jesus. He probably wanted to know if he would rule in Egypt. He was a co regent with his mother before she died. He would have been in line if the Romans did not invade Egypt and defeat our army. There are many marvelous stories here in the sacred land. Even the word 'story' comes from this time in history. Because of the different languages of visitors, the host of a home would paint his story or small scene on the landing by his stairs, maybe the baby Jesus on the first floor, maybe Khufu was painted on the second floor, maybe Jesus at the Sphinx on the third floor landing. The host may say, 'the visiter is staying on the third story of my home, the story of Jesus and the sphinx. Some people say the third floor, but the old souls seem to say the third story when referring to a level of a home or building. I am trying to concentrate, but your eyes are so blue they distract me, they are piercing, like a message from the blue heavens, like a whisper from God."

"There are as many beautiful things in this world as there are stars in the sky," I reply with a smile.

"Be still my heart, a romantic," he says as he put his hand on his heart. "You were trying to dissuade my compliment, yet, you made yourself even more delightful. I am a Security Concierge hired to protect. I accompany visitors of distinction on a journey, providing protection, guidance, courtesy and honor to all guests of prestige. I will gladly trade you, my protection for your company. You will be well cared for, a good trade if you so choose to accept. Just think about it, I will not mention it again. The ball is in your court. This place suits you, you wear it well. You are staying in the most sought after property in the world."

"Thank you, I will think about it. Could they build the Sphinx today?" I ask with curiosity.

"You cannot build the Sphinx today, the blocks that were removed weight 200 tons."

"How did they lift 200 tons?"

"It is still one of the greatest mysteries of the world. There have been many builders and crane operators that have tried to lift that equal weight."

"What happened?"

"The crane fell on its side when they tried to move the weight, man today can not accomplish the task." He smiles that big heart melting smile of his. "I would love to buy dinner for us, but I came here for a meeting in the conference room. It is my pleasure to meet you, Louise, and you also, Sharon." He kisses my hand and wishes me a lovely dinner.

Amir went to the concierge to place an order of lotus from the Upper Egyptian Valley. "I need to show respect, I want her to feel safe."

"She is in town for the wisdom conference, staying in the most romantic hotel in Egypt, smart and humorous is a dangerous combination, maybe I should be more concerned about you, my good friend! She spoke with me earlier, she is a Christian girl, I believe she is here for two weeks." The concierge replies.

"Then where does she go?"

"They fly to Luxor and stay on one of the boats, then home. Work wise, my friend! And fast! Do you know who would love her? Alexandria. Take Lady Toth to the club to meet your mother for lunch. Show her that you have nothing to hide. Meeting your mother will make her feel more secure. She will know you are proud of her. How many blue eyed people do you have as friends? They are as rare as diamonds. Of the seven continents of the world. Asia, Africa, South America, North America, Australia, Antarctica and Europe the population is predominately dark eyes and dark hair. The blue eyes and blond hair population is very rare. Take that number, then cut that number in half for the females, cut that number in half for the Christian females, cut that number in half for your age bracket, cut that number in half because you like a really smart one. You are left with some major competition for a rare prize. What is the saying? Women want to be her and men want to be with her. Treat her well, my friend."

Amir wistfully thought to himself, 'I am going to have to work for this one, I will simply try harder, that is all, just try harder, I want to know this woman. I am already under her spell, mesmerized by her azure eyes the color of the sea. In the land of Africa, Louise stands out.'

After dinner, Sharon and I decide to visit the grounds. "Come walk with me? Through the garden, across the golf course, the ancient Sphinx is sitting in a perched position guarding the secrets of the Pharaohs. Do you think the paws of the big cat hold the Hall of Records from Atlantis? I heard talk about the Hall of Records, the mythical library buried under the Great Sphinx. Does it house ancient Egyptians scrolls and history? Does the Hall of records exists? Scientists have used ground penetrating radar showing there are cavities underneath the Great Sphinx. The thoughts of a new discovery are filling my mind with wonder. What will the conference reveal? Was the Khufu family the greatest building family known to man? Was the pyramid an energy structure? Was King Tut murdered? Was Ptolemy ll, Egypt's great literary genius? I know the answers will stimulate more questions."

So much magnificence, I cannot stop smiling and taking it all in, into my heart, into my very essence. Wrapping myself in my favorite wool shawl, the desert temperatures dropping in the evening, the cool night chills my body, I feel the stillness of the desert air, the quiet of the night, the sacredness of this earth. I am humbled by the power of the past. It is what brings the thousands of people to Cairo, and to our conference, from all lands, representing all nations, the seekers of the wisdom of the soul. Everyone wants to learn the secrets of the gods.

Sleeping will be a pleasure tonight, slipping my body into the 600 thread count Egyptian cotton sheets, the luxurious down duvets and spreading out my tired bones in the sumptuous bed. Walking back to my room is pure delight, the stars twinkling in the sky, the sky so full of diamonds, the Big Dipper, and Orion. How clearly I could see the universal message of God. We are so small, He is so generous comforting us by sending His heavenly quilt to blanket the earth at night, tucking me in, saying, 'Good night my sweet child, time to sleep, and know that I love you.'

Was Jesus at the Pyramids?

In the mystical, biblical land of Egypt imagination rules!

"Is that a picture of Cleopatra's son, Ptolemy Philadelphus asking council of the young genius Jesus? I heard it was an Egyptian Pharaoh who instigated the transcribing of the books of Moses into Greek? It is true the word Bible is derived from the Greek word biblia, meaning books. Are the other men the high priests?" The early students whisper these curious questions.

The Pharaoh said to Jacob's son Joseph, "I hereby put you in charge of the whole land of Egypt." Genesis 41:41

Sharon and I are standing outside the tent when she spots Amir. "Go over and talk to him," she suggests to me. "He would be like having your own personal tutor. Imagine the discussions you could have with him. When we travel we need to be open to talking to the locals, not just to each other."

"Here he comes now, he will probably ask to sit with you and take the class. He wants to get to know you and will try whatever it takes." Sharon says, wanting his presence to be with us. "He seems to know all the professors, you can learn a lot about Egypt from him."

"May I sit with you? You gave me some thoughts to ponder when you asked me about Jesus being at the pyramid, it stirred my imagination," Amir asks with a sweet tone and a strong posture.

"I love the way you are wearing the baby lotus in your hair, beautiful and mysterious. Very delightful. I will enjoy this class very much and being with such lovely ladies is a true bonus. Shall we enter?" He says.

We take seats in the first row. Amir and the professor nod to each other as a sign of recognition. The professor turns to us, ready to introduce himself and start the class.

"My name is Doctor Christopher, I am your professor this afternoon, from the American University, here in Cairo. Our downtown campus at Tahrir Square was founded in 1919 by the American Mission in Egypt sponsored by the United Presbyterian Church of North America; which was formed in 1858 in Pittsburg, Pennsylvania. We are a university dedicated to the cultural enrichment and modernization of Egypt.

"We have a perfect number for class, that is why we were moved to the smaller tent, I believe there was a bus going to the bazaar at noon and we lost a few students. This is more intimate, it will help me, I get a bit dry by the desert Sphinx. First, I believe you all noticed the verse I wrote on the board, yes, the Lord was very connected to Egypt! Jacob's son Joseph was one of the founders of the great tribes of Israel. In about 1830 BC, he became the foremost advisor to the Pharaoh of Egypt. The ruler said to him, "I had a dream, yet no one can explain what it means. I am told you can interpret dreams." Joseph answered, "I cannot do it myself, but God can give a good meaning to your dreams." Genesis 41:15.

The Bible contains words, terms and names thought by scholars to be Egyptian in origin. The Egyptian name given to Joseph was Zaphnath Paaneah.

Jesus was in Egypt, as were many biblical heroes of the Torah. Do you know the old testament in the Christian Bible is the first five chapters of the Jewish Torah? The new testament about Jesus was written in AD.

The Christians give you old and new together in their Bible/book. The old testament or Torah is the BC, before Christ and the new testament is the AD, Anno Domini, the time of the Lord. For many people, AD represents After Death of Christ.

Do you know it was an Egyptian who instigated the transcribing of the books of Moses? Ptolemy ll Philadelphus, the Greek King of Egypt, asked seventy-two Jewish scholars to translate the Torah from Hebrew into Greek, for the great Library of Alexandria. King Ptolemy ll gathered 72 Elders, placing them in 72 chambers, asking them to write the words of God. The Torah was translated during the three centuries before Christ, starting about in 270 BC.

The 'Teaching' or Torah is the Hebrew name for the first five books of the Jewish Bible. The Greek name Pentateuchos, implies a division of the law into five parts. In the Hebrew Torah 'the beginning' is called Bereshit, when translated into the Greek 'the beginning' becomes Genesis.' Shemot becomes Exodus. 'He called' Vayikra becomes Leviticus. 'In the desert' Bamidar becomes Numbers. 'Words' Devarim becomes Deuteronmy. These are the Old Testaments.

Yes, Ptolemy ll was Cleopatra's linage. Her father was Ptolemy Xll. Her brother/husband was Ptolemy Xlll. The library in Alexandria with literary and religious history was increased by Ptolemy ll. Greek quotations from Genesis and Exodus appear in Greek literature under Ptolemy's rule. It is important to understand history.

"I want to say that many of us Coptic Christians feel that Jesus is the 'SPIRITUAL CAPSTONE OF THE PYRAMID.' Please write that down, because I think is sums it all up in that one line. That is it, we can all go to the bazaar now! We are done!" He laughs out loud at himself, which makes him even more endearing to the group.

Jesus, the spiritual capstone of the Pyramid.
"I put the figure of Christ into the tradition of one God for all people, placing him in his proper place, at the apex of the philosophical structure; the capstone of the great pyramid! In architecture one of the finishing or protective stones that form the top of an exterior masonry wall or building is the capstone.

The crowning glory, the finishing touch, the perfect place to top the greatest work of man, connecting it to Jesus the greatest work of the creator."

Picture Jesus as the capstone, the top of the pyramid with all men as blocks to hold and give structure to the body of the pyramid, as we are the body of Christ. Christ is the head of the body, and the base are the people of the body. Just as the church has a dome and we are the body. God is at the highest place.

"Is this the mystery? Man's problem of freeing his soul from the world. Is the Earth the underworld? Is the soul lost in this underworld until freed by wisdom, faith, and understanding? Do we have the soul of man, whose true home is in the heavens?" The professor poses his thoughts.

"James, I see you are waving your hand."

"Yes, sir. I just want to mention on the American dollar bill, there is a pyramid with the words, 'In God We Trust.' I believe your connection is true, since Jesus is the son of God, it makes sense to me. There is no mystery, God is ahead of everything. It is not a question, I know I am correct."

"I respect your wisdom."

"Thank you," James says as he proudly takes his seat.

Jesus was and still is the most influential figure to ever walk the earth. He had 12 legions of angels, an army of 72, 000, at His disposal if He wished to use them.

"We all know the story of Jesus being born in Bethlehem. Has any one in this room been to Bethlehem?"

"Was that you, Louise?"

When I ask, what is on most peoples bucket list to do before they die, I usually get the same answers from spiritual people. The answer is the Holy Lands and Egypt. People also tell me they want to walk where Jesus walked. Is there anyone in here that has accomplished the first request of the Holy Lands? Anyone walked where Jesus walked? Wait, before I get on a roll about Egypt, I want to hear her for a minute.

"I, too, want to hear this," says Moon Bear who is sitting quietly gathering information about the students at the conference. "I need to pick ten people out of a thousand, they need to be in possession of great gifts. I am looking for experience, awareness, compassion, intuitiveness, none judgements, inner and outer strength from wisdom. Let us hear what comes out of her mouth."

"Please stand, Louise. Have you walked where Jesus walked?"

"Yes, sir, I have walked where Jesus walked, I have sailed on the Sea of Galilee, prayed in the Garden of Gethsemane. I have stood inside the great Dome of the Rock and marveled at the architectural reverence, I have placed written prayers into the sacred spaces between the blocks of the Great Western Wall. I have friends living in Jerusalem and Bethlehem, and a family member who is a Frier stationed in Nazareth, at the Basilica of the Annunciation. The answer is, yes, sir, I have walked where Jesus walked," I nodded to him as a sign of respect and quietly went to sit down, but, before my bottom even touched the chair, I popped up again.

"Jesus lived in Egypt in his youth, the flight into Egypt is a biblical event described in the Gospel of Matthew. Baby Jesus was taken to Egypt by his parents when they learned King Herod intended to kill the infants. So, to really walk where Jesus walked, one would have to visit both countries of Israel and Egypt. Jesus would have taken his steps here on Egyptian soil. To think of little baby Jesus walking and talking right here in your great land of Egypt. Many of his words would have been the Egyptian Coptic language. This is the first time I thought of Him as a child taking his first steps, I bet He was a cute baby with big beautiful eyes!"

Jesus intimately loves you more that you have ever been loved by anybody.

"Thank you, Louise, I certainly believe you, even I did not think how cute Jesus must have been as a baby. I have grand children with their sweet little fingers and toes, I will be thinking of the Christ child with greater understanding, of the awe and wonderment of the Wise Men and how they felt when they laid eyes on his face, the baby King Jesus. For those here that have not met this young lady, her name is Louise Toth. Thoth was the Egyptian God of Wisdom, who called in the universe. How is that for a name to have in the land of Egypt?

The professor turns to Moon Bear. Did that answer your question? He whispers, then turns back to the class smiling.

"You may have noticed the Egyptian Coptic Cross, I am wearing is different from the Roman Cross, Todd is wearing. I am going to call my Coptic Cross, the Baby Jesus Cross, from now on since Louise put the idea of Jesus as a baby into my brain. Our cross is equal on all sides. The Roman Cross has a long base which was needed to support the weight of a man's legs. Crucifixion was an ancient method of a deliberate painful execution. The condemned person was nailed or tied, naked to humiliate, on a large wooden cross and left to hang until dead. It is the cross of suffering we use today as a reminder. I am an Egyptian, I prefer the Coptic Cross." He says smiling.

"Now lets talk about 'The Road to Egypt.' God told Abraham to leave the famine of Canaan. He went to Egypt and became wealthy. He defied social customs and worshipped a single God, rather than a pantheon of deities. Genesis 12. Abraham and Lot, the sons of Jacob, and Joseph, Mary and the child Jesus, all made their way along the trail from the south of the Holy lands along the shore of the Mediterranean into the land of Egypt. According to Genesis 46:8, the sons of Israel, Jacob's offspring and descendants moved to Goshen, Egypt.

"When the Holy family came into Egypt, there were dragons in the caves. What did Jesus do? Jesus told his parents not to be afraid, and do not consider him a little child; for he is and always has been perfect and all the beasts in the forest must be tamed before him. The lions, panthers and other wild beasts of the desert now walked with Jesus as a sign of respect showing their submission, wagging their tails and showing him love. "Be not afraid, they have not come to harm, they come to serve me." Please use this energy of love. The lions were important to the child, like the Sphinx, they were magnificent to behold. Remember on the third day, God made the trees, nuts and fruits. Nature was to feed the family on their journey into Egypt, the trees bowed down, laden with fruits to feed his mother and father. Their roots gave the earth a tug and water rose, cool clear water bubbled from the spring for Mary to drink. It was easy for Jesus to command nature, because nature was created by his father and he who loves the father will love the son.

"I would like if all of you visit the Coptic Orthodox Church of the Holy Virgin in Maadi. You can take a taxi, go in a small group, it is about eleven miles south. The Orthodox have the best history of the Holy Family in Egypt," the professor declares with certainty.

"Every time from now on when I think of baby Jesus in Egypt, I will have the image Louise put into my brain of Him playing as only a child can with His mother on the banks of the Nile River, dipping his toes in the water, giggling like the joyous creation God made him to be. Sitting on Mary's lap putting His cold wet hands on both sides of his cheeks like my grand children do, smiling at me with their big brown eyes. Yet, I can picture Jesus at five years of age talking with great wisdom to the priests at the Church of Saint Sergius and Baccus in Old Cairo. He was also at the old cathedral of St. Mark in the Azbekiya district of Cairo. Picture Joseph drawing water to wash Jesus at the well, now a holy sight called the 'Well of Jesus' across the street. Whenever and wherever Jesus laid His head, had a meal, talked to a priest, it became a holy site and what do you do with holy sites? Build churches for all to come see where Jesus walked. The Synagogue of Ben Ezar, was built on the site where baby Moses was found, they are known for their Library of Jewish Heritage of Egypt in old Cairo, because Jesus, Mary, Joseph and Moses were Hebrew. During the time of Jesus there were over 40,000 Jewish people living along the length of the beautiful Nile River.

Thoth was the God power who built the pyramids without slaves, he was a spirit deeply connected to God's wisdom and His great wonderment of the heavenly universe. Men came from all over Egypt, Africa and the Middle East to be involved with the working of energy structures.

The God Thoth had turned his back on the Egyptian Pharaohs because the latter Pharaohs chose to take slaves. He did this long before Moses led the Hebrews Exodus.

One of Thoth's rules; man is not to have slaves, man is not to own another man. Egypt has not been the same since Thoth turned his back on the slave kings and man fell away from the soul's purpose and wanted to control other men, setting up slavery and idol worship. Even when the Slave War ended in America and the slaves were set free, the God Thoth did not free Egypt for introducing slavery. No other nation involved went bankrupt after the Slave War in America, only Egypt. A nation cannot run from it's sin.

You call it the Civil War, yet, there is nothing civil about war.

'The truth shall bear witness of itself.' Thoth said as did Jesus, happy are you that search and have hunger for truth, for I will satisfy you with the bread of Wisdom. Thoth was the God of Wisdom, as was Jesus. We are wisdom, energy structures with the Holy Spirit in us. Even a small blade of grass has energy, providing chlorophyll, amino acids, minerals and vitamins. We must be aware of the nature around us, it connects us to a path of peace.

Please feel free to copy the timeline, I thought you might enjoy this information.

The God Thoth prescribed roots, greens, seeds and nuts, this is medicine, giving green plants of living food. The Egyptian medication has been around for more than 12,000 years.

5,000 BC. Please eat these roots, greens, seeds and nuts, it is medicine.

5 CE. Jesus gave herbs, greens, seeds nuts and prayers for healing.

1800 A.D. That prayer is superstition. Take this potion instead.

1950 A.D. That potion is snake oil. Here, swallow this pill.

1990 A.D. If you have side effects from all the pills, we have pills for each of the side effects. If you get yeast from all the pills, take this antibiotic.

2013 A.D. Please eat these roots, greens, seeds and nuts, it is medicine.

Jesus had many followers. Jesus was a young philosopher who told you where to draw your line in the sand, he talked about truth and taxes.

Egypt had papyrus paper, Israel had papyrus paper, why was the rest of the knowledge a mystery and not history?

"Was Jesus at the pyramids? Jesus' father, Joseph worked at the Babylon Fortress, today it is called Coptic Cairo. Abu Serghis was the home of Jesus when His family lived in Egypt. They traveled to visit the plateau of the pyramids. The answer is yes. Could you keep him away when his family was in Cairo? Does that even make sense to you? A man child not going to the greatest spiritual structure of old Egypt? His favorites in the animal kingdom were the lions. Do you think he would not want to touch the grandest lion in all of Egypt, with the power of nature in his body and the intelligence of man in his face? A lion is the king of the beasts, He is the King of the universe.

"Jesus would attract people who wanted to listen to the wise words of the holy boy. How would he have so much wisdom? Where did he come from? Is he like our God Thoth?" The professor pondered as if he was living 2,000 years ago, asking the questions of the locals.

Jesus can reveal himself to anybody!

"When Jesus was sitting with the priests at the Sphinx he may have heard the story of Thutmose III whose name means "Thoth Is Born." He was the sixth pharaoh of the 18th dynasty. The Sphinx was originally built in 2500 BC and was a very smooth cat with the long tail. A thousand years later in 1500 BC the New Kingdom emerged. The sands of time were drowning the mighty Sphinx. Thutmose could see a shoulder and head, he wanted the earth to reveal more. He asked the God Thoth and Horus the national patron god, the falcon headed king who ruled over the entire kingdom of Egypt for help clearing the sand. So grateful was the Sphinx he rewarded Thutmose the next position as pharaoh. The pharaoh pleased with himself decided to give the giant cat a face lift. He had the skin of the lion painted a reddish color and his pharaonic head piece was adorned with stripes of blue and yellow." He smirks as he tell us.

Jesus would have been beside the Sphinx approximately 1480 years after Pharaoh Thutmose III cleared and painted the majestic lion.

"Back ground information to understand why the pharaohs wanted to meet with Jesus. At the age of three Cleopatra's son Ptolemy Philadelphus was proclaimed Co-ruler with his mother. She killed herself when Marc Antony was defeated by Octavian, and Egypt became a province of Rome in 30 BC. The Ptolemaic Dynasty ended even though Cleopatra VII had infant sons. Octavian became Emperor Augustus in 27 BC. He was the first and greatest of the Roman rulers. He ruled with wisdom and power and kept peace in Rome. The Roman Emperors were accorded the title of Pharaoh while in Egypt. Do you know there were six other Egyptian Queen Cleopatras before Cleopatra Vll? Plus Alexander the Great's sister, the Greek Cleopatra. It gets confusing," says the teacher.

Even though Rome now ruled Egypt, the Ptolemy family would still have a political following. Do you think they would want to know if they would rule again? Do you think they would be curious to hear the wisdom of the young genius named Jesus, who escaped from the rule of the Roman King Herod?

"Love is my religion." Professor Christopher says, "Everything my father made for me is alive, it is all alive, the air is alive it is linked around the whole planet of earth and beyond. When I breathe, I inhale the air of my fathers, of Moses, of Noah, of Enoch. 99 percent of the genes of humans are identical to the genes of our pets, our dogs, cats and lions, the same as the trees. Celebrate the air. Just being here now is cause to celebrate, celebrate life! It is called quantum entanglement. It is a 'Mystical Ideal' that we are all connected, not separate. Thoth the God of Wisdom taught this principle from the beginning of time, the mystical ideal in Egypt's 'Mystical land!'

Egypt once was lush and beautiful. Please close your eyes, take three deep breaths. I hold the breath for the count of ten then I release into the image of the Garden of Eden, the way Egypt used to be. Picture the sound and smell of the luxurious Blue Nile born high in Ethiopia, where the river was considered holy, the Gihon River was mentioned in the first chapter of the Bible as the river flowing out of the Garden of Eden with its thick vegetation and magnificent waterfalls, so romantic are the pictures in my mind, I fall into a restful state. Think of this often, Thoth like Jesus taught everything that has life is the written law. It is in a blade of grass, in the trees which give you fruit, in the Nile River, in the mountains, in each bird that flies, in the fish in the rivers and the seas, most of all it is in your body. All living things are closer to God. The scripture is without life, it is like the books of the dead, go and praise God in the land of the living, the laws of God are written in your hearts. The River Nile brought black soil to enrich all the valley to the sea. The Indians knew better than the city dwellers, love your Father in Heaven, look to the stars to see his face, love the earth mother, walk with grass under your feet and feel her energy. This was the creation of Thoth. In your sacred mind, picture Jesus playing with his mother in the Nile River, laughing, and enjoying the deep love of a boy to his mother, his very first love.

"The Nile Valley is a rich fertile biblical land. Like Jesus, Thoth expected a life with honor, the golden rule, he hand wrote magical formulas in the Thoth Books of the Dead. The Bedouins say Jesus learned much of his magic from Thoth's books. A holy foot print relic of the boy Jesus was found at Sakha, on the back of the stone. It was found in 1984, imagine that, by sewer workers. The men drank the water because of the sweet smell, one man had a miracle healing of his eye when he washed his face. Miracles are forever, there are visions at many of the Coptic Churches. The Virgin Mary Church in Zeitoun glowed and the Virgin Mary made her appearance in 1968. In the Coptic, the Arabic word is Bab ila On, or gateway to On, we say Babylon. Saint Virgin Mary's Coptic Orthodox Hanging Church is one of the oldest churches in Egypt. The Suspended Church has it's nave suspended over a passage way above the gatehouse of the Babylon fortress in old Coptic Cairo. The nave is the main alter of the church. It is a city of churches, residents include 2,000 Muslims, 20,000 Copts and 50 Hebrews. Remember, originally Jesus was a Hebrew. Some Hebrews feel Jesus came to fulfill the law. Many Hebrews say part of that law was the Kabbalah, the secret doctrine of the Jews. Was it their version of the mysteries?" He asks us.

"Many of you have seen an obelisk familiar to Joseph and to Moses. The red granite shaft, together with three others like it, once stood before the royal priestly school at On. Moses, as a foster son of the Pharaoh's daughter, would have been educated at the school. We know the piece of which I speak as one of "Cleopatra's Needles," and one stood at the entrance to Central Park in New York City. It was brought to America from Egypt and erected in 1881. Height about 68 feet, weight about 224 tons. It is inscribed with Egyptian hieroglyphs invented by the God Thoth. They were originally erected in the Egyptian City of Heliopolis on the orders of Pharaoh Thutmose, (Thoth born) around 1450 BC. His father's great royal wife was Queen Hatshepsut. The monuments were falsely named 'Cleopatra's needle.' Which shows how complicated history becomes when stories are false, because the obelisks were already over a thousand years old in Cleopatra VII's lifetime?

"Question, Ginger?"
"I have a question about the importance of the city of On?"

"Remember the story of Joseph and the Amazing Dream Coat? The city of On is now Heliopolis, next to Cairo. Joseph's father Jacob, also called Israel, favored Joseph his eleventh child, and gave the 17 year old son a coat made of many colored pieces of cloth. His jealous brothers plotted against him, and sold him for 20 shekels to Ishmaelite merchants. The merchants sold Joseph as a slave to Potiphar, one of Pharaoh's officials, and the captain of the guard. He ended up having a very high ranking position in the Egyptian Kingdom, Joseph became the governor of all Egypt, Genesis 41:41. Joseph married the daughter of the chief priest of the school in On. Later when Alexander the Great invaded Egypt in 332 BC, they changed the Egyptian name of On to a Greek name, Heliopolis, meaning, 'Eye of the Sun.'

Pharaoh gave to Joseph, Asenath, daughter of Potiphera, priest of On, to be Joseph's wife. Genesis 41:45

The tribe of Joseph came out of the womb of the Egyptian mother Asenath. Many Israelites were a composite of Egyptians, through their two sons, Manasseh and Ephraim.

"Genesis records nothing more about Asenath. Some she was a virgin who rejected many worthy suitors in favor of Joseph, but Joseph could not have a pagan wife. Frustrated, she locks herself in a tower until she knows Yahweh. She rejects her idolatry in favor of Joseph's God. She then receives a visit from an angel who accepts her conversion to the one God. Bees cover her head and sting her lips to remove false prayers to the pagan gods of her past." I believe that is a myth, the professor declares.

"I will explain the rest of the story for those of you that did not see the play. The great famine came just as Joseph said it would when he translated the pharaoh's dreams. Egypt was well prepared for the famine, they stored grain, more than enough for their own nation, enough to sell to neighboring nations, including Joseph's brothers who came to Egypt to buy food. Joseph was not recognized by them, but after a bit of psychological revenge, he revealed his identity. Genesis chapters 42. Joseph had the power to execute them, yet he forgave them for what they had done to him. Joseph knew God had a plan for the entire series of events." Doctor Christopher says. "The pharaoh was generous with

Joseph, providing a large county of land for his family and friends in the Goshen delta."

The old testament section of the Torah traces the tribes of Israel back to Jacob, the grandson of Abraham. Jacob's sons were, Reuben, Simeon, Levi, Judah, Dan, Naphtali, Gad, Asher, Issachar, Zebulun, Joseph and Benjamin.

"The question of sibling rivalry presents itself to us. These older brothers were overwhelmed with jealousy. Jealous of Joseph's relationship with his father. To think they put their half brother into a hole in the ground, then sold him to merchants, upsets me to my core. Picture the frustration in the family. Jacob's children had many mothers. Reuben, Simeon, Levi, Issachar and Zebulun were born of his first wife, Leah. Her maid servant, Zilpah bore Gad and Asher. Rachael's maid servant, Bilhah bore Dan and Naphtali. The youngest, Joseph and Benjamin were sons of Jacob's love, the woman he waited so long for, his wife Rachel. Here is the story, Leah was the older sister of Rachel, the girl whom Jacob wanted to marry. On the wedding night, the girl's father switched daughters. The father claimed it was not the custom to give the younger daughter away in marriage before the older one. The father then make an offer to Jacob. He can have Rachel in marriage if he works another seven years. Genesis 29.

"Jealousy is an emotional feeling full of the negative thoughts of one's own insecurity, one's own fear, and one's own anxiety. Jealousy is a combination of emotions such as inadequacy, resentment, anger and helplessness." The professor proclaims. Fortunately the famine brought the brothers to Egypt and they asked for forgiveness from Joseph.

Yet, God had a plan for Joseph, as he did for all the 12 sons of Jacob. The linage of these 12 sons became the 12 tribes of Israel.

"What was the date of the Exodus, please?"
"The Jews settled in the land of Goshen, the place in Egypt given to the Hebrews by the pharaoh of Joseph located in the eastern delta and the Jews lived there for 400 years; then Moses led them out of bondage. Rabbinic Judaism traditional date is 1313 BC, they use the Seder Olam Rabbah, 2nd century AD to determine this religious fact. Yet, I have seen many different dates ranging about a one hundred year span."

"Jason, you have a question?"

"Yes, was Passover celebrated the week of the Exodus?"

"Yes, the tenth plague brought upon the Pharaoh was the death of the first born. The Hebrews were instructed to mark their doorposts with the blood of a sacrificial spring lamb. The angel of death would see this marking and "Pass Over" the first born in these homes. Hence the celebration of Passover. The angel of death took the lives of the first born who did not have the markings of a Hebrew home.

"Yes, Meagan?"

Please speak about Exodus. The amount of people vary dramatically. What is your opinion, professor?"

"The Hebrews were led by Moses out of Egypt. Exodus is a Latin word derived from the Greek word Exodos, meaning to go out, depart or exit. In Exodus 12:37 of the Torah and Old Testament, the Israelites numbered about six hundred thousand men on foot, besides women and children, plus many non-Israelites and livestock. The 600,000, plus wives, children, elderly, and non-Israelites would have numbered 2 million people, the entire Egyptian population in 1315 BC of around 3 million. Therefore if they walked ten abreast, not counting livestock, the line would be 150 miles long. Exodus originates not as history, but to demonstrate God's purpose and deeds with his Chosen People, leaving memorials of God's triumph behind.

"Your next question will be who was the pharaoh? Pharaoh Horemheb was known as the Pharaoh of the Oppression 1319 to 1292 BC. The next Pharaoh Ramesses I was known to some as the Pharaoh of the Exodus reigning from 1292 to1290 BC. Remember the soldiers of the pharaoh died in the Red Sea chasing the Israelites.

"How did Ramesses the second, who was the third Egyptian Pharaoh, 1279 to 1213 BC of the nineteen dynasty, become regarded as the greatest, most celebrated, and most powerful pharaoh of the Egyptian Empire. How did Ramesses II become so powerful if the work force and soldiers were destroyed? He was the greatest builder after the pyramid era. Where did he get the man power to establish a skilled, trained team to build the monuments that he built? The more you know the more questions you will have?"

"Believe not the movie version of handsome Yul Brynner in his prime, but an older version of Ramesses ll nearly eighty years of age, retiring turning the ruling power over to his sons. It is noted that later there was chaos in Egypt, which would make sense after plagues and an exodus of the work force. Who would be left to build the monuments? Not the angels." He laughs.

"Yes, Anastasia?"
"Do we become angels when we die?"
"No, we are not angels and can never become angels. Only angels are angels. When we die, we do not become angels, as sweet as the vision my appear to our hearts. Angels are a unique creation of their own, very different from humans. They are intermediaries between God and the men of the earth. The angel Gabriel appeared to Zechariah, telling him he would become the father of John the Baptist. Letting him know his son, John would be the prophet preparing the way for Jesus. Also, Mary and Joseph were prepared by personal visits from an angel. The shepherds learned about the birth of Jesus from angels. There are many angelic appearances throughout the bible, but, we can not become angels. Only angels are angels!

"Ginger, question?"
"Yes, sir, do we have guardian angels?"
"Many of us believe we each have a special angel to watch over us during our life. I like the idea, it is comforting. I do not know the answer. I can quote Matthew 18:10. "Do not be cruel to any of the little ones. I promise you, their angels are always with my father in heaven." I believe it meant that angels stand before God on behalf of those they protect.

"I, like you, picture the angels appearing around me or swooping down to catch a falling child. These mysteries are so powerful to our hearts. I believe, when the disciples asked about who would be the greatest in the kingdom, Jesus answered pulling a child into the circle, saying to enter the kingdom of God, one must have child like humility and faith. Always influence the innocents of the world in a positive way.

"Many people choose professions with the attributes of angels. Healing professions, doctors and nurses, teachers, ministers, care takers, providers, social workers, people that inspire, people in the arts, all those that assist in natural disasters, fire men and women, police and many more. Life is a tough school house, for me, I do picture a guardian angel watching over me and my family, protecting us. When I pray for people I ask for God's strongest angels to comfort and protect. Hebrews has a quote I live by.

Hebrews 13:2 Be sure to welcome strangers into your home. By doing this, some people have welcomed angels as guests, without even knowing it.

'By home,' I believe it means wherever you are, your private space. Always tell people, they are welcome, it shows a graciousness of spirit. Angels play a role as God's servants and messengers. These are not illusions, people have talked with angels, and walked with angels.

"Daniel, last question?"

"Gabriel is one name, I want to know the other names, please?"

"The others that come to mind are Michael, Raphael, Jeremiel, and Uriel, plus the seraphim and cherubim. God's heavenly host may be composed of many different groups. Again, I believe if the angels can move in and out of the old and new testament, they can move in and out of our lives as well. I believe God whispers to us all the time. Why would He not have his legend of angels whisper to us as well. It is a lovely way to end our time today. May God have whispering angels telling you the secrets of His universe, and the secrets of His infinite love.

"Wait, just one more question, please?"

"Yes, Jheri, I know it will be deep. Go ahead, ask me."

"Can you please give me your favorite bible story that exemplifies cowardliness and courage?"

"My favorite, Jonah and the whale." It is a tale of cowardliness and courage. God called Jonah to preach to the people of Nineveh. What did Jonah do? He took a boat going in the opposite direction, on purpose! Do not waste your time running from God, you will only make things worse. God made a sudden storm on the sea, reminding Jonah to obey. The crew grew upset. John 1:15 'Then they threw him overboard and the sea became calm.'

"Jonah did not want to go to Nineveh. What good does it do to preach to the most dangerous of enemies? This ancient city was located on the

Tigris River in northern Iraq. Nineveh is across from the city of Mosul, the homeland of Jonah. It was the capital of the Assyrian Empire.

"Jonah could not hide from God, the Lord brought him back in the belly of a whale. We, like Jonah have traveled through the same enemy territory warning people of their impending doom. 2,772 years later, we still suffer preaching to this war torn country.

"I like ending on a happier note, about the angels. Yet, I bet many, many powerful stories are seen, felt, and told about the angels helping the soldiers, children and families in Iraq. Pray that the soldiers will be comforted by the ethereal forms and even the human forms of these heavenly creatures, walking with the light of the Lord, illuminating their steps.

"One more question, James?"

"When you say the Lord's prayer do you say debts or trespasses? We have a bet for dinner, I am curious.

"I am a traditionalist, I use the King James version, so I say debts. The NIV version changed the word debts to trespasses. Let me say it for you, join in if you would like. It is a simple prayer written by Matthew.

Our father which art in heaven, Hallowed be thy name. Thy kingdom come, Thy will be done in earth as it is in heaven. Give us this day our daily bread. And forgive us our debts, as we forgive our debtors. And lead us not into temptation, but deliver us from evil: For thine is the kingdom, and the power, and the glory, forever. Amen.

"Todd, question?"

"I want to say something that came to me about Cleopatra's son?"

"We will talk about the Queen later this week," the professor says, "but, you may have the floor. Please come up front and introduce yourself."

"My name is Todd. Being an extrovert, I seem to get clarity when I say my thoughts and information out loud, so bear with me, I will give you the history that lays the background for my thoughts."

"The Ptolemaic Dynasty was the last linage of Egyptian Rulers. I am trying to put myself into their time of history, using my knowledge and my common sense. Rome took over Alexandria. I get that picture. Caesar was already killed in the Roman Senate. They hated him for having a child with Cleopatra. I believe his wife was very influential and very upset when her husband flaunted his mistress and her entourage in Rome on March 15, 44 BC. Cleopatra was claiming Caesar was the father of her son, this offend the Roman officials. To save face in Rome, Caesar refused to claim the boy, choosing his grandnephew Octavian to be his heir to the Roman throne. Yet, the senate was afraid and took matters into their own hands and assassinated Caesar. Cleopatra quietly slipped back into Egypt after the murder." Todd says.

"Ptolemy XIV also, died that year, shortly after Cleopatra returned to her capitol, Alexandria. Coincidence? Or did Cleopatra poison her co-ruler brother, before the Romans chased him? She did want to replace him with his nephew Caesarion, her son by Caesar? Then the Romans took Egypt from the Greeks. The Roman Octavian wanted to rule the Mediterranean world and Alexandria's harbor was perfect for Roman ships. He then rose to supreme power changing his name, Octavian, to Augustus. This occurred in 30 BC.

"Augustus would want to kill the son of Cleopatra and Caesar because he would be an adult and could claim his rights, because he was next in line to the Egyptian throne. So, he was killed right away. The children of Cleopatra and Mark Anthony were youngsters, and killing them would make the Romans look like barbarians. Cleopatra had twins that were taken to Rome." Todd fascinates us with his fluid history as he discusses his thoughts.

"Cleopatra and Mark also had a legal child, Ptolemy Philadelphus, the great, great, great, great, great, great, great, great grandson of Ptolemy Philadelphus II. Mark Anthony was married to Cleopatra according to the Egyptian rite. That rite was written in a letter quoted in the Roman Suetonius. Although, he was still married to Octavian's sister, Octavia Minor." Todd laughs. The royal soap opera continues.

"I read somewhere that the boy, Ptolemy Philadelphus was named King of Syria and Asia Minor at the age of two.

"Those of you who know me, know I love history. I am almost to my point. The boys disappeared. I agree with the professor, I believe the powerful forces of Cleopatra's secret service brought the boys back to Egypt. The Romans spread rumors that they died, but if they died in their youth, it would have been written. "The last of the male linage of the Egyptian Pharaoh is dead." Advertising their death would have been note worthy, since Cleopatra was a member of the long linage of the Ptolemaic dynasty.

"Here is my point. Jesus was a child of Hebrew parents. I am picturing Jesus speaking to the linage of Ptolemy II. Jesus would have know about the Torah, Genesis and the other four books, because the Septuagint, the 70 Jewish scholars transcribed the Hebrew to Greek 300 years earlier. My whole point being, I understand from the side of Jesus, why he might enjoy meeting Cleopatra's son. It was a great thing Pharaoh Ptolemy II did for the history of religion, ordering the transcribing of the Ancient Hebrew Scriptures. Picture the pharaoh commanding, "Write for me the Torah of Moshe (Moses)." My question. If the translation had not been called by the pharaoh, would we have an old testament?"

"Todd, it is a thought provoking question and I do not know the answer. I thank you for the summary of Roman history, I truly appreciate your interest and knowledge," the professor states. "You laid the story for my next class."

"Thank you, Doctor Christopher."

"Have a wonderful evening. I will remember this day fondly. I enjoyed being with you in this tent under the watchful eye of the great Sphinx and pyramids on this famous Giza plateau. This is a special event for me also, thank you so much for coming."

Give thanks to the Lord for He is good his love endures forever. Psalm 107:1

The class gave the professor a standing ovation, everyone was pleased with the information and the length of the seminar.

Amir turns to us wearing a big grin, "Do you ladies have time for dinner this evening at your hotel, I would love to escort you?"

"Yes, we do have time," answers Sharon. "We certainly do and would enjoy your company very much."

As we walk out of the tent, I overhear Dr Amon asking if Amir's driver could please drop him off at the museum. Amir signals to me to wait a minute, please, "I need to find David." He returns in a few minutes red faced, "I do not have a car at the moment, I will take the hotel shuttle back with you, if that is all right?"

Sharon whispers, "Does Amir have his own driver?"

We pile into the Mena House shuttle for a three minute ride to the hotel. Walking into the lobby is a treat with stylish ambiance awaiting every turn.

"It is five, Amir and I are going for a Turkish tea drink, why don't you take our notebooks back to the room and get ready for dinner, I will keep him company, I think I will join the others for dinner and let the two of you have some time to talk. Meet us back here." Sharon orders as she points at me to leave.

Amir smiles, "I will be right here with the boss."

I walk back to my room thinking about an appropriate dress code for our evening dinner. It is such an exciting hotel, so many interesting people, such diversity, it will be best if I wear my black outfit and low heels, always sophisticated in any land. I lay out my clothes and organize my dressing area. Wash my face, light make up, tan hose is more casual since he is wearing a sport coat, black skirt, black top, breasts covered, open toe heels, African turquoise necklace with Coptic cross, bracelet, earrings, ring, nails are done, take a breath, stand up straight, comb out hair and voila! I pick up my little black bag and out the door I go. I stand for a minute before I turn the corner to the lobby, taking a breath, standing up straight, hips under, stomach in and smile. Now the long walk through the lobby, nodding to the concierge, smiling at the bell captain, being careful not to slip on the marble flooring, breathing and finally turning slowly into the lounge.

Sharon grabs my arm, "He is a Security Concierge, no worries, we had a long talk. Have a wonderful dinner, you are perfectly safe eating in the lovely dining room. See you tomorrow morning for class. You do look great, you clean up well and fast, even early. Pray we get picked tomorrow for the private ceremony." She waves as she walks away.

The Maitre d' escorts us to a private area, to a lovely table with a bottle of red wine already properly uncorked, breathing and waiting for us. I am pleased that I did not pass out from nervousness when I notice the little gift box on my plate.

"Are you wearing a different shirt and you are wearing a tie, did you stop into the men's shop?" I inquire.

"Yes, thank you for noticing. I bought a new shirt and Sharon picked the tie for me to wear, I spilled my drink. The gift on your plate is something simple, I bought one for her also, for helping me. Open it, you will see it is a non obligation gift, if there is such a thing."

I lift the lid to the little box. "A money clip."

"To keep your Egyptian currency separate from your American money." He leans into me, "it is a men's shop with man type gifts."

"I love it."

"Here is your first Egyptian pound to put in your new money clip."

"I like the way you take care of the details."

"I have something else for you to make your time in Cairo easier."

He pulls a cell phone from his pocket. "I have many of these, they are disposable, prepaid Egyptian cell phones. You can call me anytime with this local phone number, you will not have the hassle of using your American overseas roaming charges. I can program my cell number into the top spot, the police if there is trouble, the hospital and then your hotel number."

"That is the kindest thing to do for anyone who is in a foreign land. Thank you so much, Amir. You are so organized and thoughtful."

"I have a selfish motive, I want you to call me. I want you to be one of the lucky ten to be honored for the pyramid ceremony. Call me if you want to brag about it. Shout it from the roof, I believe you will be one of the chosen, I just feel it."

"Thank you for the kind thoughts, there are about 986 people here, it would be the luck of the draw."

"Louise, you are a tour de force. Sharon told me all about your life. Your God given talents make you who you are. Egypt relates to you. You were called here for a reason more powerful than you can imagine at this time. The fact that you are in receipt of your husband's name is not an accident. His and your parents deaths were not accidents. It allowed you the freedom, as harsh as it sounds, to be able to find yourself and Jesus of Egypt. That is your story, that is the power inside of yourself that must be told. Being in this ancient land will bring you to a life with such depth and responsibility. This is not a whimsical trip made by a curious woman. You have a calling, to transform the world permanently for the better. You were born with tools to accomplish this, you have a stable personality, intelligence, courage and charisma. I suggest you read out loud words of ancient texts, these writings will resonate very strongly with your noble aspirations. You have an awareness and an openness to universal consciousness, it is so apparent in the fact that you are not defensive when dealing with others. That is why you were born to the parents you had, to become the woman you are today. Why you married the man you did, why the Lord took your parents and husband. You see without the attachments you are available to do God's work." Amir says with a powerful conviction.

You are a shield around me,
O Lord; you bestow glory on me
and I lift my head.
Psalm 3:3

Ceremony Inside the Giza Pyramid

"Let's hurry to the morning seminar, we do not want to be late for Black Elk and Moon Bear." I say with excitement. Outside the tent a clever sign: '2560. Pyramid building in Giza. 20,000 workers needed. Housing under the stars, Wage: one loaf of bread and one gallon of beer daily. Applications available. Apply within. Dress code, Ancient Egyptian.' Professor Amon, Thursday 7 PM.

"Is that creative and enticing? Was your professor fun like that? I cannot wait to meet Professor Amon. Sharon, I want to hear this lecture, let us sign on the list for seating early before the class gets full." I declare.

Then we enter the tent of Chief Black Elk the Lakota renowned Indian chief and world-class speaker. Black Elk's grandfather traveled Europe with the famous Bill Cody Wild West Show. I am so impressed with his information, and his heart caring attitude, it feels marvelous to enter the world of such a knowledgable speaker.

Chief Black Elk is holding a very long list of the names of all the registrants at the conference, the chief privately chose ten for his group from his audience to be with him and his partner Moon Bear in the Great Pyramid for the entire afternoon ceremony.

The chief sighs, "We want people who are clear channels, people who were open to receiving."

Both of us girls are shocked to be chosen, yet, at the same time we know it is our hearts destiny, to be appreciated in such a manner is an honor that fills every cell of our being. This is an experience of a lifetime, and we are in our element. When can you ever get a group this size all interested in the same thing. All diverse ages, a campus of sand beneath your feet and a multi cultural people with a zest to inhale all the knowledge. All wanting what is best for each other.

Sharon keeps saying thank you, it means more to her then they could ever realize. This was always such a deep seated dream of hers, Egypt and the pyramids, in fourth grade both of us wanted to be Egyptologists.

I dial my new cell phone, "Amir, I appreciate your prayers, Sharon and I am going to be entering the pyramid this afternoon. I have always dreamed of being at the pyramid. To be inside for a private ceremony was never in my dream, God added that."

"You deserve it. You were called for a reason."

"Thank you, and thank you for the wonderful time I had last evening, you are so polite, and smart, I appreciate your helpfulness"

He laughs, "Go, have fun. I will talk to you later. I have a dinner meeting that will run until about nine. I will talk to you then. You are now going to walk in the footsteps of the Great Khufu, the ruler of the once greatest nation in the world, plus having a meeting just as he did so many generations ago in his chamber. Very Good, Lady Louise. Enjoy, we will have much to talk about this week."

After a bite we take the shuttle from the hotel to the Giza Plateau. That in itself is exciting. As we are getting ready to enter the Great Pyramid, I see each of the people in the group checking themselves to make sure this is not a dream.

What a powerful journey back in time!

We line up to enter the long, narrow, solid granite hallway, the excitement gurgles in my stomach as I move where the great pharaohs walked before me. My steps are so carefully taken. You could hear a pin drop. Me, in the Great Pyramid that is closed to the public; just the 11 of us following the great Chief Black Elk up the 153 foot Grand Gallery, a rising corridor with a 28 foot high corbeled roof. Beyond lay the ceremonial resting place for the great King Khufu, a simple room roofed by 400 tons of granite. We are told there were relieving chambers built to deflect the enormous load bearing down from the pyramid's vertical axis. We are now in the King's Chamber, an out of body experience. There is so much enthusiasm, as if this is a movie, yet it is real.

This is an in your body experience, I have to focus, 'mind, body and spirit must always be as one,' I keep repeating to myself. My blood is pulsating, my skin tingling with the excitement, the prayers of a lifetime, this is truly my hearts destiny to be here at this moment to experience every sensation. My eyes wide open, my pupils dilating, so much power unfolding.

When we enter the King's Chamber, we all find seats along the walls. I move to the last position by the entry doorway. The air is very still, I know that I will need some air movement and the shaft could provide the most cooling. It is a large room with an empty stone sarcophagus, a sarcophagus that held a sovereign's body at one time. Now it is an empty granite space waiting for our presence.

Chief Black Elk sits to my left, wearing one of his best ceremonial outfits, with fringe hanging from the arms of his leather tunic adorned with intricate bead work. He wears a bear claw necklace around his neck as a testimony to his strength, killing a bear is revered in his culture. In front of him is a space for his ritual with an assortment of large rose, and amethyst quarts crystals. This is an experience beyond any other.

I am thinking to myself, 'Is Indiana Jones going to be coming up the sacred gallery passage way? The doorway is next to my right shoulder. Am I going to wake up?' I can not believe this is really happening to me.

'Who am I going to tell about this event? Who will believe that I am sitting in the King's Chamber with the famous Indian Chief Black Elk and Moon Bear playing his drums?'

It is such a high level experience. 'Nobody's going to believe this. I imagine it is just as awesome for the Indians, they have never done this before either. I better be in the moment every moment, because this will never happen again in my lifetime. This is an experience so serious I have to inhale every ounce of energy, every emotion that's going on in here because I'll never go through anything like this again!'

Most people come to Egypt on some type of sacred journey, but they travel in tours or groups. They buy the public ticket, or a private group with a minimum of 40 and enter the pyramid with the crowds but our group of twelve have the pyramid to ourselves for a three hour ceremony, a concept beyond everyone's wildest imagination. Twelve of us, like the apostles having a sacred meeting place.

The chief starts the ceremony with the people on the other side of the room. I watch carefully, each of them stand in front of the sarcophagus. 'Why do they have their backs to the chief and face the sarcophagus?' I can not understand, it feels disrespectful to the chief, yet, that is what each one of the guests chose to do, to face away from chief, they face the granite, then each person moves to lay down in the empty King's Sarcophagus. When they were ready, they rise and go back to their place along the wall. I can see they have an uncomfortable look on their faces. 'Feel this, this is not ever going to occur again in our life. This is a moment so precious in time. Feel the power of the moment, this is where the power is, in each moment. Be in it.'

I turn to look at Moon Bear sitting on the other side of the entry way, with his drums between his legs, his hand made high quality wooden bongo with its snugly fitted tuning ring set to begin a journey that will bring creative fulfillment and rhythmic joy. The rhythm of the beat haunts me, the earthy connection of his hands playing on the animal skin draws me into the feeling of his native custom.

The chief is in his full headdress, the feathers trailing down his back to the granite, such a magnificent portrayal of the heroic American Indian. I am sitting on the granite floor looking with marvel at Black Elk, watching the chief praying to the spirit of his grandfathers, his one grandfather was a great warrior and peacemaker who had fought at Little Big Horn.

We spoke earlier about our similarities in the Christian faiths, and about his grandfather, Black Elk who was buried in Saint Agnes Catholic Cemetery in South Dakota. The emotion of this journey is intense, watching him as he is moving his arms and saying a Lakota prayer to his ancestors. He is a perfect stature for a chief, a large tall man, a powerfully strong figure wearing a huge feathered headdress, full Indian attire, with drums playing, crystals on the ground, and the chief singing a Lakota hymn. I sit here in awe and wonderment, watching every move the chief makes, my heart is swelling with pride and respect.

I am one of the most logical, reasonable, practical people on the planet. Sitting with my back against the wall, my body burning from the energy, I have to lift up the back of my shirt to press my skin against the cool Egyptian stones. Slipping my shirt up in the darkness, putting my entire back against the very grounding walls of the pyramid is the most curious experience I have ever felt. It will soon be my turn, quietly slipping my shirt back down, I ready to stand in front of the chief.

Now Chief Black Elk nods to me to come. As I rise, I think, 'no way will I turn my back on such a magnificent character.' Standing facing him is not courage, it was just part of a circle of friendship, the crystals in front of us, the chief with his arms up saying the prayers in his native Lakota tongue, talking longer with me than with any of the others because I am facing him, we both feel beauty and love radiating from his heart. Then he nods, letting me know that it is now time to lay in the Great Sarcophagus.

As I lay in the sarcophagus, thoughts race, 'I am laying where great kings have lain in this very sarcophagus in the king's chamber,' I cross my arms keeping the energy in me, holding all that energy in like a personal hug, keeping it close to my heart.

In less than a second I experience a vision beyond anything I have ever felt. Friends are coming close, a joyous feeling, a proud community lovingly laying large lotus blossoms, saying kind words. They are in a small procession very close to my body, in the sun light I am lying on a bed of flowers, the exotic fragrances filling the air. Musical instruments are playing in my dream, compassion and peace rest in my mind, like a child floating in the pool without a care in the world. I understand love knowing that God is always present and He lives in truth and light. We are holy beings in an earthly body, the body is the house for the wisdom of the soul.

Chief Black Elk slowly speaks a Lakota prayer to calm and ground us. We feel his peace and gentleness.

We gather ourselves and in silence follow the chief down the long corridor shaft to the bright shimmering light of the entrance. The memory of this experience will live in our minds forever.

"Let us all ride back to the hotel, you are so blessed today, I am proud of each of you. Remember never put a question mark where God has placed a period." Black Elk says in his strong comforting authoritative voice.

Is there a Giza Pyramid Code?

I walk with the chief into the hotel, my deep intensity lifts the moment I enter the lobby. I absolutely love being in beautiful hotels, and this hotel with its cultural exotic foods, and romantic architecture near the Sphinx is enchanting to say the least.

"How about if we clean up and gather in the conference room, I would like if our group from the pyramid has dinner together privately," the chief suggests with a more relaxed voice. We all want to be with him again to extend the bonding experience we all so deeply felt.

He went to the concierge to ask the hotel to arrange a feast for the twelve of us in the meeting room. So much better than the private dining room of small tables, the conference room had one large mahogany table seating twelve comfortably. "Thirty minutes and we will meet in the Ramesses Room," he instructs with a more relaxed tone. I am so mesmerized by the majestic Indian chief.

"I would be honored just to carry his books home from school," I say, whispering to Sharon.

"I know what you mean, awesome is the only word that can describe a force like his. Watch him as he walks through the hotel, granted he is still wearing his ceremonial attire, carrying an enormous headdress of feathers in his hand, I guess it is how one must have felt after a private Elvis concert, these men have so much charisma. I am sorry for the analogy, but you know what an Elvis fan I am," says Sharon.

The afterglow shows on our skin, we girls clean up in our rooms, dressing in fresh clothing, I try on my new light ivory tunic with gold embroidered flowers and a tender baby lotus blossom in my hair. Sharon picks the same outfit in a deep purple hue with her dark hair giving a more sophisticated appearance.

As we enter the Rameses Room, the waiters have already set the table with a crisp cream color Egyptian cotton table cloth, with oversized matching napkins. The silverware is a reed motif, large with a properly balanced weight. Moon Bear holds out his finger and rests the spoon over it to check the weight. It is a perfect balance. His mind is always curious.

"Everyone shows me such kindness, more than I ever felt before. Is something going on that I need to know," I smile at him with curiosity.

"It is your name, you have one of the most famous names in Egypt. The God Thoth, was 'the mind behind the cosmic order.' You would be like the father to all the gods. "You and Phah, then you gave life to Ra, you were his tongue, he had you translate his ideas into printed words, so you had to invent hieroglyphics, you were the God of Writing. Thoth wrote over 40 books, beside their bible, he wrote eight medical book kept in the Library of Alexandria. The city of Alexandria, became the medical and intellectual capital of the Mediterranean world. Thoth wrote books on ethics, geography and the mysteries of life. He was the author of all works of science, astronomy, astrology, mathematics, religion, geometry, philosophy, theology and magic. The Egyptians claimed he was the true author of every work of every branch of knowledge, human and divine."

"I am telling her about her name," Moon Bear says as Black Elk enters the room.

"You must listen to him. Thoth was the God of the Moon, a god very sacred to my partner, Moon Bear," says the chief.

"I always thought the Sun God Ra was the biggest god in the land," asks Jason, the quiet scientist in the group.

"Yes, you are correct, Amun Ra was the biggest god that the people worshiped, because they could see the sun. Someone had to say the words to call in the creation, to set the world in order, or chaos would be everywhere, that was Thoth. He protected Ra. You are absolutely right, the people knew the sun was the great source of light energy. Let me tell you about the sun, the core of the sun is 27 million degrees Fahrenheit, and 93 million miles from earth, it releases more energy in one second than a billion cities could in one year. The Egyptians did not know this, yet, they instinctively knew its power. They must have worried when the sun would set and Ra would go through the underworld each night. Ra would take his two best friends, Ma'at and Thoth to go on his solar barge with him, it is good that his companions were married to each other, they did the trip every night, and 3,000 years is a long time. Imagine the joy each morning when the sun would rise in the East, maybe we might learn to be more joyful," instructs the chief.

"Let me make this easier to understand on a simple level, by the way this is an interesting entry to what I wanted to discuss. You all have a tablet and pen on the table in front of you, this is one reason I like to have a dinner meeting in a conference room. Of the ten of you that I have chosen to be in the pyramid today, which one of the group faced me?" Each person wrote the same name, Louise. Who of the ten of you do you think would want to be the Egyptian cosmic creator, and who do you think would want to be Ra? Why? Remember the sex of the person would not be an influence.

The majority of the group wrote Lou to be Thoth and Dan to be Ra. Why? Jason says, "Lou is the most organized."

"Who would be Ra?" asks Anastasia. I pick Dan to be Ra. I think he has a big ego. Dan wants to be on stage, as the Sun God Ra would want to be center stage, and the world revolves around Ra, we are the planets revolving around the sun."

He laughs, "I am a singer and I love the stage."

"Dan would not want the job of Thoth, it would require being in the background, he would think that a thankless job, he would want to be the star, not the one that holds it all together, he would not be interested in inventing hieroglyphics, that is to detail oriented."

Dan would be a great Ra." speaks the elder of our team, Jheri continues, "I would choose for myself to be Maat, the Goddess of Truth, I am a writer and I understand the importance of truth, it is the basis of all self esteem. Words are powerful, words seem to come from God. In the beginning there was the Word, and the Word is God. It is through my words that I express my creative power. It is through my words that I manifest my world into being. I love being a writer, and I love words. I see myself as Maat, being the wife of the God of Wisdom would be the best combination, Truth and Wisdom."

"Lou, you are writing a novel, would you want to write it as if you are Thoth." the chief is asking sweetly in his fatherly way.

"I would like to be myself in this life."

I see what the chief is doing, how our different personalities would coincide with the personalities of the gods giving us each a role to play in the growing of a great nation, the growing of the greatest nation of the ancient times," Jason speaks with deep thought, thinking of whom he would pick.

"Later in the week, we will meet here again, I will ask for a reservation for this room. Each of you think about which god you feel would represent an aspect of your personality. We will have a portrayal of your information. Be bold. By the way, Abdul, the concierge at the front desk laughs with me when I ask for a reservation. He thinks it is very funny, coming from an Indian Chief." Black Elk declares with a hardy laugh.

"Chief, do you and Moon Bear believe the stones in the pyramid had healing properties?" Jason inquires.

"I believe that, the chief and I come from a culture that is comfortable believing in energy," Moon Bear answers with a smile as the chief gathers his papers, "we have great knowledge about mother earth, her quarries have great power, I believe you will learn about the energies in Doctor Amon's lectures. Do you believe stones have healing properties?"

"Yes, and there are minerals in the earth," adds Daniel.

"We all saw the little sparks of light move, my people have seen this many times. We were invited to speak at this conference because we are respected, do you agree?"

"Yes, the teachers here are professionals and very learned men and women. I am proud to have met you," Todd confirms. We are all shaking our heads in agreement.

"There is much of life that we do not know, yet it is real. Many say the Giza Pyramid was built according to a secret code with the power to perform miracles, the building now called Gizeh was also called the Hall of the Initiates. I believe it was built from the inside. When I think of things simple or complicated, I relate them to how I would handle the situation. I would build it from the inside out. Similar to a spiral with right angle galleries, a seven degree incline, with notches at four angles to allow the stones to be turned and to allow ventilation. The high chief left ideas, the black dorite ball, notches, one Egyptian inch."

"An Egyptian inch is a bit smaller than an inch," Todd states, "there must be a clue.

Black Elk grins, "I believe it is a big clue to decoding one of man's mysteries. If one Egyptian inch is equal to one year, then the length of the corridors add up to 2012 years. The Grand Gallery comes into play, dramatically raising the height of the roof named Ascending Passage. Have any of you been to the Spring equinox in Teotihuacán? The annual event which takes place around the March 20, 21 at the Old Mayan site of Teotihuacan, Mexico. Thousands of people visit for the event, they dance, burn incense and chant climbing to stand at the top of the Pyramid of the Sun, arms outstretched facing the sun in the morning on the eastern horizon. What does this sound like? Compare the length of the base of the Pyramid of the Sun with the base of the Giza Pyramid and are they the same? Yes, they are the same dimensions at the base. Both have calendars that have the year 2012. Interesting.

"Inside the pyramid here is a Seal or Boss, it looks like a small rainbow arcing three inches over an eight inch line. Is it a new sunrise code, a new day is coming? It is the only inscription found so far in the Giza Pyramid." Black Elk ponders these questions.

"Prophecy inside the pyramid? Wait, the Mayans calendar stops at 2012, they believed it was the end of the world, or did they?" wonders Daniel. "It is something to consider."

Maybe they believed it was the end of the world as they knew it, and the birth of a new day, a spiritual awakening calling people to prayer and worship. Could it be the return of the Men of Wisdom?

"What do you think about this? I think I may put my book idea aside and bring it back to finish after 2012," I say very seriously. "I will publish it in the new era. I am going to write down some questions."

Will we witness a birth of a new era where the people are protected by cameras and communication devices like cell phones instead of guns?

Will it be an era of peace? A new world of gratitude.

Will we see Moslems praying over Christians, and Christians praying over Moslems?

Will the power of the people become greater than the people in power?

Could 2012 be the year of the end of the dictatorship Mubarak?

Could the pyramid prophecy code be a new independent thought process similar to the original ancient Egyptian philosophy of equality when men and women are educated and equal?

"I believe this year is a turning point that will be a new kindness in humanity. We will again teach through the whole body, not just the brain, but the heart and intuition. A dawning of new possibilities, the end of closed minded egos, an openness to peace, an illumination, and age of enlightenment to God's love," Jheri adds with enthusiasm. "Many modern scientists regard DNA as a waveform able to be modified by light, radiation, magnetic fields and sonic pulses. The legacy of Thoth/Enoch suggests this language of Light, or ancient harmonic science, could affect DNA. The longer the wave, the lower the frequency. Sound is the same, the longer the wave, the lower the sound. Waves at the low end would be radio waves, microwaves, infrared waves, invisible light, ultraviolet light, x rays and the high frequency the gamma waves. Could they use Waveform Mapping and Time-Frequency Processing of DNA and Protein?"

Ancient Egyptians declare, "If you would speak with the gods, you must learn the language of the gods." The language of Thoth/Enoch/Jesus connection implies humans were meant to evolve to the highest present form.' May we sing with the glory of the most High God? Could the harmonic language be intertwined with the waveform properties of light? The Keys of Enoch are sound and light keys, the mythic power of the world described sonic sounds encoded within the ancient mantras and god's names, capable of directly affecting the health system in a positive way. It produces profound healing and a higher consciousness state. Frequencies of relaxation." The chief reiterates.

"Meanwhile doesn't anyone wonder how Louise got a name like Thoth." Black Elk is looking at me with a curious gaze, "You have blue eyes and blond hair, very rare in this part of the land. How did you get to have such a famous Egyptian name?"

"Be careful what words you speak. It was my husband's last name. I was putting him through college when I married him. He was beyond broke and he said, 'Maybe the only thing you're going to get from me at the end of the day, is my name.' It would have been best if he had not have said those words. He became a builder and retained the shopping centers and office buildings, but the last recession when people could not pay for their rent, he still had to pay the big mortgages until we gave all our savings. No one is in the habit of financing their delinquent clients for such long periods of time, finally it affected our bottom line. Giving the buildings back to the banks was bad enough, but laying off our office team and labors was also a real sadness, because they had families to care for and depended on us for jobs.

"I had nightmares. In my vision I felt the pain so deeply, I compared it to a news story I saw on TV of a hard working African American lady in South Philly that came home one day to find her brick house was on fire and her children were trapped inside and the flames were so severe that the fire department roped off the area. Everyone was trying their best but no matter what they would do, they could not save her babies. To us the buildings were also our babies, from the moment of conception through birth, staying up nights worrying about all their problems, from zoning board meetings to designing to digging foundations, from plumbing to wiring, from interior build outs to leasing. We put just as much time into them as our own babies, the emotion was not quite the same, I love my children much more but the work was the same. We suffered terribly and I learned I can endure great pain, then both my parents and husband died right in a row, the expression, it comes in threes."

"You lost your wealth, your years of hard work, then your family, that is more than one should have to carry, yet, you have one of the best personalities. You seem to have a fearless and determined heart. How does that happen?" Anastasia inquires with a sadness in her voice.

"I believe it is the breaking of life that produces the strength, the true blessings of life. Remember when Jesus turned the two fish and five loaves of bread into enough to feed thousands, he took something that was not enough and blessed it. The two fish and five loaves were not enough? No, and we are not enough. It was the breaking of the bread that caused the blessings to occur. If you are to prideful to be broken then how can you be internally blessed and spread your blessings among thousands? I am not talking about material blessings, I mean the blessing of the spirit, the peace within the soul. When one is in the EGO he is far from God. It is called Edging God Out. My husband listened to the banks when they kept saying take the money, buy more land, here is the loan, sign on the line. When was it ever enough? How many buildings did he need to build and own?

"The Bible tells us in the story of the feeding of thousands, Jesus' attitude was one of gratitude or thankfulness. He took a child's lunch of five loaves and two fish, gave thanks and had them distributed. He gave thanks! He did not complain, He gave thanks! Not only did He feed the people he had twelve baskets left over.

I decided to dedicate myself to the Lord by faith. I asked Him where I should sow my seed so that I could be a blessing to others. I have been wealthy on paper and I have been broke, yet I find fulfillment and I am satisfied with my life. I have a peace even in low times. I know that life is like a highway under construction, some sections are smooth and some sections are under serious repair.

"The Lord's Prayer must have hit you hard. Forgive your debtors. Your renters must have owed you an enormous amount of money." Black Elk says with much concern.

"Yes, but their businesses were going under and they could not pay, we let them stay until we found someone new, but everyone was downsizing. We had a lot of vacancies. We signed personally, so all the banks were paid; we sold the two industrial parks at a small profit, we sold eight office buildings at cost and they took back the remaining three. Life is a learning experience.

"I gave a testimony in church and I can remember saying with tears streaming down my face, that my Bible study teacher told me, we were going to study 'minor prophets' and I said, I do not want any more minor profits, I want my major profits back."

The beauty of the spirit comes from the attitude.

"I learned to be grateful for each day. When my second son was born, my baby and I almost died. He was an emergency cesarean, the fetal monitoring unit was not detecting a heart beat. The team of doctors rushed me into the operating room, put me on the table, stretched out my arms like a cross, strapped down my wrists, and tried to be calm in the middle of a state of panic. When I finally woke in the recovery room, I was so cold, I could hear the doctors talking, but I could not get them to come to me, I could not utter a grunt or any type of sound to get attention and I was shaking on the inside, I was as cold as if my body was kept in a refrigerator, it was a horrible experience. I felt as if my brain was the only part of me that was alive."

"Is that when your spiritually grew?" Anastasia asks.

"Yes. I always believed in God, yet, I never really studied His Word. I did not know the facts. Proverbs should be taught in schools. Among other sections of wisdom." I say slowly, reflecting.

Don't worry about anything, instead pray about everything; tell God your needs and don't forget to thank him for His answers. Philippians 4:6

They all sat back on their chairs thinking about the experience.

"How is your son today?" Todd asks.

"Perfect, I laid in the hospital bed trying to make deals with God, I will go to church more, study your Word. Please Lord, breathe oxygen into my little baby's brain and his sad blue body. The Lord answered my prayers and I made a decision to find gratitude in all things. I took my son everywhere with me, constantly teaching him because of the lack of oxygen to his brain, I wanted to enrich that little brain."

"In an instant life can be changed," says Jason, "no wonder you feel grateful."

Our heads turned toward Moon Bear as he sat tapping on our information forms.

"Louise, I see by reading the registration forms you were born on the day of Thoth in the Egyptian Calendar, called the day of Tehuti, Djehut and it is your last name. That is the Egyptian name for Thoth. I see your ancestor dropped a consonant. 'Toth, Thoth, Tothe'. It depends if it's being translated into English or Roman or Greek, they each spell it a little differently," Moon Bear confirms. "We are giving you extra attention because of your name being the God of Wisdom and all that. It is very curious to us, blue eyes. That could be your Indian name, 'Eyes of the Sky."

"Eyes of the Sky' has more," I say as the group sits back listening with an encouraging curiosity. "Years ago I designed vacation homes called the Blue Heron Resort, the blue heron and ibis are brothers and the ibis is the sacred bird of the God Thoth."

"Fate," says Jheri. We are supposed to meet here, all of us, here in Egypt, to have this experience together. It is giving me chills, my arms are wearing goose bumps."

"Wait a minute. Is that in the Pocono Mountains in Pennsylvania?"

"Yes."

"Near the Pocono 500 Raceway?" Daniel questions.

"Yes," I answer with a bit of surprise.

"I stayed there! I am from New York, I went to see Paul Newman race." Daniel says with excitment.

"Yes, Paul rented my condo on the lake." I giggle.

"Black Elk, he stayed right next to me. So, I stayed next door to your home that you designed?"

"Yes, my husband built the development and I furnished the units."

"Builder talk, everyone else would say, my houses, you say units."

"Black Elk, do you know who else was there? Mario Andretti. Mario was 'Driver of the Century." This is amazing Daniel exclaims.

"I, too, am a fan." Moon Bear says nodding his head.

"Mario has his own home in the mountains, a big one, not in our development." I chuckle, "his family lived in Nazareth, I lived in Bethlehem and as a child I would swim in the Jordan River. Imagine that! Never thinking I would stand in the great Jordan River someday."

"Aren't you impressed with your accomplishments?" Daniel wonders.

"It is different on my end, when we build, we start with raw land, then we have to get permits. When we broke ground we still did not have electricity. We had to dig up the existing road and build a new road deeper into the woods to give all the units waterfront views. There were no water lines when we started, we had to bring buckets from the lake to clean the condos. I sat with a blank piece of grid paper when I was designing the units, deciding on the exterior, then the interior, thinking how I would back up the plumbing to cut costs, stacking the bathrooms and fireplaces. It is years of work before a project is finished and the twinkle lights are on the trees.

"Then my husband told me to set up three model houses. It was so remote, I thought how are the new owners going to deal with the frustration of waiting for furniture deliveries. I wanted them to have a vacation. So, I put together furniture packages with a price so low they could not refuse. I went into the wholesale furniture business and ended doing the work for all the homes. Then I hired the local craftsmen to make the clocks, lamps and designer windows.

"You did as your name sake," Black Elk interjects, "you brought 'Chaos into Order.' That is what the God Thoth did with the universe. You, my dear, have the ability to cut right through and get to the point. You can see the big picture, then cut it into pie shapes and feed it to the people."

"Thank you, I am proud. It was fun when I think about it. Eleven acres in the woods and 126 condos, which equates to 504 beds, 504 bed spreads, 1008 pillows, 504 headboards, 378 drapes, 126 custom chandeliers, 378 oak wall clocks, 200 stain glass windows, 126 dining room tables, 1004 chairs, 252 sofas, 300 dressers, 1004 end tables, 126 coffee tables, 1025 lamps plus kitchen supplies times 126 and 470 towels for the bathrooms. Ha ha, I laugh, yes, it did turn out beautifully, I am very delighted."

"You should be, I never even built one house. I am remembering all the blue herons, the lake and the stain glass windows that were in the condo." Daniel says sitting back on his chair full of pride. "What a small world, what a small world!"

"Stain glass windows?" Moon Bear questions, wrinkling his brow.

"Ever since I was a child, I love the way the light comes through the colors in glass and I had a window designed for each unit. Every home had at least one stained glass window. It was my gift to the people that bought the units. I strongly believe that everyone deserves a special piece of art gifted to them in their lifetime. It is a connection I have with God that I want to share. I put art into everything I do. If my name is connected to a project, you will see the hand of God through the art. Thank you, Daniel for caring. I forgot about all the beauty we created." I say with pride in our teamwork. "It was teamwork."

"I had an extra 5 houses of furniture in our storage warehouse. Years later, I was on the West Coast, the warehouse was on the East Coast and I did not want to ship everything to California. So, I decided to give it away, I asked two people, who told me they did not want my furniture. I could not give it away. I felt so rejected. Finally, I put an ad in the Bethlehem, Pennsylvania newspaper, 'Bedroom sets, Dining room sets, in factory boxes, $250 a set, includes oak table with 2 leaves, 8 chairs.' I had to get it out of the warehouse, we no longer own the building." I say sadly.

"Offering a free house of furniture, is extremely gracious," Sharon states, "she is used to doing things in a big way, it is perfectly normal for her, but people are thrown off by her generosity. I have seen her be rejected many times, yet she is only trying to help. People do not understand her heart."

"No good deed goes unpunished." quotes Daniel. "I would love to visit you in California."

"Where I live now I am visited by the sweetest young white heron birds that stand in the light surf, on the docks, and swim in the salt water pool. The drawings I have seen of the Thoth God, with the head of an ibis bird, looks just like the heads of my precious visitors. This is now giving me goose bumps, there are so many coincidences. Our group is so unique to be chosen. How many are here at the conference? You hand picked ten to have a once in a lifetime experience in a private ceremony in the Great Giza Pyramid. How awesome is this?" I giggle.

"Fate is the Egyptian word for coincidence" repeats Jheri. "We all need to pray God will show Louise in His timing what she is to do with this new information. I believe He has a divine purpose for her and is clearly letting her know she has an unusual connection to Egyptology."

"The part that fascinates me is that she does not have much of an ego. She knows life itself is a gift. We do not even own ourselves. How can we have an EGO? Who wrote the history of the Emerald Tablets? Their antiquity dates back some 36,000 years B.C. The author is Thoth, an Atlantean King-Priest who founded a colony in ancient Egypt, he was the one that wrote the Emerald Tablets in his native Atlantean language. Most people would have an ego, she is so calm. I love that quality, Louise, you have a very peaceful nature about you. I believe your calmness is from God." Yasuko expresses. "Those who know the truth have been set free."

"EGO is self pity, a method of gaining attention. It is the 'i' in bitter. We need to turn bitter into better." Sharon adds.

As the waiters finish setting up a plentiful buffet in the back of the room the chief speaks, "Before we have our meal, I would like to ask Lou if she would honor me with the English words to this prayer?" the chief thinks for a moment, then says "you can read the prayer and I will translate your words into my Lakota language, we will be a duet of prayer to Mother earth and Grandfather spirit.

"Oh great Creator of the Universe, hear our prayer,"
"Oh Great Spirit. Whose voice I heard in the winds.
Whose breath gives life to all the world.
Hear Me. I thank you for the gift of life, for your love,
your strength and wisdom.
Thank you for living inside of me and all around me,
for walking with me in beauty, and in reverence.
You are my radiant light.
Thank you for the gift of abundant life.
I ask you Great One to bring your energy to our
hearts, and in to our food so it may nourish us with
Your love. Amen"

The room is silent when we finish, duets are so lovely when reverently portrayed, I hug the chief and feel my heart warm with a love. Everyone gets up to hold each other in silence, it is a deep and mysterious feeling, without words we each hold, touch, look and feel the others needs and respect for the sacred space. I did not desire to speak for the rest of the evening, I want to keep all the energy from the moment inside my soul, I also want to hear what the others experienced during this one of the greatest days of my life.

I am thinking to myself, 'what did you do today young lady? Well, I followed a great Indian Chief into the King's Chamber of the Giza Pyramid, had a vision, said a prayer with the shaman, and received a huge bouquet of flowers.' This is the most unusual day, I feel as if I am in a film of the life I want to live, and I may be wearing this grin for a very long time, I suppose my entire lifetime. My brain and my heart are so incredibly full of gratitude.

The group decides to surrender to the fragrant aroma of the spices coming from the buffet dinner table, culinary delights, new Aramaic dishes. "Feel free to continue the discussion," Moon Bear suggests. "We have learned much, please share."

Daniel spoke up to let us know he researched the ibis bird and asks for the floor, he reads the words from the computer in the conference room, "the African Sacred Ibis was an object of religious veneration associated with the God, Thoth. At the town of Hermopolis, ibis birds were reared specifically for sacrificial purposes and at Saqqara where the world famous Step Pyramid of Djoser is located, archaeologists found over a million ibis mummies.

"These are very sacred birds, listen to this," he says, "there is a myth that tells about a tale which starts in the beginning of spring, winged serpents from Arabia flew towards Egypt, the birds called ibises meet them at the entrance, they did not let the winged serpents enter Egypt. The ibises killed all the serpents and because of this deed the ibis has become greatly honored.

"The paper tells of the ibis legendary bravery during hurricanes and storms. The ibis bird is the last sign of wildlife to take shelter before a hurricane or storm and the first to reappear once the storm has passed, and the ibis is the logo of the Maglan, an Israeli Special Forces unit."

"I have information," Meagan whispers, "I did a paper on birds. The ibis is a long legged marsh bird that walks along slowly and deliberately, scanning for small fish and other food hidden beneath the water's surface, like the God of Wisdom, seeing deeper than most. Also, in ancient Egypt, after the seasonal Nile flood, fertile mud would pile upon the riverbanks, the king's scribes would fan out across Egypt, resurveying the fields and assigning boundaries, measuring the land one stride at a time. To the ancient Egyptians, the wise old scribes looked and walked like the ibis birds surveying the riverbanks! The God Thoth chose the head of the wise ibis and the body of a superior man.

Daniel says, "I am personally requesting to be Osiris, the God of the Underworld, the God of Love and the God of Beer. He made the grains sacred, he was in charge of the sprouting of the vegetation."

"I want to be Isis, I want to be Hathor, I want to be Seth, I want to be Anubis, Horus, Bastet, I will take Nut, we all claim our special heroes."

Anastasia says, "What a creative way to learn about Egypt."

'I am enjoying the enthusiasm and easy rapport. I have a sense of peace and love for the people that love this land, the chief taught me the wisdom of the earth, the ancient minerals for healing and the powers of grounding, and it's connection to all peoples.' I think to myself.

In this country worshiping the gods was sacred; it provided fruits of prosperity and it was the law. Ancient Egyptian Gods had all the power, magic and wisdom. The Sun God Ra brought light and warmth for all the land. Without Ra, the land would fall into darkness. Crops would wither, life itself would vanish without the light of the sun. The gods were the Egyptian's true belief system for thousands of years, and they appreciated the gifts the gods bestowed upon them. This is what they knew.

Our group finishes and is reluctant to leave each other. How could we ever have another day as unusual as this day?

I walk slowly back to my room, what a day, my feet may never touch the floor. As I open the door I notice the hotel phone light is blinking and the maid placed a note under my door. Opening the letter, my eyes are playing with my heart, a request typed on the gold embossed stationary of the Mena House Oberi. 'Professor Doctor Amir invites you for a private tour of Cairo. My limo will arrive at 12:00, after your class with Doctor Zahi Hawass. If you would like to invite a guest, you will feel more comfortable, it will be my pleasure to escort them. At your service, graciously, Doctor Amir.'

Can this day get any better? I pick up the phone to listen to the same message. Then I call Amir, We will be ready at 12 sharp, in the lobby. "How am I going to get this smile off my face?"

"Keep it, it is God's gift to you. We will talk later, have a wonderful sleep, sweet dreams."

"You as well, Amir, may the Lord hold you in his arms all evening, and walk beside you each day. Good night."

Meeting Doctor Zahi Hawass

Amir stops by our table after our breakfast meeting. "I thought some of you might like to have illustrations of the original sphinx and Giza pyramid. They looked quite different 5,000 years ago, but, so would we standing in the sun, wind and weathering the earthquakes." He says as he passes out the drawings to those of us at the table.

"Professor Amir, this is a very rare picture of the pyramid, it looks like a white shining energy structure, gleaming in the sun. Polished limestone, I believe. Good work. May we keep these?" Jason asks.

"Yes, they are for you, they are just copies, I have the originals. Ancient Egyptians called the Great Pyramid, the 'Glorious Light.' This pyramid with its casing stones acted like gigantic mirrors and reflected light so powerfully it would be seen by some as a shining star on earth. Egypt is a magical place to draw. I have to get back to my office." He comes over to me and gently hands me the extra drawings for the other students. "Louise, I will be back for you at noon. Anyone else interested in joining us on a tour of Cairo?"

"Thank you, but we have an engineering class." They say together, then we all rose, walking outside together gathering in front of the hotel showing the drawings to the others waiting for the mini bus to the tent for class.

I had been an educator after college. I admire great instructors and I am proud of great teachers because accurate teaching has healing properties, for knowledge is power. Truth is the greatest healing medicine.

I want to speak with Doctor Zahi Hawass before his class morning seminar, as I am standing in line waiting to meet him, I overheard the others mention he studied in America. "I am originally from the Philadelphia area, from Bethlehem," I announce to him proudly.

"I received my PHD at the University of Pennsylvania in Philadelphia, we may have seen each other." He says with a gleeful smile.

I chuckle to myself, "Today I live outside Los Angeles in Newport Beach."

"A location of distinction. Can you really see the beach?" He asks in a pleasing manner.

"Yes, I am about 65 feet from the sand, on the sunrise side is the ocean, and the sunset side is the harbor. Have you been to one of our famous Newport Beach Christmas Boat Parades? It passes in front of my view, it is magnificent. Did you teach Egyptology in L.A?"

"Interesting. I taught archaeology at the University in California in Los Angeles. It takes a conference in Cairo to bring you to my class," he says letting out a hearty laugh. We both chuckle, "I find when I talk to people we are more alike than different. Laughing is great medicine and very bonding." We both agree! (He became the Secretary General of the Egyptian Supreme Council of Antiquities.)

"I will see you in the tent," he says with a sweet smile and twinkling eyes. He shakes his head laughing to himself.

The professor arranges his papers and maps and turns to the group. "Hello class, please find a seat, there are a few seats left in the front row. My name is Doctor Zahi Hawass, I am the Chief Inspector of the Giza Pyramid Plateau."

We sit admiring his display of large maps before our eyes, the pyramid prints. "You are looking at the plans of the Great Giza Pyramid of King Khufu. Rather complex isn't it? The modern passage goes down through the pyramid and then connects to another corridor that ascends to the King's and Queen's Chambers. The original passage continues downward into an unfinished chamber directly under the pyramid." He says.

"There cannot be mistakes. Imagine the genius minds coming up with these calculations? Do you think some of the shafts are a mystery? You are correct. The shafts are not connected to the outer faces of the pyramid or the Queen's Chamber, their purposes are unknown. At the end of one of the king's shafts is a black diorite ball and a bronze implement of unknown purpose. Diorite is a volcanic, subvolcanic or plutonic rock. Diorite is an extremely hard rock, Egyptians used diorite balls to polish. The hardness makes it a perfect stone to make a high polish, and to provide a durable finished work which is very important for making inscriptions. Do you think it may have been placed there for us to find to learn about their ways of working these massive stones?" He questions us.

The Great Giza Pyramid of Khufu, Constructed from 2560 to 2540 BCE (Before Christian Era)

"Imagine the pyramid casing of polished limestone, gleaming in the sun light in the day and reflecting the stars and moon light in the evening. Now you know why it was named one of the Wonders of the World." When Professor Hawass said these words his face beamed with pride, all his feelings show on his face and he lights the room with his enthusiasm. Do you possess X-ray vision? Is it possible for you to see into the great pyramid? Are you the holder of a mystical super power? Can you see the grand gallery inside King Khufu's pyramid? If so come with us as we enter the North side ascending the passage to the sacred room of mystical ceremonies.

"I love the illustration of the pyramid gleaming in the sun. What beauty the Giza plateau held for the Egyptians. Now it really does look like an energy structure, I could not imagine it before I saw this drawing, they were just words, now I get it," whispers James to Sacia as they both nod their heads.

"Do you know that we have not found the body of Pharaoh Khufu? Nor have we located any of his treasure rooms. If you have x-ray vision, would you please tell us where the treasure can be found?"

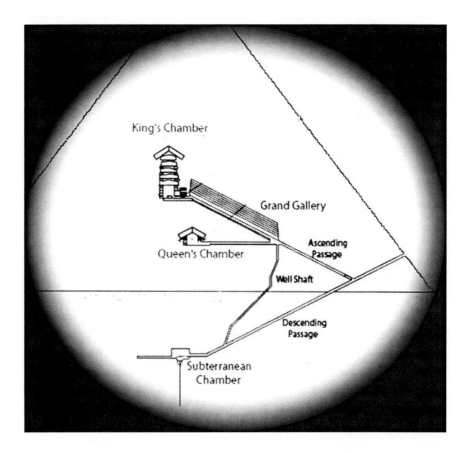

"The King's Chamber is 34 feet from east to west and 17 feet north to south with a flat roof 20 feet above the floor. Three feet above the floor there are two narrow shafts in the north and south walls. What is the purpose of these shafts? It is not clear: they appear to be aligned on stars or areas of the northern and southern skies, we thought they were air shafts for ventilation, but one of them follows a dog leg course through the masonry," says Doctor Hawass.

"The Great Pyramid needed to be completed before King Khufu died. The largest granite stones in the pyramid are located in the King's chamber, weighing 25 to 80 tons transported from Aswan more than 500 miles away. Ancient Egyptians cut stone blocks by hammering wooden wedges into the stone. They soaked the wedges with water. As the water was absorbed, the wedges expanded, causing the rocks to crack. Once they were cut, they were carried by boat on the Nile River to the pyramid. It is estimated that 5.5 million tons of limestone, 8,000 tons of granite, imported from Aswan, and 500,000 tons of mortar were used in the construction.

"Pharaoh King Khufu, learned practical experience from his father Pharaoh Sneferu, who was quite prolific at pyramid building. These are Egypt's largest pyramids and are the most massive ever built. As a young pharaoh's son, Khufu would take one of the chariots to visit the Red Pyramid that his father designed and was building for own his tomb."

Stories of adventure were blazing through my mind as fast as Egyptian horses chasing a runaway chariot. Father and son riding though the desert on their golden chariot to the Bent Pyramid at Dahshur.

"Quarrying, transporting, and placing the seven million cubic yards of stone for the three pyramids and adjoining structures at Giza was accomplished with a workforce of about 30,000 men. Each pyramid complex was started when a pharaoh assumed the throne. Of the Seven Wonders of the ancient world, the Giza monument is the sole surviving wonder. It was constructed during the 4th-dynasty for King Khufu, and his male heirs, Khafre and Menkaura. You understand for me being the Chief Inspector of the Giza Pyramid Plateau is an honor. Imagine Khufu's pyramid, smooth like glass, the polished limestone reflecting the sun's energy. King Khufu's pyramids will stand through eternity, to rise to the heavens, to the mighty Sun God Ra, to pierce the clouds and project rays of light for all to see the greatness of their pharaoh.

"These pyramids were not built by slaves to feed the egos of the pharaohs. No, the workers were willing builders, farmers, stone cutters and carvers, skilled artisans who wanted to do something great. The Great Pyramid, is built on 14 acres. Imagine 480 feet tall. Each base side, 755 feet long. The Giza pyramid weighs 5.9 million tons. Building this in 20 years was a difficult feat, installing 800 tons of stone each day. Picture the construction, 2.3 million blocks, involved moving more than 12 of the blocks into place each hour, night and day for 20 years." The professor declares.

Think about that fact. 2.3 million blocks, involved moving more than 12 of the blocks into place each hour, night and day for 20 years. Talk about a spirit of cooperation; just imagine the teamwork needed to build one level of the pyramid.

"The greatest architect Imhotep was the genius of all the engineers. The Greeks still honor him as a healing god, showing the level of his power." Imagine, how the boat building business grew during this time of building, many barges 130 feet long transported granite diorite blocks weighing up to 80 tons down the Nile River from Aswan. The pulleys and levers to load and unload the blocks from the barges. It took a decade to clear and prepare the 14 acres called the Giza pyramid plateau designed for the Khufu families pyramids and their sphinx to guard the secrets."

"I have a question, how did they cut the stones?" Sharon asks with great sincerity.

"Granite has a naturally occurring fault line, Dolomite is harder than granite therefore they needed to build a fire heating the stone to expand it. Find the fault line. Once it expanded, they poured water to contract along the fault line and the stone was easier to break apart.

"Dolomite's high magnesium content conducts electricity. Dolomite granite is a transmission stone, and the sealed shafts of granite keep the electrical charges present in the shafts, like an insulated wire. The charge was in the ground, and spread across the base of the Great Pyramid, concentrated up to the tip. Then the capstone was gold which facilitated the negative ions acting as a conductive path to move the electrical charges to the atmosphere. This was an energy structure." Doctor Hawass continues.

"There are limestone aquifers and porous rocks under the pyramid. When the rain fell, the water drained into those porous rocks and produced electrical charges. There was an increase in ground current and a change in the magnetic field when the water runs in, and the movement of water, like the Nile River rising and falling, creates a mild electrical charge. When there was a concentration of negative ground charge, added to a concentration of positive ions above, a discharge similar to a little ball of lightning was created.

"On the south side are the queen's pyramids. Three remain standing to nearly full height. The fourth is an empty tomb hidden beneath the paving around the pyramid, it is the tomb of Queen Hetepheres the sister-wife of Sneferu and mother of Khufu. It is a recent find, it was not suspected until the first course of stones and the remains of the capstone were looked at carefully.

"You must look around very slowly may discover interesting artifacts. A visitor was horseback riding, minding his own business and all of a sudden his horse caught his hoof in a hole in the sand. They reported it immediately to the authorities. It was a historic discovery!" Doctor Hawass says with a grin like a Cheshire cat and a twinkle in his eye. "This was such an important find."

The class wants to go horseback riding, to take a historic ride like that one, to be present to the moment, to be aware of holes in the sand by the rocks. For decades Egyptologists spent their time studying the great megalithic structures. This one hole in the sand led to discoveries of new tombs of numerous workers of the three pyramids of Giza. The scientists first found an inscription that was carved on the wall of the tomb that read, 'acquaintance of the king.' The man's bones indicated he was an overseer, with healthy amounts of tetracycline in the bones of his mummy. Imagine! That antibiotic was not even discovered until 1948, but it was in the Egyptian diet because of the recipe for beer. Ancient beer became medicine with its nutrient rich soil complete with algae and minerals.

"Did Khufu's son build the Sphinx?" questions James.

"Yes, the whole family were the strongest pyramid building family in Egypt, and the Sphinx is the largest statue in all of Egypt. Do you know if you could put it in a football stadium, it would take up the whole field. This was a different stone than the granite used in Sharon's question. The Sphinx is carved from limestone. Limestone was formed millions of years ago when Egypt was under the sea. Giza had coral reefs and sea bottom sand drying in different layers forming the sediment we call rock. One layer was hard and strong, then the next layer could be sand base, soft and weaker, more vulnerable to sand storms and earth water. When the ground water rises under the Sphinx it bleeds into the salt and then the body and causes deterioration. When Pharaoh looked at this magnificent piece of land, I believe he could have thought of building a Pharaonic family headquarters. It took 10 years to survey the 14 acres and carve the underground tunnels. Of course there would be underground passage ways. The infrastructure was an enormous project, and all builders know the foundation is the most important thought process, because you cannot go back and decide to add a deeper basement into a house that is already built. Do your diligence!

"Khafre, like all sons loved to be part of his father's greatness. I believe he build the Sphinx to say, 'we are the power of a lion and the mental power of a pharaoh, together we are a God.' The lion is power under control and the head of the man wearing the head piece of a pharaoh. I want to make this clear, the Egyptian Sphinx was a protector, not like the Greek legendary Oedipus Sphinx that ate people."

"What?" Todd questions with great enthusiasm.

"Yes, the legend describes a winged living sphinx with the body of a lion and the head of a woman. She would sit on the road to Thebes, now Luxor. When a traveler would pass she would ask the answer to her riddle or she would eat them. Oedipus cleverly thought of the answer to satisfy this crazy woman sphinx. 'Question. What animal is it that in the morning goes on four feet, at noon on two feet and in the evening on three feet?' Answer. The animal was man who in the morning of his youth is crawling on all fours, in the noon of his life he walks straight on his two feet and in the evening his old age he adds a cane and he limps on three legs.' The crazy sphinx in mental defeat, throws herself off the cliff to her death. We say that the Greeks were frustrated because the Egyptians were superior in mathematics, architecture, and astronomy. We were the superior builders of the world and all nations copied our beauty. The Giza Plateau represented the power and energetic possibilities of Egypt.

"Question, Jason?"

"The old pictures look to me to be a huge rock sitting on the sand. I can understand the rock being carved into a head, but where did the body come from?"

"Good question. The Egyptians quarried a horseshoe shaped ditch. The head of the Sphinx was an enormous rock above ground which they did use as the head. The rest of the body sits in a ditch the size of a football field made of limestone, and one day at a time they chiseled out the 20,000 tons of stone to make the Sphinx Temple in front of the Sphinx statue. You will hear more about this fascinating lion statue later."

"Also, Jason, you asked me about tombs earlier. Yes, in 2010 we discovered a double tomb of Shendwas and his son, Khonsu. They are from the 6th dynasty of Pepi ll, 4,300 years old. The tombs are west of Saqqara's Step Pyramid of King Djoser. This may be the largest cemetery of Ancient Egypt containing tombs from Egypt's earliest history up through Roman times." Professor Hawass states.

James says, "If you go to Torin, Italy, go to the Egyptian Museum in Torin, it is the only museum other than your Cairo Museum dedicated solely to Egyptian art. The collections were excavated in Egypt by the Museum's archaeological mission between 1900 and 1935. In those days the findings of the excavators were divided between the excavators and Egypt. I found the scans fascinating."

"Yes, James, I must to tell you about the amazing work we are doing here also with body scans. When Princess Ahmose-Meryet-Amon died 3,500 years ago in Luxor, she died because she needed bypass surgery to treat calcified arteries. She died in her 40s due to heart disease. She is the oldest known victim of heart disease. Researchers on the Horus study investigated 52 ancient Egyptian mummies, and found evidence of atherosclerosis in half of the mummies. Fascinating, isn't it? Even back then, with all their healthy fruits and grains. Maybe too much inflammation from a lifetime of beer?" He laughs.

"She was the sister and wife of Amunhotep I. She is buried at Deir el-Bahari." The brilliant professor adds.

Doctor Hawass receives a standing ovation, the crowd loves him. "I do not have time for more questions today. I truly enjoyed myself, make the most of the wonderful speakers available for you at this conference. I am sure I will see many of you walking around the area. Enjoy a healthy day, there is much to see in this mystical land. Do not just study, remember to play and you will have a trip of a lifetime to tell your grand children someday."

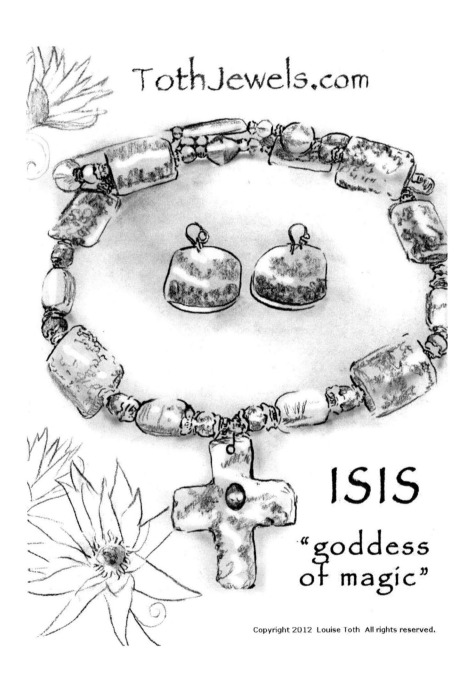

TothJewels.com

ISIS

"goddess of magic"

Doctor Amir's Cairo

'Rushing back to the hotel to change is so exciting, imagine a date with Cairo! Amir will be here at noon, that means lunch at the bazaar, best if I am covered out of respect for the Muslim traditions.'

I cover my head, pinning my scarf into place, taking a deep breath, standing up straight, closing the door of my hotel room and strolling through the lobby.

David opens the car door for us, "I am so pleased that Amir is taking you to church, what a treat!"

"You will enjoy the church, it is St. Mark's Coptic Orthodox Cathedral in Abbassia, we used to have ten here, but eight have been destroyed. First we have lunch, I need to stop at the club for a minute." Amir smiles.

The driver takes us just a stones throw from Tahrir Square to a lush island in the Nile, a 150 acre refuge for the Egyptian society, a country club, the Gezira Sporting Club. Gezira is Arabic for island. We arrive at the impressive long circular driveway, pass the tallest flag pole holding the country's red, white and black banded Egyptian flag.

Amir escorts us to the terrace where Cairo's elite would dine, the tycoons, intellectuals, diplomats and men of letters who made their fortunes through savvy business dealings and personal contacts with the British.

We walk to a table where a fashionably dressed elderly woman is waiting. He reaches over to kiss her and says, "I would like you to meet my mother, Alexandria, mother these are the women I was telling you about, Louise and Sharon."

"A pleasure to meet you, what a lovely accent, Egyptian, Arabic and British," I declare feeling the excitement of the terrace over looking the waters of the Nile River.

Alexandria laughs, "Many of my Egyptian friends have attached some British accent. The British have a monarchy as do we. This club was founded in 1882 and was reserved for the exclusive use of the British Army. The Viceroy of Egypt became part of the British sphere of influence in this region. In my forty years here I have developed the accent, it does sound quite proper and very 007. We have had some of the most exclusive James Bond party's here, the tuxedos and ball gowns, gambling, card games, it was an era of intrigue."

My mind is picturing all types of intriguing romances and business dealings. "I bet you have the most exciting stories of meeting in the shadows of this magnificent island country club." I am enchanted with the mother as well as the son. "I could see the British influence as we drove into the club, there is a very large croquet or lawn ball game going on as we speak."

"Oh, I like her, son, she is charming and has an observing mind." Alexandria adds with an classy flair. "Please stay for lunch."

"I cannot think of anything I would like more, your son was cared for very well, he has your sincerity and graciousness and I am proud to be in the company of such a kind family."

Amir orders for everyone at the table. "Thank you for allowing us to join you, Mother. It will be part of the Cairo tour, today."

"I miss my club in Pennsylvania, I used to belong to Saucon Valley Country Club. It also has a lovely winding driveway to a gracious colonial club house on over 800 acres. You would love it, there are three championship golf courses with a six whole short course for kids." I smile at Amir's mother.

"I would love it, I do love the country, I believe it is in the country if it has three courses."

"Yes, Alexandria, and the best thing is we had plenty of caddies."

"Now, I am jealous," Amir expresses, "I play a better game when I can walk up on the ball and a caddie clubs me. The winters? My mind is picturing 800 acres with virgin snow, ice covered trees, frozen water holes and rolling links, it would be a photographer's dream."

"Pennsylvania is a beautiful state, full of green rolling farm land." I am proud to say.

Alexandria questions, "How did you grow up? I am just curious? I noticed your cross. You are a Christian woman. Yes?" Did you go to church?"

"I grew up going to the Cathedral of Saint Catherine of Sienna. At high mass we had bishops, incense and plenty of pomp and circumstance. I am still attracted to details, because love is in the details. Beauty is all around us, in everything we do we can see beauty and beauty is love."

"We are Christians also, my son and I, and we attend the Coptic Orthodox Church, and we have a Pope. I, too, enjoy the splendid pomp and circumstance. I have been admiring your necklace with the Coptic cross. Did you get it at your hotel jewelry store?"

"I designed it. I love turquoise and I mix it with other stones and I do love the cross. I will design one for you. You simply tell me what you like and it will be in the mail to you. Your son was generous enough to offer me some private tours." I say with a heartfelt appreciation. "Actually, I want you to have this one," I take the necklace off my neck, stand in back of Alexandria and hook it around her neck. "It is lovely on you, I am very proud to know you will be my Egyptian model. Thank you," I kiss her on the cheek.

"Son, she is charming and talented, I am so pleased, I did not expect such a delightful day."

Sharon and Amir come to know each other, while Alexandria and I sit looking into each others eyes, with greatest sincerity, noticing how different our looks are on the outside and how similar our hearts are on the inside. "After brunch, and the church we will go to the Khan Al Khalili bazaar." I lean in to tell her.

We kiss Alexandria goodbye and walk through the exclusive club past the lobby, through the grand entrance to where Amir's car is waiting, as the driver opens the door I could hear smooth graceful music.

"What a wonderful voice," I comment. "Music so different from the American music, the sound tells me, I am in an exotic land."

"We will enjoy the bazaar, then the church and the Coptic area, then we can get to the Professor's Beer Party on time."

"We are going to have the best day," Sharon is wide eyed.

"Now let me tell you about this old Turkish bazaar, it was founded by the Emir Djaharks al Khalili in 1382. Because of his controlling nature, one of your heroes emerged. The Khan was responsible for a stranglehold on goods between the East to the Western world. The spice markets in the Khan, were controlled by a monopoly and forced explorers such as Columbus to find alternate routes for goods coming from the East, thus directly responsible for the discovery of the American continent." Amir discusses with great pride, "When man tries to control, someone will be forced to take leadership and find a new way, a new discovery will be born."

"We are going through it now, I am concerned. There is great frustration in the air." He says pensively.

"Do you have holdings in America," Sharon asks feeling his worry. "I do not mean to pry, I am concerned."

"No, the only things I own outside of Egypt are things in Dubai, which I bought years ago. I feel safe there, they knew my father when he was in the gold business. He sure spoiled my mother, she does have exquisite gold," he shakes his head and she rarely wears it. "You should have seen her in her day, when dad would take her to the club; it was completely exclusive, the ladies would feel safe dressing in diamonds, rubies and sapphires. Today she keeps everything in the safe, she says it is only safe in the safe."

The bazaar with all the shapes of brass, exotic fragrances, delicate cobalt blue perfume bottles, tantalizing essential oils, fine Alabaster, rose crystal, hard and soft leather goods, and Egyptian traditional water pipes, the Khan Al Khalili is a delight for the senses.

"Goods from all over the world arrive here, with our alley ways and off streets, you can find more Egyptian shoppers then tourists, buying everything from American jeans to fine gold jewelry. There are no shortages of souvenirs and tee shirts, but, you can also buy them at your hotel, in the airport and at all the sites on your itinerary," Amir smiles. "I am curious, where do you attend church on the west coast?"

"In California, I belong Mariners Church. It has the most amazing campus, with a chapel, school, worship center, great cafe, book store, and more, everything you need. I also drive to Saddleback Church for their amazing pastor and speakers. When I joined they were regular size, now they are called mega churches, prayer centers for all people. They hold about two and a half thousand a service with a number of services.

"We have an expression that translates to, 'there is nothing more beautiful then a passionate heart." Amir says respectfully.

"Where did Sharon go, we must stay together, we must, Sharon? Sharon where are you," he calls. "It can be worrisome here depending on the crowds. Sometimes we get gangs in town looking for trouble."

"How so?"

"You light skinned women are a prime target. Let's say you are a man and have a stable of fine black Arabian stallions that you love to ride and to show off to everyone 'how rich you are.' Then you see a magnificent white horse, would you not want to have it? A man riding a strong white horse has a real prize. Think how that horse stands out in his stable, his friends would want one. Where can I get a horse like yours, they would ask? I want a strong and beautiful white one, they would have to come up with a great deal of money, they are rare, especially the ones with blue eyes, yes?" Amir states feeling frustration.

"I do not like where this is going, the answer is, if they do not have the money to buy this beautiful strong white horse, they steal one, except now we are not talking about horses any more," I understand. Sharon was standing near us, hearing everything.

Amir excuses himself and walks across the street to a young man in the tobacco shop. As Amir gives the young man a note, they both stand with their backs to us, "I know who you are," the young man says, "my father, Miles Kalil, worked with your father in Dubai. I must talk with you, we have problems since the revolution. Can we talk?"

"Yes, tell me your thoughts, I am eager to hear," he replies.

"Have you liquidated your real estate, taking your money out of Cairo, keeping it in cash? We need you to protect our countries history. The artifacts, if we have another act like the one in Tunisia our ancestors words will be wiped off the earth. Some of the police here do not care about history, it would demoralize us, they did it in Baghdad, we must protect the Cairo Museum, it is Egypt's past. There are mob assaults by radicals against Copts, causing them to flee their homes."

"First I want to say your father, Miles, was a good man, I am so sorry he got shot by a coward sniper. Bad enough to be killed, but to be shot in the back by a cowardly sniper upsets me to my core. I remember in Marsa Matrouh when a mob of a thousand radicals, attacked the city's Coptic population. The 400 Copts barricaded themselves in their church while the mob was destroying 18 of their homes, 23 shops and 16 cars. I understand and believe as you said, many of my friends have liquidated. I agree, protect the artifacts, I am a professor, it is my sacred duty to the history of my Egypt." Amir smiles at the young man, and shakes his hand, "Good bye, it is important to meet you, it is fate to meet you, I know this to be true."

"Let's look around here then go to the Coptic area about 4? Amir suggests.
"What does Coptic mean?" asks Sharon, "I am Jewish."
"The word Copt is one of the names for Memphis, that was the first capital of ancient Egypt. Today Coptic describes Egyptian Christians, as well as the last stage of the ancient Egyptian language script. It was the language that was spoken in Egypt until the end of the ninth century AD, they held on to it for 250 years after the Arab conquest of Egypt. Gradually, it started to phase out and was replaced by the Arabic language. Even though you are of a different religion than Louise and myself, you will enjoy the Coptic area, Jesus was a Hebrew." Amir smiles, "Louise, did you see the Coptic Altar of the Church of the Holy Sepulchre in Jerusalem?"

"It is a sacred and magnificent site, it commemorates the death and resurrection of Jesus, just as the Church of the Nativity in Bethlehem commemorates His birth. I must tell you the truth, I did not originally travel there with a group for a spiritual journey. My son was sent to France by his snowboarding sponsor and he was a minor, I went along until he was picked up at the Paris airport and I met the French team. Then I flew to Jerusalem and I was picked up by my friends, the Barakat family who showed me around their city.

"I stayed at the King David Hotel and it just happened the Spanish King Juan Carlos was there and you know how one event leads to another."

"You are a fascinating little adventurer."

"What I really want to get is a belly dancing outfit, they have some in the shop next door." Sharon proclaims.

"Let's get one for you, how about you Louise, I know you would be great with a bit of ooh la la dancing gear?"

"I was quite good really, I took Belly Dancing for Flexibility classes. Does that qualify me to be a talented beginner in your country?" I am laughing at the ridiculousness of my comment.

"I think so." Amir graciously responds with a confusing look.

Sharon is trying on some conservative styles. The fabrics here are magnificent. "I am going to look at the hotel boutique, so I will concentrate on you, Sharon." I comment wanting to give her my full attention.

The store clerk offers Sharon a great price, she says, "I saw you talking with Amir, and I give good prices to his friends."

"You cannot be making any money on this outfit at all?" I ask her.

"You are correct, but when Amir has a dinner, he will buy 10 or 20 outfits for the guests and he gives me a big tip to have everything in order. All the store clerks know him, I have many special clients because of him. Handsome, generous, and a very good family. We respect his word. Here he comes now."

"Hello, Anka, how is your family?"

"Very well, thank you. I gave Sharon a deal, she is your friend."

"Thank you, tell Ata, your little princess, Amir gives her kisses."

"She will be seven next month, she is growing so fast. Give your mother a hello from me. She may secretly wish you were still seven, all mothers do." Anka responds with a warm smile.

"I ran into Amon, he is with a large group of his students. I guess you could call it a bazaar field trip. That sounded better in my head." Amir laughs to himself.

"We are getting tired, could we please go into the Coptic area at another time? Maybe we should have done that before the bazaar?" Sharon asks him very sweetly.

"Your wish is my command, we will see the Coptic area another time. There is so much to do and so little time," he jokes. "I will call my driver right now to pick us up on Bab Zuwayla Street at the corner of the triangle. He will take us to your hotel. God will put a magnificent sunset in the sky tonight. You need to have a sunset camel ride, later this week, I will take you both to the camel camp, it is just left after the Sphinx, then right on Gamal Abdul Nasser Street.

"Have either of you ever ridden a camel?"

We both shook our heads, no. "This may help, camels rest with their knees tucked under their bodies. Carefully watch the others to learn the movements of the huge animal. When you throw your leg over the back of the camel, the camel straightens his hind right leg, jerking you to the front left, then the camel straightens his hind left leg, jerking you to the front right.

You may feel like a rag doll being thrown about. I want them to please put up a sign. '#1, Camel Ride, #2, Doctor next door for Chiropractic Adjustments.' The doctor would make a fortune. You will have something unique to think of me riding with you, yes? We can be riding the ancient way, with the pyramids and the spectacular orange blazing sun as our backdrop." He chuckles to himself. "Would you girls like me to meet you at the party tonight?"

"Yes, Sharon exclaims, "I am going to have to think of a clever outfit and Cleopatra hair."

"I will drop you off and meet you at the party at 8. I have to go home to get something dashing to wear, also." Amir says with a smirk.

"Thank you, I do want to see the Coptic Museum in Cairo, later in the week, I understand it houses some of the world's most important examples of Christian Coptic art." I say with seriousness and respect.

"Yes, it is a great mix of native Egyptian and Hellenistic influences. You would also enjoy the Church of Alexandria, it was founded by Saint Mark the Evangelist in 42 AD and claims jurisdiction over all Christians in the continent of Africa. It spread Coptic art to Sudan and Ethiopia. Saint Mark is the author of the Gospel of Mark. There is so much to see. I must focus on impressing you with my Egyptian flair tonight." He laughs. "It is unfortunate David is busy, he would enjoy the lecture/party."

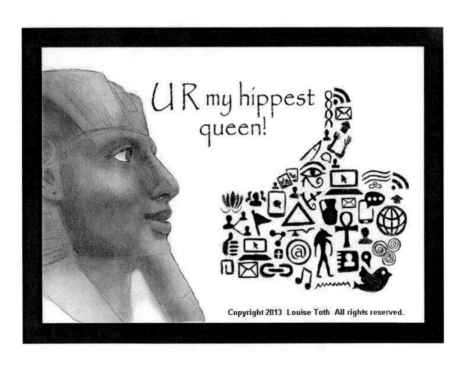

U R my hippest queen!

Beer, the Drink that Built the Pyramids

I look into the gift shop and find an 'Egyptian Queen Headpiece', a shimmery gold crown with gold braid trim, gold embellishment accents with a pearl jewel and a cobra snake with black jewel eyes over the forehead. I buy it and a gaudy fake gold bracelet. Then I walk by the hotel boutique when I see the sale sign on the door. There is a beautiful long light colored silk turquoise dress calling my name. I return the gaudy pieces.

Later, I am chatting with some of the members in my group as we walk through the hotel admiring everyone's outfit. It feels like an event just going to the event. We take the hotel shuttle to the tent. Then I enter the tent and see Amir across the room. He looks like Yul Brynner in The Ten Commandments, wearing an interesting Egyptian golden necklace.

"I am speechless." I keep looking at him with all his courage wearing a half naked Egyptian outfit. Even though he is an Egyptian man, it still takes courage. 'Beautiful necklace,' I think to myself.
"We have seats saved on the end of the row," he replies laughing. "Welcome to old Egypt, 2560 BC." He winks, "great dress."

The tent is packed, everyone is early for Professor Amon's lecture. Egyptian parties on the desert sands with camels, pyramids and the ancient Sphinx as a back drop. The sultry music vibrating through the tent, the high quality sounds of the orchestra, the gentle strings of the guitar, the cries of the violin, and the light sweet airy flute. Sharon looks comfortable in her outfit passing out warm baked flat onion bread on decorated trays while twenty Egyptian men in dark woven wigs are walking around, each holding large clay containers, carefully pouring us the special soupy drink. "Would you like the barley flavored with dates? Would you enjoy the emmer wheat sweetened with figs and honey? Would you like the original thick drink with residue of barley? Would you rather taste the filtered and strained translucent type?" It is an exciting opportunity to taste the beers of ancient Egypt.

"My favorite is the date beer," I encourage the young man to pour a second cup. It tastes like dates in liquid oatmeal.

"My name is Dr. Amon, I will be your instructor today. He holds his plastic cup high, this is the Nectar of the Egyptian Gods, the golden color of the rays of the Great Sun God Ra. Before it was a brew, a Bud, a Miller, Coors, a Heineken, a Corona, a Sam Adams, before Ben Franklin laid claim to his famous statement, 'Beer is proof that God loves us and wants us to be happy,' this beer was considered to be the gift from the Sun God Ra.

"Imagine you are a gatherer, and you fill your clay buckets with wild barley. Rain water falls into your jars, you do not give it a second thought, as time goes by that rain water moistens the grain, it starts to sprout beginning to produce sugar, as more rains come the wild yeasts convert the sugars to alcohol. You return to discover your clay jars are holding a tempting soup. The warmth of the Sun God Ra fermented your grain, and you now very are happy gatherers. You accidentally discovered the greatest drink in history, a drink made from barley.

"Let us raise our glasses and toast the majesty of the god. For it is you great God Ra who have produced the grain, warmed the land, and have filtered love through this beer, the truth is, every potential partner looks more desirable, yes, Ra is love."

Amir and I drank the soupy drink and soon are laughing, completely relaxed by the wonderful manner the professor introduces his topic. The young German gentleman next to Sharon stands, raising his mug toasting the teacher in his native tongue, soon everyone is joining in, each in their native voices, so happy to have such a interesting ambience in a learning situation.

Professor Amon laughs, "The sounds of all the languages is a melody to my ears, we are all having a joyous time, yet the Egyptian beer is only 3 percent alcohol and this really is young beer, not fermented yet, so at this time there is no alcohol content."

He continues, "7,000 years ago, the Mesopotamians and Egyptians were the barley growers, and where there is barley, there is beer. Beer is the world's most widely consumed and oldest alcoholic drink. It is produced by the fermentation of barley, and wheat sugars. It was known to be a rich source of nutrients, and is sometimes referred to as liquid bread. Because beer was low in alcohol and high in vitamins and minerals it was drunk from the cradle to the grave. Northern Africans were hunters and gatherers before the big drought, then all tribes from the Sahara moved to the Nile and its fertile valley for survival, they became agricultural farmers of wheat, barley, flax, and cotton. The delta became the pharaohs hunting ground for hippos and relocated wild animals.

"Long live Ra," the sun worshipers in the fields would sing joyous praises to his name. Let the Sun God rise again another day, so our fields produce, and we can have beer. Men are not complicated creatures.

How do you get the young men to come and work for you? The Great Khufu knew, "You promise them a beer." Isn't that tradition still used today, a young man needs help moving his apartment belongings, he calls a buddy and promises, "If you help me, I will give you a six pack. Beer was money and favor. It was currency to pay the workers, priests, tradesman and those that held a public office, everyone was entitled to a beer. Beer drinking had become an integral part of life for every man, woman and child, including the Pharaohs, they had our own royal breweries."

"In ancient time, the Sun God Ra's daughter infused the alcoholic drink. Yes, Hathor's sacred brew opened the imbibers minds to be in direct contact with the world beyond, it created the link between the heavens and the earth and the mystery of life and death were revealed. The Sycamore tree was the enchanting Goddess Hathor's sacred tree, friends and lovers would meet there to have a beer flavored with her special aphrodisiac, mandrake Mandragora, a plant whose bark contains an alkaloid, a narcotic, soon everyone was drunk, and their minds seeking the knowledge of the heavenly stars. The Egyptians were familiar with drug preparation from plants and herbs. Besides mandrake, they had cannabis and lotus blossoms, a powerful narcotic. Dropping a lotus flower into a cup of wine would release the narcotic." The professor states.

The burning of sacred incense often brought the energy of the ancient gods to mind, I am imagining the God Thoth standing in back of Khufu dressed in his native Egyptian attire, saying "Drinking beer was brought to its knees during the Arabic conquest of 640 A.D. when Egypt became part of the Moslem world. The Koran became law and the Koran states that holy Moslems practice sobriety. Egyptian brewing was outlawed. Previously the pharaohs turned brewing into a state monopoly and gave license brewing rights to entrepreneurs and priests. Many temples opened their own breweries and pubs, all in the service of the Sun God Ra but, that was before the sobriety of the new religion and the outlaw beer act, for that reason buying one of my beer labels was outlawed."

Soon I am picturing Steve Martin on the beer label in his Tut outfit, selling the brew from his 'condo made of stona, King Tut,' I am singing that catchy song, 'walk like an Egyptian.' Does this ever happen to you, when people talk about serious subjects, my mind goes to the absurd?

I began to day dream of my imaginary yacht on the Nile River sailing from the highlands of Ethiopia flowing into the delta emptying into the lowlands of the Mediterranean Sea, by the bustling city of Alexandria.

"I have to talk about the great drought, wind and sandstorms which devastated the Egyptian Old Kingdom in 2,150 BCE." The professor says. "So desperate were some they turned to Cannibalism. That is true, it is a fact of survival. In later times, not to long ago, when the Essex was sunk by a sperm whale in the Pacific Ocean in 1820, the survivors spent three months in the small whaling boat before being rescued. When the boat was found there were two members remaining, the members who died had to be eaten, they had made a pact. The tale is the famous novel Moby Dick, the name of the whale that started the terrible journey. Desperation changes our view of what we are capable of doing. The ancient Egyptian people were so poor, the crops dried up, and the crime rate went sky high. We had a well organized Mafia in Egypt, the police and guards that once protected the tombs were now robbing them of all the gold and jewels.

Crime does pay, in many cases. If you complained, do you think they would blame it on you? Even the priests that hid the mummies in caves removed all the gold and jewels they could from the sacred bodies."

"Let's change the subject." The class is feeling queasy. "Let me tell you about the Nile River Valley, it will be more relaxing for you to hear." Dr Amon says as he looks over the class.

"The Nile is the longest river in the world, flowing over 4,000 miles," Amon tells the group, **"the White Nile is the longer of the tributaries, but the Blue Nile is the main source of water and fertile soil. The White Nile was named from the light colored clay sediment in the water. The origins of the White Nile are in deep central Africa, as far south as southern Rwanda. The river flows north through Tanzania into Southern Sudan. The Blue Nile starts in Ethiopian, during the rainy season in the summer the rich deposits of black silt are washed along the river, it is the nutrients in this soil that covered Egypt with the best fields for growing barley, making the best and most healthy beer. It was the Nile River which enabled the Ancient Egyptian civilization to become what it was, the greatest of ancient civilizations known to man. The river would flood every summer, bringing Egypt rich black soil, and life giving resources to the desert. The Egyptians revered the Nile, and even had a celestial counterpart for it in the night sky, the Milky Way.**

"The life blood of Africa's commerce. Africa; diamonds, gold, and oil, the river brought the builders and the granite to the pharaohs, the Giza plateau was a lush tropical paradise, surrounded by their own waterways, moats and boat lanes."

At the time of the Nile's summer flooding, the local farmers could not till their fields, that was the time they went to help build the pyramids, the stairways to heaven, it must have been such an adventure.

"How many of you know it took a decade to prepare the land under the great Giza plateau? They cut boat channels to bring goods, a moat for work and a lake so the boats could turn around. The farmers joined the full time workers who came from all over the continent following the call of the great pharaoh. The Egyptians developed a calendar to predict the seasons of flooding, because they needed to store their barley and wheat, to sell to the overseers, to feed the pyramid builders."

"No more barley for me, it was quite tasty, thank you very much." The waiter comes beside Amir to fill our glasses and he responds with a warm smile.

"Remember the Egyptians did not invent beer, they had learned the art of brewing from the world's first known brewers, the Sumerians, Babylonian, and Assyrians in Iraq. The Egyptians gave us the best documentation of ancient brewing practices. Egyptian brewing was painted on murals in vaults, pyramids, and sacrificial chambers showing the importance and high esteem in which the art of beer making was held in Egyptian society.

I love the smell of the smoky incense, I am imagining King Khufu speaking, "It was lush and splendid with swaying palms. I am here to ask you to be aware, there are still about 50 percent of undiscovered treasures buried under the sands of time, waiting for you to find their locations and reveal their mysteries." I am imagining him on stage in a Broadway play.

"You all know the best vitamin for friendship?" Doctor Amon states.
"B 1"
"Ha ha, we will continue this lecture next week. I love your response to the party theme, and I want you to invite your friends that may have missed today's class. Same time, same station, good bye, I will answer questions after our next class," the clever professor has our attention, and knew when to leave us wanting more.

He receives a standing ovation from all of us well dressed Egyptian 2560 BC students. "Bravo. bravo."

**The Lord will fight for you;
you need only to be still.
Exodus 14:14 NIV**

Moon Bears Sacred Ceremony

After we over indulge during the scrumptious buffet, Sharon and I are ready for a long walk around the beautiful hotel gardens.

We notice Chief Black Elk and Moon Bear deep in conversation under the strong Persea tree. These wise Indian Shamans just knowingly gravitate to a comfortable place to sit in the morning light. They are under a tree that had a particular solar meaning associated with the rising sun, it is protected by Ra, the Sun God. We smile as we stroll quietly by, careful not to distract or disturb them. Tonight we stand in front of the mighty pyramid and hold hands around the Giza Pyramid, an experience of awe.

"I am going to enjoy this magnificent hotel today and just rest. I believe I will take a book to the pool, sit in the sun and hopefully catch a cat nap." I say, thinking, 'I wish I was as good as the others at riding, but I am not.' "Yes, I really need to unwind. The pool is calling my name. I will meet you at sunset. Enjoy your horseback riding, please go and have a blast. See you out front at 5:30."

We take the shuttle at sunset to meet the others already at the 'Great House of Eternity.' Moon Bear is standing next to the Giza Pyramid sweeping his clearing feather over each of the many groups, clearing their negativity, as he says a Lakota blessing. "Form a circle around the Great

Pyramid. What a special ritual, holding hands in prayer, around this Great Pyramid, each one lighting our own candle and repeating the words. It is an amazing dance of the souls in prayer." We all respect him and do exactly as he asks. The sun is setting and the evening sky is a hazy shade of awesome. This alone would be worth the trip. "Is that a picture of Moon Bear and Louise with the others at the pyramid ceremony?"

Talk about a high frequency! Imagine a thousand people from all nations joining hands in prayer around the Great Giza Pyramid. The magnificence of spirit, the power of God, the unity of energy fills each of us with anticipation.

I stand in front of the great pyramid with my lighted candle, my eyes wide as saucers imagining the great Pharaohs and kings of all lands, looking at this very same pyramid. Each one thinking the very same thought, how did they do this? Let me walk up the steps to God. It takes something like this to get such a large crowd quiet. I could see each person having an inner dialog with themselves. What have I done with my sacred life? Is it conceived by God, man's stairway to the heavens. Who will understand this emotion? How does mortal man conceive this? What is my purpose, what am I here for, little me, how can I make a difference, what shall I do?

"No matter what is happening around me, I will have strength, confidence and rest knowing that He will keep me safe. Challenges may come my way, but I won't be worried about them. I know that ultimately things are going to work out for my good. I know that no weapon formed against me shall prosper. People may be talking, trying to make me look bad, but I do not even give it a second thought. I know that my future is too bright to be distracted. I know they don't control my destiny. I just keep on being my best, walking in integrity, and meditating on the Word."

Amir says these words with the strong confidence of a man who has been through battles of his own.

"When the night is dark and the moon is the only light I see, I won't be afraid, as long as you stand by me." As long as you stand by me. I found myself saying the words out loud. "Yes, that is right, God, as long as you stand by me!" Many are leaving, I did not realize how long I am standing here, under the Great Khufu, 'House of Eternity.'

"Each time I am here to see the structure I think the only way to build the pyramid is if electromagnetism can nullify gravity. There are world geomagnetic energy grids and the ancient Egyptian megalith builders understood energy," Amon states in his official manner.

Professor Amon joins us, "Let us go back to the hotel for tea and discuss these ideas."

Ginger throws her arms up and declares, "Turkish tea in Egypt, I love it!"

"Let us hurry before the night air makes your cheeks a lovely shade of pink." Amir declares in his clear open way protecting me.

The Professor Amon, Daniel and Ginger are walking in front of us, "An entire population was inspired by these megalithic structures that had energy in the huge stones. The Great Pyramid was built in an area that had electromagnetic fluctuations, telluric currents that are generated in the land, when these lines cross, it is considered a sacred energy.

"The currents are similar to the dragon lines in China, where only a ruler can be buried, and temples and sacred sites are most often built there." Daniel lived in China for a year.

"Telluric currents are a phenomena observed in the Earth's crust. The currents are primarily induced by changes in the outer part of the earth's magnetic field. The electric potential on the Earth's surface can be measured at different points; the general direction of flow is towards the sun." Amon continues.

He took a breath, "Telluric currents can be harnessed to produce a useful low voltage current by means of earth batteries. Egyptians knew how to control energy, since the earth's geomagnetic field rushes back powerfully, just before dawn."

Professor Amon declares with pride, "Dolomite's high magnesium content conducts electricity. Did you know that electrical magnetism accelerates sounds? Picture the Great Pyramid sheathed in white calcium limestone so highly polished it shined like a mirror honoring the rays of the sun. The top cap was made of gold and silver, just picture it glistening in

the noon day sun for all of Cairo to see the power connecting the mighty universe. The casting stones were broken by the big earth quake in the 14th century that destroyed much of Cairo. After that the limestone was removed for mosques and building in the area. The pyramid had a limestone sheathing with a highly conductive core, the sheath was an insulator and the passageways of granite, which are slightly radio active, ionize and electrify the air. Fascinating, isn't it? When there is a change in a magnetic field, electrical power occurs."

As we enter the Mogul Room lounge our group is escorted to a reserved area. I think it best to enjoy the formality of the distinctive Turkish tea ceremony in an Indian Restaurant in an Egyptian country. The impressive tea set is next to our table, beautiful sterling silver engraved tea pots. The tea master asks if I would like sweet tea, and pours an entertaining long pour of the strong sweet tea. "When" he says with an English accent, as he moves the flow farther from the cup without spilling a drop. We are pleased, enjoying all the pampering, so welcoming and comforting it feels to be in the company of elegant manners.

"Would you please bring me a proper piece of stationary," Professor Amir asks the waiter. He takes the pen from his shirt pocket, "I have something for you, let me write down the recipe for the latest rage in beer, the King Tut Beer.

The Legendary Recipe: Ingredients

8.0 lbs. (3.6 kg) liquid wheat or barley malt extract
⅓ oz. (10 g) coriander seeds
⅓ oz. (10 g) juniper berries, dates or yeast

Mix extract with 5.0 gallons hot water, boil for 15 minutes. Crush coriander and juniper, boil 10 minutes, then switch off heat. Cool to fermentation temperature add yeast. Ferment at 65 °F (18 °C) for 5-7 days before racking for a further 1 or 2 weeks.

"That would have been fun fact to tell the class," I am impressed with the interesting information even though I know I will never try to ferment my own brew.

"I did not want to break Professor Amon's lecture, I am sure he knows, this information. The first bottle sold at auction for over $7,600.00 at Harrods, London. How fun, some went for $500, the rest of the bottles were about $70.00.

"How did they know what to do?" Ginger questions.

"Tutankhamun Ale was made from his mother Queen Nefertiti's secret kitchen in the Sun Temple in her city of Amarna. Egyptologists and University of Cambridge archaeologists have made 'Tutankhamun Ale' the most expensive brand of beer. They found several breweries, including the royal brewery when they unearthed 10 rooms meant for brewing plus they found the ingredients." Amir smirks, "They made 1,000 bottles of this exclusive and expensive beer.

"Our atmosphere is so dry in the desert towns traces of bread, grain and beer residues were preserved in the breweries at Amarna, Tut's childhood home built by Tut's father Pharaoh Akhenaten in 1350 B.C."

Ginger asks, "Professor Amon, you were talking about magnesium? I am low in that mineral, it is a mineral, right?"

Amon is thrilled to teach her, "Yes, most women's bodies are low in the mineral magnesium. An ion is a molecule or atom in which the total number of electrons is not equal to the total number of protons, therefore giving it a net positive or negative electrical charge. Magnesium is a common ion and necessary for the human body."

"We will leave you men to work out your details for tomorrows class," Sharon exclaims with an uplifting energy. "It will be exciting to have you as our teacher, Amir."

Amir quickly turns to me, "Louise, I almost forgot to tell you, I already bought the tickets for a concert at the Sphinx tomorrow night. It is excellent timing, you do not have a class. I will call after I check with the others. It will be a real treat, it does not happen often it is special, you must come and enjoy yourself."

Houses of Eternity

'Our God has put eternity in our hearts,' Ephesians 3:11.'

"Hello, My name is Professor Amir, your scheduled Professor Amon was called away, and I am substituting for him. I brought the pyramid prints with me and the drawings of King Khufu's boat. Best I call it a ship, I have a boat, this is a ship. I am going to use the notes he gave me, if you have questions please ask, this will be very informal."

"The great 'Houses of Eternity' were the energy vessels by which the pharaohs ascended to the heavens, the gateway to the stars. The Egyptians were focussed on creating a higher level of human consciousness. Building for the ages was not sufficient for the Egyptians, they were preoccupied with their Pharaoh's afterlife, the goal was eternity! They were responding to the spirit. The need for spiritual expression on a massive scale, with works of beauty that were in harmony with the land pushing through their limits to develop the most creative ideas and magnificent structures that were ever built. Dedicated to the worship of their gods, these pyramids are the best technology known to man. The surveyors laid out straight sides 750 feet long that differ by only a few inches. Think about that. Off by only a few inches. Could our engineers accomplish the tasks today?

"The Khufu family were the pyramid builders for generations. We do not know the number of men, some Egyptologists believe that the labor was organized into a hierarchy, consisting of two large groups of 100,000 men, divided into five groups of 20,000 men each, which may have been further divided into smaller groups according to the skills of the workers. What we do know is that the skilled craftsmen and engineers probably had to do the work from the inside out. That is my theory, anyway."

"Louise, you have a question?"

"Why do you think the pyramid was built from the inside out, when all others say from the outside with ramps around the pyramid?"

"Because the Egyptian designers received information from Thoth. I apologize for chuckling. It is charming you have the name of our great god. You were in the King's chamber. The base of the hard granite sarcophagus, in the chamber of Khufu's pyramid, measures 98 x 105 x 227 cm. Because of its size the sarcophagus must have been transported during construction of the chamber. This pyramid has the most complicated inner structures of all pyramids. It would have been impossible to haul it through the passages, through Grand Gallery and specially past the low entrance into the chamber. Louise, I was hoping you received some secret information? Remember how small the door was when you entered the Kings room? What do you think?"

"I agree, I would have enjoyed secret mathematical wisdom from the ceremony in the King's Chamber, or at least, some information about the treasure. But, I was wondering the same thing, the sarcophagus is one block of carved granite, way too large to fit through the doorway."

"Jason, you have a question?"

"Yes, I am having trouble understanding how they could pull the enormous blocks? They weighed two tons."

"Since we do not have a personal record of family history from the pyramid builders, we have to try different scientific principles. The stone block was laid on a wooden sledge tied down with ropes. The sledge was installed on tracks lubricated with watered oil. Sledges on tracks were used for transporting the stones. Tracks came from the harbor to the foot of the pyramid. The engineers built the tracts with different degrees. Four would be the average incline, some would be eight degrees up to 24 degrees up the flank of the pyramid. You needed about fifty haulers if the incline was five degrees using a rope roll. The rope roll is the only way the gradients are possible.

"Yes, James?"

"They had to use a grease. Copper grease is used today as a lubricant for car brakes. They had copper then, do you think that is the oil they would have used?"

"Great question, James. Possibly copper grease was used for the rope roll. The copper would have been grounded very fine. The copper abrasion would have been mixed with oil to make the copper grease. The ancient Egyptians did grind copper to an abrasive to polish marble."

"Yes, Jheri."

"How did they get the stones to the pyramid?"

"I have always owned boats on the Nile. I believe they used two boats with a raft in the middle between the boats, or the boats could capsize due to the weight of the stones on the barge raft type of floating device. The bigger the boats, the bigger the rafts, the more they could carry, but, that poses the problem of steering. I would have kept the weight about 50 tons, that would have been a very reasonable weight to maneuver. You know there was a harbor here and like any harbor there were loading ramps that sloped into the water."

"Yes, Yasuko?"

"How come we never see pictures of the pyramids of olden days in front of a harbor, that makes perfect sense." Of course, they would have boat lanes.

"I have asked myself that question many times. Yes, there were boat lanes. Maybe all the drawings were burned by accident when the library in Alexandria was seized by the Romans in the time of Cleopatra and Mark Anthony. The Ancient Library of Alexandria, in Egypt, was the largest and most significant house of knowledge holding ancient Egyptian texts. As hard as Ptolemy 1 Soter in 320 BC worked to preserve written works, most was lost in the fire accident during the Roman conquest in 30 BC. Let me finish the notes I have here from Professor Amon then I can sit after class.

"Were Pharaoh Khufu's bones in his tomb?" Daniel wants to know. "Truth is, the pyramids never did house the bones of King Khufu. There are underground tunnels between the Khufu pyramid on the southern side and his son Khrafre's pyramid on the eastern side, and

the entrance door to the northern side of the Sphinx Temple Complex, a network of shafts and only the engineers, labors and high priests had the secret knowledge. Both of his sons built pyramids next to their fathers. Khrafre finished the Sphinx Temple Complex. Could we even remove the 200 tons blocks today?

"He had his great ship sealed into a pit at the foot of his Great Giza Pyramid. For 4400 years the ship was safe, then in 1954 it was discovered, dug up and relocated! It must shake the rulers confidence to the core, as though he was being robbed of his sacred burial secrets." Amir states.

As he is touching the pyramid plans, I am imagining 'in my play I would have the professor do a calling to bring in the ancient heat, wind, smoke, and a trumpeting vibration, then the young King Khufu would stand on stage before our eyes.' Khufu would speak, "I came to the Egyptian throne in my twenties, and immediately started my plans for this, the greatest of all pyramids. I, the Great Khufu reigned for 23 years. I wanted my sailboat with me in the afterlife, that is why I requested it was buried at the foot of my "House of Eternity." I needed my 143 foot wooden yacht for when I would be sailing on the stars, on the Milky Way. Can you picture my boat with its tall strong masts and full sails etched into the sunsets and the orange colors of the desert sky? Can you picture me sailing on the stars? Yes, I know you can. You have an imagination as sharp as mine. Look up to the stars, and you will see me sailing on the Milky Way, the Nile of the heavens."

Khufu speaks. "Let me tell you; the Khufu ship is one of the oldest, largest, and best preserved boats from all antiquity. My boat is the world's oldest intact ship, I commissioned a masterpiece of woodcraft. Do you believe me if I told you it could sail today? Believe me, it could! By the way, so that you will not be confused, some refer to me as Cheops.

"Over 4,000 years old, it was my ritual vessel, a solar barge style, to carry me, the resurrected king along with the Sun God Ra across the evening heavens. The ship was my funerary barge to transport my embalmed body from Memphis to Giza. I used it as a pilgrimage ship when I would visit holy places. My barge was then buried for me to use in the afterlife." The pharaoh says in my day dream.

I would have the winds blow, incense burn and the thunderous sounds high above the stage, as if to come from the heavens, as great Pharaoh Khufu disappears.

Can you imagine, you are in your twenties, you are king, the Nile is bountiful, a beautiful sailboat is yours for the asking. The Nile River with all its lush blossoming meadows, the beautiful Nubian princesses, the palms swaying, dates dropping at your feet. It is good to be king?

"The ship is now housed in the Khufu Solar Boat Museum, a small modern building next to the Great Pyramid. It was discovered in 1954 in 1,224 separate parts." Professor Amir lectures.

"Question, Todd."
"How long did it take to assemble the 1,224 parts?"
"The reconstruction took 14 years, the boat had U-shaped holes allowing for the boat to be stitched together by ropes or vegetable fibers. It appears that the boat was deliberately dismantled. There are several boat pits near the pyramid of Khufu, five to the east and two to the south."

"James, you have a question?"
"What material did they use to build?"
"Cedar was the building wood of choice. The cedar was shipped to Egypt from Mesopotamia for use in building ships and homes. The Phoenicians established trading alliances and brought back gold, ivory, grain, paper, and turquoise from the generous Nile Valley. The Egyptian culture was also trading to the south with Nubia, and Kush. Ship building prospered and the flowing Nile River with it's date palm groves and fertile fragrance was the true highway of the Egyptian life. The designers of the pyramid complex designed it all as a port for the Netherworld. The boats would bring the pharaoh and the royal family on the eternal journey of the sun, which they embarked upon in the world beneath the surface of the world. Very impressive, indeed. The building of the pyramids brought many other businesses to Cairo. If the Egyptians only offered a commodities market. I could have made a bundle of money because the grain dried up and became very valuable. Who would have invested in grain and gold futures?"

"One more, Meagan?"

"Was it a drought that destroyed the spiritual integrity of Egypt?"

"It was the drought 4,200 years ago that was the demise of the spiritual integrity of Egypt's great civilization, and the central government weakened." The professor agrees.

"Lake Tana varied with differing sediments registering lush tones and drought during the previous 15,000 years. The rains stopped, the lake dried, there was not an abundance of water to flow into Egypt. Without water the agriculture dried, the plants were not healthy enough to grow vegetables and fruits, the cattle died without grain and grass to eat. The fish in the Nile were eaten, the tombs robbed for gold to buy food. You now have a dehydrated, starving country that was dry for nine decades. Seismic investigations with sound waves and carbon dating verified that fact. Scientists measured sediment from the high bed of Lake Tana in Ethiopia, where the Blue Nile is born and flows north joining with the White Nile at Khartoum in Sudan flowing through the lowlands of Egypt to the Nile Delta at Alexandria. Without the heavens giving rain, the earth will dry and the people die. That time line is about 2200-2100 BC. Good question, Meagan, I hope you kept your grain futures during the drought." Dr Amir laughs to himself.

"Please copy the list of kings and their pyramids on the back of the prints I handed out in the beginning of class. If any of you want to sit with me for a few minutes, you are welcome to ask me uncomplicated questions. Thank you, it is a pleasure to teach this class, I enjoy it as much as you."

Pyramids of the Great Pharaohs

King Djoser 2624-2605 Saqqara
King Sneferu 2575-2551 Bent Pyramid, Red Pyramid, Saqqara
King Khufu 2551-2528 Giza
King Djedefra 2528-2520 Abu Rawash
King Khafre 2520-2494 Giza
King Menkaure 2490-2472 Giza
King Shepseska 2472-2467 Dahshur
King Neferirkare 2446-2427 Abusir

These are the pharaohs of the early dynasties. Their possessions are the most studied artifacts in the world. The dynasty dates differ, because there is overlapping.

Protodynastic Period, Naqada III, Dynasty 0.
Early Dynastic Period 3400-2980, 1&2.
Old Kingdom 2980-2475, 3 to 6.
First Intermediate Period, 2475-2160, 7 to 10.
Middle Kingdom Period, 2160-1788, 11 & 12.
Second Intermediate Period, 1780-1580, 13 to 17.
New Kingdom of Egypt, 1580-1090, 18 to 20.
Third Intermediate Period, 1090-663, 21 to 25.
Early Period of Ancient Egypt, 663-641, 26.
Arab Conquest—641-now. The Egyptian power is in the hands of the Muslims.

Professor Amir is swamped with beautiful admirers. "Tell us about the radar?"

"The SIRA radar was deployed in Egypt for mapping subterranean complexes beneath the Egyptian pyramids. Arrangements made with President Sadat of Egypt resulted in three decades of top secret excavations to penetrate the system. Chambers of the Deep?" Amir acknowledges.

"Yes, Sacia?"

"Is it the legendary City of the Gods that is sprawled beneath? Complete with an underground waterways. Are there massive chambers the size of churches with enormous statues, the size of the Valley of the Nile? Will men enter the subterranean rivers and lakes looking to penetrate sealed chambers?"

"If things are top secret Sacia, I do not have permission to discuss it. Great questions though."

"Ginger?'

"Do you think the scientific examination of the world's key pyramid sites would reveal them to be sophisticated harmonic structures? Do they mirror positions of the planets? Are the stones in the Great Pyramid harmonically tuned to a specific frequency or musical tone? Could the sarcophagus in the centre of the Great Pyramid be tuned to the frequency of the human heart beat?"

"I did not have toning forks to test this theory. Many people believe as you do about harmonic freguencies." Amir adds.

"Hello, my name is Anastasia, I have a question about the vale of tears and the Ka of the soul?"

"This is complicated and may be the only question. The phrase vale of tears, or valley of tears is a Christian phrase referring to life and its earthly sorrows, which are left behind when we leave the world and enter the kingdom of God or heaven. The world as we know it is a vale of tears, to die and be with God as a better existence than an earthly one, was relatively unknown among the ancient Egyptians. They thought they were coming back again, that is why they mummified their bodies for their return. They loved the religion, culture, and customs of their daily lives so much that they wanted to continue them in the next life.

"The ancient Egyptian pyramids are the most famous historical monuments devoted to the dead. The ancient Egyptian society was an intelligent society that made elaborate tombs and mummification rituals. The tombs were houses for the hereafter and were carefully constructed and decorated, just as homes for the living were. Mummification was a way to preserve the corpse so the soul, Ka, of the deceased could return to receive offerings of the things they enjoyed in the present life.

"The process by which a Ka, or soul, became an akh was not automatic upon death, it took a 70 day journey through the duat, or Otherworld. There was judgment before Osiris, Lord of the Dead where the heart would be weighed on a scale against the Truth Feather of Ma'at. If the Ka, or soul, was not properly educated for the journey, it would be fraught with dangerous pitfalls and strange demons. They needed to study Thoth's Book of the Dead to learn the secrets or knowledge as we do today from the wisdom of our Bible. These books were written as guides to help the deceased successfully navigate the duat journey to the other world, for us, heaven.

"If the heart was in balance with the Truth Feather of Ma'at, the Ka or soul, passed the judgment and was granted access to the West as an

Akh who was ma'a heru "true of voice" to dwell among the gods and other akhu. At this point only was the Ka, soul was deemed worthy to be venerated by the living through rites and offerings. Those who became lost in the duat or tried to avoid judgment became the unfortunate mutu, the Restless Dead. The hearts that were heavy with evil and weighted more than the Truth Feather, the Goddess Ammit waited patiently behind Osiris's judgment seat to consume them. She was a combination of the deadliest animals in Egypt: the crocodile, the hippopotamus and the lion. Even today the hippopotamus is the leading cause of human deaths by animals in Africa. Being fed to Ammit was to be consigned to the Eternal Void." Amir continues.

The Giza pyramid was a place where men become gods to awaken the memory of the spirit life. Their spiritual training started in childhood, they had master craftsmen carve and paint the murals on the walls of their tombs in the Valley of the Kings. The hieroglyphs in the books of Thoth were the magical spiritual words to guide them to their afterlife. Thoth's books were their bible, their book of knowledge. The bible guided them on their spiritual journey. Imagine writing the words and pictures of the bible on the walls of your burial tomb. This process took years to do, in checking the work and reading the words they learned the importance of Thoth's magic. The magic of wisdom of their creator. These were the highly evolved citizens of the greatest culture in the world, why, because they were originally a society of truth and beauty. Many were seekers of the knowledge their god's purpose for them for the first thousand years. Only later did they fall into a darkness due to the great famine. Their anger from the pain of generations of famine, caused them to become an idol worshiping warring nation using slaves to work the pyramids.

"Come, we have another class," Sharon says as she pulls me away.

Concert at the Sphinx

"You will be mesmerized tonight, 'An Evening Under the Stars,' in front of the Sphinx. I have the very best tickets for the show. My mother insists I take her, and her cousin Kasha. Are you available? We will wait in the lobby for you to come, unless Mother wants to have a drink in the lounge, I will look for you.

As I stroll in the lounge, I pause a moment to watch Alexandria and her old neighbor Omar leaning in to each other, elbows on the bar, intently listening to each others words. The moment they saw me, they break into song. "Every little breeze seems to whisper, Louise."

I stand here laughing. What a fun memory. Charming people in a delightful atmosphere.

It is a beautiful moon lit night, walking to our seats under the blanket of winking stars, the peacefulness of the open air, an appreciative crowd, the wonderment of the pyramids and the giant Sphinx is a sight that will be embedded into my mind, and soul forever. A body of a lion with the head of a man, the symbol of animal power and of human intellect. A whipping tail wrapped around a giant of a lion, his back paws ready to pounce.

All of a sudden Alexandria screams like a teenager as the show starts. Ali stood on the Giza plateau looking at the crowd, the Sphinx, and the pyramids. The audience stands and applauds his love. What an energy force standing in front of the last Wonder of the World. The stage goes dark for a split second, two laser lights radiate from the side of the platform, soon smoke roses from the center as if to command the Pharaoh's revival forces, a hologram of the Ancient Nile Valley covers the stage, the light show begins. I sit in awe being transformed by a wild ride of lightwave energy.

"I heard the Millennium celebration with dancers, fireworks, lights and lasers woke up the crouched lion." I laugh to myself. "My friends Melinda and Jim told me to watch it on television, even with lavish electronics and an extravaganza of music, it was still so much more than an artistic spectacle. They kept telling me how surreal it felt to be dressed in elegant attire standing next to the pyramids during the light show." I whisper leaning quietly toward Anastasia. "They are my neighbors from Newport beach."

"Oh, my dear, I wish you were here. We enjoyed dining in white, carpeted tents catered by the best hotels. I talked with some of America's Millennium Society. They had 500 of their members in attendance. They checked all over the world to find the perfect site. They considered Machu Picchu, Stonehenge, the lost city of the Incas in the Andes, but nothing could compare to our last surviving monuments of the ancient world. Our pyramids are man's testimony to the greatness of the human vision.

"We Coptic Christians loved the idea. We had some opposition from the Islamic groups because we celebrated a milestone on a Christian calendar. The party did cost at least nine million dollars, but selling the international rights to TV stations around the world balanced the price." Amir stated. "You should have seen mother and her friends. The marvel of the concert was intensified by the fireworks exploding over the pyramids."

Alexandria says wearing a contented grin. "Louise, they had a giant image of my favorite Egyptian diva's face projected onto the side of the pyramid. The French musician created an electronic opera inspired by the great Sun God Ra traveling from dusk to dawn. A thousand artists preformed the dreams of Ra while dancing on a four tiered stage. It was an extravaganza of a lifetime. Across the Nile there was a flotilla of sailing boats wearing white lights and white balloons. I will not live long enough to ever see anything like that again."

"God has set signs and wonders in the land of Egypt." Jeremiah **32:20**

It is a reminder that only the most stubborn of man would have an ego, step out of your world, and sit near a Sphinx the size of a football field. If that does not humble the spirit, the milky way overhead may be the message from God, telling us that we need to be in astonishment of His mighty works. Have less about us and more about God. It is not about us!

The mysteries, events, prophecies and people of the ancient sacred texts have invited me to ponder secrets. Egypt challenges me to explore the life I see with my heart. Every circumstance whispers to me when I take the time to listen. Here in Egypt, I am forced to listen. The magnitude of the events shake me to my core.

'What a day for a girl born near the quiet Amish country. The stars tell a story of peace and gentleness when viewed from afar, how lucky we are.' I think to myself, what moments in my life can compare.

Amir woke me from my trance. I was deep into myself, relaxed in the moments of contemplating the universe.

"Wake up sleepy head. I will pick you up for lunch at the club tomorrow, how about one o'clock? I have to get the other ladies home. Good night." Amir is so pleased with the evening. "I will see you tomorrow."

He has a grin on his face, knowing how much I respect him for his efforts. Great to have my own private Security. I smile at the ambiance of the evening and walk into the hotel.

"We all heard the concert from here, the lights were very cool, something very special, yes," they ask me about the laser lights.

"You will read about it in the morning paper, I will let it be a surprise. Good evening." I walk toward my suite, ready for some hot tea.

Sharon calls the next day. "I heard all about the concert, I wish I had been there."

"I just woke up, is it 10 am? I was really tired. Sensational, just like everything on this trip. What are you doing today?" I inquire passively.

"I am helping set up for the Pyramid Party. Professor Amon, 8:00. Part 2." I expect to see you there."

GREETINGS

Beer Party II

I dress in a proper teal knit suit, very appropriate for the country club, a green turquoise necklace, earrings and bracelet to match. Light lipstick. I rarely wear much makeup or concealer, I like being natural, pulling my golden locks straight back into a pony tail. I pride myself on being the clean cut girl next door, able to dress in a flash and look smashing. I check myself in the mirror and am ready to walk through the lovely hotel corridor to the lobby.

Are my eyes playing tricks, I walk close to the gentleman hoping he would feel my presence and if I am right he will say hello.

"Louise, is that you?" He looks at me with surprise, hugging me, laughing and giving me a warm embrace.

"Michael when did you arrive?" I feel so happy.

"We checked in last night," he says so pleased to run into me again.

Just then Amir walks into the lobby.

"Amir, I would like you to meet some of my friends from London." Amir could see the happiness I am feeling running into old friends in a foreign land.

"I would love if you could please find it in your hearts to join us on such a short notice, I would enjoy your company, I am taking Louise for lunch at the island. Please join us," Amir's training and graciousness impress me.

"Yes, we would be delighted, we were just going to the dining room for lunch and being with friends would be better, this is so unexpected. How wonderful." Michael rejoices at the thought of new things.

As we walk outside, Amir's driver opens the doors for us, he grins at me saying, "My lady." Off we all go to the island in the Nile, to the impressive Gezira Sporting Club.

Alexandria is outside waiting, her car pulling up a minute before her son arrives. "Mother, I am excited to introduce you to Louise's friends."

"I am in heaven," mother cries, "I am having the best time since Weezie came into my life, she is quite funny you know. Let us order a feast, I will make this lunch last a long time. I have all of you to myself. Let's order everything! When did you arrive?" she asks Michael and his wife.

"Last night and it was a celebration landing, I saw a wild light show from the air. We were circling the area, the airport was backed up. What a gift for us to see this event, timing is everything. First let me tell you, you have a breathtaking city to fly into at night, the monuments magnificently lighted, I was appreciating the beauty of the Sphinx when all of a sudden two laser beams shot up at us, I could see the smoke, then a hologram of vegetation, palm trees, reeds, the way Egypt must have looked in the olden days, then I saw the crowd cheering?" Michael conveys his image.

"An awesome laser show, lifted our spirits, I am fascinated by laser shows, I am like a kid whenever I see them," Alexandria says with great pride in her Egypt. She continues walking toward the terrace.

"What a view of the Nile, so relaxing, I love the water, I miss the smell of the water, it feels comforting to my soul, I am home." Michael lives near the Thames River. "Thank you, Amir for inviting us."

"I enjoy the peacefulness of water. I live on the Island of Zamalek full time now, this city is a garden of plants, cool leafy streets lined with villas and 19th-century apartment blocks. I love the harmony, this area is one of the most attractive parts of Cairo and a home for many European expatriates, very British and French. I enjoy walking down the street and sitting outside for my coffee, in Egypt, we have open air ahwas, or coffee houses. You are British, you fit right in." Alexandria says full of joy.

"Your table is ready, right this way," the gentleman seats us at the corner for the best view of the sailboats on the Nile.

"Mother loves living here on the island. She has plenty of culture, Egyptian Opera House, art galleries and museums, performing arts at the El Sawy Culture Wheel Center. She is so proud of her heritage and all the history of her native Egypt." Amir shows his love for the woman who raised him so well.

"Has my son taken you to the Napoleon Bar. The French invaded us also, the Emperor Napoleon had his private quarters at the unique Shepheard Hotel in the heart of downtown Cairo. The hotel was the romantic rendezvous place for allied officers, politicians and spies during World War II. It had what I loved, a famous terrace, with a shaded view of the comings and goings of the people on Ibrahim Pasha Street below. It was the playground for international aristocrats having their laced tea, speaking of business deals, affairs and trading political secrets.

"Someone burned down the hotel, what kind of example does that show the world. Destruction to our heritage that cannot be replaced, it is my biggest fear today. That someone will bring harm to our museums and destroy our artifacts. We must have a spiritual calling to protect the artifacts of Egypt!" Mother fumes.

"How can we have a drink there if it burned down?" Michael teases.
"You are funny, they built a new one, silly." She laughs.
"Excuse me, Alexandria, you will like the buffet," the waiter suggests, "it is the lamb dish that you enjoy so much."
"Thank you, we were all admiring the abundance." We each agree, and off we go like hungry school children after recess. How lovely to be standing here in this spot deciding upon the tasty array of gourmet foods while watching the boats passing.

I thought, 'it is just like home, I love the smell of the sea, watching the boats pass by, the light dancing on the water, the gentle current.' I look at Amir, "I could stand here all day and watch the water."
"It is my favorite thing to do also, it is mesmerizing to me. Takes us back to the womb. Being near water feels like peace and comfort in the womb of nature." He says sincerely. "I would appreciate a hammock under this tree or rocking chairs. All the stress is leaving my body, I may fall over."

"Michael, you seem like the kind of man that likes to travel, what cities and countries do you love and have you had any problems in this area?" Alexandria asks of him.

"We have always loved traveling, and have traveled extensively, but when we were in Tunisia, we had some uncomfortable experiences."

"President Ben Ali stepped down after 23 years of corruption. It was immoral the way his wife went shopping in Paris, using the country's presidential jet. White collar political criminals, that was what they were, the money alone for the jet fuel for her personal shopping trips could feed a nation," Alexandria proclaims upset at the scandal.

"Mr Abdul, could you please bring me a large ice water and a screwdriver," she laughs, "I need a screw driver and a hammer and I could do with a few hours at the shooting range."

"Why do they protest?" Michael's wife wants to understand.

"Look into the French Revolution. Absolute monarchy ruled France for centuries. They had extreme poverty, inflation, government corruption, dissatisfied youth, unemployment and human rights violations." Alexandria declares. "Today we have economic conditions of poverty, many people are hungry and scared. They want to have human rights, they want a roof over their head and food on their table, they want democracy with a free and fair election, they are tired of corrupt dictators."

The French people revolted, the needs are the same basic human rights, but now many Arab Muslims put their demands under the umbrella of their religion. We have the frustrated poor Arab families wanting respect, wanting to have democracy. The revolution started in Tunisia. The name given to the revolutionary wave of protests in the Arab world is called the Arab Spring.

Alexandria continues, "Here in Egypt, as in Tunisia, we are having many poor men finding their identity in their rage. What frightens me is fact; young men can get carried away in mob situations and damage is done when they are fueled by the organized extremists whose specific job is to cause chaos! It is the extremists spurring the violence, it is manufactured violence. A group can be relatively small and restrained, but rapidly go out of control when groups of extremists are brought in to specifically rile up the crowd to target diplomatic compounds. Mainly, US. and Israel Embassies. We see medieval attacks in the 21th century. Shameful."

"Alexandria, what do you think can be done to end this anger. The cost to life, property, and the human soul, I am sick of the fighting in this world. You live here, this is not the Middle East, yet, you all are neighbors. How would you handles some of these problems?" Michael asks with a heavy heart.

"The Arab nations need to spend time focusing on their own countries. Our former ruler stole 70 billion from our countries budget, we do not have money now, but we do have man power eager to work. Put down the weapons. Respect women. The new government spoke of equality for women. I do not see any equality." She continues. "As for Israel, I say leave them alone."

"The State of Israel, is a parliamentary republic in the Middle East. It is surrounded by Arab countries, Egypt, Lebanon, Syria, and Jordan. I believe, if the Jewish people would put down all their weapons they would be destroyed. But, if the Arab surrounding countries would put down their weapons, there would be peace. I feel it is as simple as that! Israel is a small country, the size of Vancouver Island." She states.

Jesus taught peace and respect. A healthy spirit thrives in peace.

We all chuckle at her quick mind and easy way of defusing the topic. "I love these conversations Michael, I want to die someday with a brilliant mind and a truly passionate life but, I do want to apologize for my rude conversation. Did you ever have a Déjà vu, Michael?"

"Yes, I have had some Deja vu feelings."

"I am a very fast read of people, I had to be, my life depended on it, a very long time ago."

'That is the first time I heard my mother speak of what I long suspected, before my birth, when she was young. She must feel so comfortable to utter such words. She has a kinship with the good doctor. Michael looks exactly like the photo of the British officer mother was so close to. My mother always has an infinite amount of knowledge, I always wondered how she could know so much, as if she worked for the British Intelligence. My mother, yes, of course, she was thinking of herself sitting across from the handsome gentleman in the uniform of the British military.' Amir thinks to himself, 'I wonder? Is there more to this? I do not have an Egyptian nose?'

I know exactly what is going on. I stand and ask if we could be excused for a few minutes, "I would like to see the grounds of the club and the flower garden." I say eager to calm and support Amir.

"Louise, do you remember mother telling you this club was founded in 1882 and built for an exclusive resort for the British Army when they took over Egypt? I am trying to piece the events together. In 1922 Egypt became independent, in 1943, the British Army surrounded Abdeen Palace and threatened to overthrow the government because there were reports that King Farouk openly supported the German Army. Therefore the British troops remained in the country until 1952 when Nasser rose to power. Even if I write a time line, I am so thankful for the British and I dearly love my mother, so I will just be grateful for all things and let my mind rest." Amir empathizes with his mother, and decides to not question.

"Let's go to the Pyramid party tonight." I suggest.

"That is just what I need, some mindless fun," he smiles tenderly. "Let's finish our food then say good bye to mother and head back. Mother will want to stay, she has a bridge game later with her friends." We sat down, Amir's heart is racing and his sharp mind has a dull numb feeling. Did you ever feel that sensation as if you were in shock at news that overwhelmed all your senses and you could not function? That is what Amir is going through, it is getting worse as the moments were turning into minutes, yet, time is standing still. He could not speak.

I took over, gave mother a kiss as some of the ladies came in to invite her to play bridge. Perfect, I hug each of them reminding them to play for costume jewelry, they giggle and all is well.

"Michael, we have a fun beer party event tonight, you will love it, I do want to invite you and your wife. The professor did say we could bring guests, you will love the history of the pyramid in the unique way Professor Amon does his presentation. It is at 8:00 tonight in the big tent. We have to dress in Egyptian attire similar to the year 2560 when they were hiring for the workers to build the Giza Pyramid. Let's stop at the hotel gift shop, they have some Khaleegies, the long sheath dress that men and women wear."

As we saunter into the gift store, we notice there were only a few left. "There is a big party tonight," the store clerk expresses friendliness.

"They are not expensive, let's just do it now," Michael says as he signs the bill to his room. "This does not even cover that lunch your mother picked up. I am grateful to know you. Let's meet in the lobby at 7:30. I would enjoy having an Egyptian party at home," says Michael to his wife. "Cultural creativity."

"You are so sweet, you will get very interesting ideas at this party, Amir gave me the recipe for Tut beer, I will give you some copies for fun, not that I will ever brew any." I reveal to her.

It is charming watching the guests strolling around the Mena House Hotel in the Ancient Egyptian clothing. As we walk through the gardens to the area closer to the great Pyramid, Michael saw the sign and read it out loud, "2560 Pyramid building in Giza. 20,000 workers needed. Housing under the stars, Wage: one loaf of bread and one gallon of beer daily. How fun is this, my college professors were not creative as Professor Amon, yet, we drank on campus anyway?"

Everyone was early for Professor Amon's lecture. It is an authentic Egyptian party, with the desert sands, pyramids and sphinx in the back ground, the voice of Umm Kulthum, 'the star of the east,' vibrating through the tent, the high quality sounds of a full orchestra, the gentle strings of the guitar, and the cries of the violin. Doctor Michael could not stop grinning. We take our glass, thanking them for their kindness and we find the good seats Sharon reserved for us.

"I wanted you to hear my favorite Egyptian music while you mingled. The songs of this singer have a full symphony, it comforts and inspires me. Now let me concentrate on the lecture." The professor speaks with the pride of his country through the tone of his deep voice. We raise our glass, toast each other, thanking the host for his kindness, chatting with our friends, making introductions and finally taking our seats.

"Before I start, I want to personally thank Professor Amir for making me a copy of his pyramid prints to hang in back of me as I speak to you. Some of you missed my first lecture, you will have to borrow the notes from your good looking Egyptian well dressed friends sitting near you. We all know each other well enough now after some of the experiences I have been told. You are truly my most blessed students ever. What a trip we had holding hands around the pyramid, thank you to Chief Black Elk and to Moon Bear for your prayers in your wonderful Lakota language. I heard there were ten of you in the Great Giza Pyramid for an afternoon, a private meditation. Do you each know what a sacred experience that was, will the ten that were chosen please stand." We looked around the room, ten is a very small number.

"You are ten of the luckiest people I know, what a gift. Record it now in your brain so that it will be set securely for your whole life because you will never have this experience again. Thank you Chief Black Elk and Moon Bear for working with the Egyptian authorities to allow you this private time to walk where the pharaohs walked.

"If that meditation does not set you ten on a course of empowerment, I do not know what will. You have accomplished one of the most requested journeys of a lifetime, to have a sacred meditation in the Giza Pyramid, the last wonder of the Ancient World." Amon is grinning ear to ear.

"What a night. Now you all can feel what joyous energy is present when like hearted people are together sharing inspiring experiences. I am honored to have met each one of you. Let us toast to health and since we are under Islamic law of sobriety, we shall refer to the drink as barley soup," my name is Doctor Amon from the American University here in Cairo. "The Nectar of the Egyptian Gods, the golden color of the rays of the Great Sun God Ra. Before it was a brew, a Bud, a Miller, Coors, a Heineken, a Corona, a Sam Adams, before Ben Franklin laid claim to his famous statement, 'Beer is proof that God loves us and wants us to be happy,' this beer was considered to be the gift from the Sun God Ra.

"I said those words more fluidly last week," he chuckles, "now a mini recap of my lecture, for those of you who missed the first class. I will give you a review. Imagine 7,000 years ago, you are a gatherer, and you fill your clay buckets with wild barley. Rain water falls into your jars, you do not give it a second thought, as time goes by that rain water moistens the grain and it starts to sprout and it begins to produce sugar, as more rains come the wild yeasts convert the sugars to alcohol. You return to discover your clay jars are holding a tempting soup. The warmth of the Sun God Ra fermented your grain, and you are now very happy gatherers. It is produced by the brewing and fermentation of barley, and wheat sugars.

It was known to be a rich source of nutrients, and is sometimes referred to as liquid bread. Because beer was low in alcohol and high in vitamins and minerals it was drunk from the cradle to the grave. Northern Africans were hunters and gathers before the big drought, then all tribes had to move to the Nile and its fertile valley for survival, they became agricultural farmers of barley, flax, wheat and cotton. Production increased and Egypt became a major producer of linen and cotton cloth.

"All Pharaohs had their own royal breweries as did Tut's family, and I have 250 copies of the recipe of Tutankhamun Beer. They will be handed to you on the way out of the tent, if you each take only one please, I think we will have enough to go around." Professor Amon says.

"There are still 50 percent of undiscovered treasures buried under the sands of time, waiting for you to find their locations and reveal their mysteries. The tourists riding south of the pyramid had a most valuable episode when one of the horses stepped upon a hole. How exciting, 5,000 years of history revealed by an accident of a tourist riding a rented horse!

"The scientists have since found thousands of worker's tombs of mud, brick and stone. The higher up the hill they went, the more prestigious were the ranks of the overseers of the building project. They found hieroglyphics explaining who they were, and carvings of people making large vats of beer and bread.

"Just imagine, the smells of hundreds of loves of bread baking outdoors in open ovens all day long. Beer brewing, wine making, and the all time favorite, homemade onion bread. We have delicious warm onion bread coming through the aisles now, and please have more barley soup." The teacher smiles.

In Egypt, beer was regarded as food. The old Egyptian hieroglyph for the word 'meal' was a combination of the words 'beer' and 'bread.' Onions, dried fish and the soupy beer bread was the standard diet of the common people along the Nile. Egyptian beer was also made with emmer and flavored with honey and ginger. The most expensive beers were brewed to a darker amber or red color with a higher alcoholic strength and dominant flavor much like an ale today.

Hundreds of bakeries were found, hundreds of bakeries for thousands of workers, who were cutting, pulling, polishing thousands of stones. This was not a camp of slave workers. The bones that were found indicated equal numbers of men and women. Small towns of whole families. They were fed well with their beer, meat, duck, fish and loaves of bread and wine for the managers.

"Let me do the math on the amount of beer you needed to keep the promise of a gallon a day for each man. I guess it would be about 230 million gallons a year. In the future beer will be a 28 billion dollar business. Love that wheat and barley!" He laughs.

I imagine Professor Amon touching the pyramid prints as he did many times, rubbing the incense on his hands, soon he has the four winds swirling, the northern wind following the path of the river, of the Nile delta, the breeze of the raising light of the East, the setting of the winds of the West and the southern breeze of the Nubian golden wind. Peace and Unification. My imagination is taking me back in time.

The lights flicker in my mind and the great God Thoth and Pharaoh Khufu stand in the tent, in the foreground of their mighty works. The God Thoth laughs. "The pharaohs want to be Gods. Let me tell you about this great Pharaoh's son Khafre, he built the pyramid next to his fathers, the second largest in the Giza plateau, just three meters shorter than his fathers. Calculate the beer for the job. Yes, you can do it, don't forget the chambers below ground." If only the group could see the lights twirling, papers levitating. "Khufu's family was a pyramid building family and Pharaoh Khafre tops everyone by adding the Sphinx, the greatest statue on earth, the keeper of secrets, the guardian of mysteries a megalithic structure, the largest in the world, the Abu al Hol, the 'father of terror,' the Arabic name for the protector of the pyramids. Carved out of a single block of limestone, the crouching lion, a mythical creature with the head of a human man and the body of a lion, this enormous cat like sculpture has mesmerized millions of visitors. A bit of father and son competition, what do you think?"

"Khafre, means, 'Appearing like the great Sun God Ra.' Choose a name wisely, it is more precious than gold."

The Japanese math team is busy calculating the amount of beer needed for that project. "If the Sphinx is 240 feet long, 20 wide and 60 high. Do they get more watery, extra light beer in the summer months?" Yasuko asks. "Also, some of the blocks weighed 200 tons that were removed around the big cat and used to build the Sphinx temple. I heard there are chambers under the Sphinx, am I correct and how do I account for them?"

"You are correct, the ground penetrating radar used today has uncovered nine underground chambers with metallic objects under the ground of the Lion Sphinx. Let us agree they needed mass amounts of beer and barley grain to make the bread, onions, honey, duck, meat, fish, fruit, everything to feed such a hungry crowd."

The class toasts the project and agrees on the massive feat laid before the workers who carved the Lion from one earth stone. We students shake our heads saying, "how it boggles the mind."

There is always controversy about the time frame of the building of these structures, some historians calculate Egyptian life at 10,500 BC. The glorious magnitude of these structures stand as a reminder of the immortality of the soul. There is a higher spiritual knowledge and purpose. Egypt is a mysterious land.

Could the chamber in the Leo Sphinx house the informational books, the books of the God Thoth?

"Would you like to learn an interesting fact?" Amon says with the innocence of a young man teaching his first class. His eyes light like he has a precious bit of sacred wisdom worth repeating. "Beware of the Sphinx, the 'father of terror' the Abu al Hol." Professor continues. "He is protecting the secrets of the pharaohs. I will end here. Have a wonderful time in Egypt, travel the direction of your heart, it is the wisdom of your body."

The class feels delight in Doctor Amon's presentations. We are all so pleased to have this unusual experience. We applaud him, "bravo, bravo."

We walk out of the tent and stand marveling at the lights reflecting on the ancient wonders of the world.

Again, we applaud, "Bravo, bravo."

Do you like my QR Code?

Take a picture of it with your phone...

See the magic!

U R my hippest queen!

Social Media Call for Awareness

Faith makes us sure of what we hope for and gives us proof of what we cannot see. Hebrews 11:1

I want to give you quick background of our religious backgrounds. When Jesus left Egypt, He went back to the Holy Lands. In the first chapter of the Torah, and Genesis, the Lord God talks with Abraham. 'Abrahamic' religions each have a linage from a single patriarch. Abraham is the patriarch father of the world's major religions; Judaism, Christianity, and Islamic. God made the covenant with Abraham through his son Isaac. Abraham was married to Sarah, and Judaism began.

Let me first explain the proximity of these ancient religions that are all located in the Old City of Jerusalem. Just imagine the beauty and possibilities of the four sections of the ancient walled area, located in the city of Jerusalem.

The oldest quarter is the Jewish Quarter, containing the Western Wall which is a portion of the retaining wall built by King Herod in the first century BC. The Temple Mount once was the home of the first temple built by David's son King Solomon in 957 BC. Less that 400 years later it was destroyed by the Babylonians. Then Herod's Temple was built in 516 BCE and destroyed by the Romans 400 plus years later in 70 BC. Today only the famous wall remains. A sacred site to the Hebrews.

The Muslims also consider the Mount a sacred site. The Dome of the Rock was built on it after the Muslims invaded Jerusalem in 637AD. The Noble Sanctuary is the site of the binding of the Hebrew Isaac, Abraham's son. It is the location of the Muslim Muhammad's ascent to heaven. This makes it one of the oldest Hebrew sites and one of the oldest Islamic sites. Abraham's other son Ishmael settled in Mecca. The Al- Aqsa Mosque in the Old City of Jerusalem rests on the far South side of the Mount, facing Mecca.

The Muslim Quarter is the largest and most populated, extending from the Lions Gate in the East, along the North wall of the Temple Mount, in the South, to the Western Wall-Damascus Gate. It covers 76 acres. There are many Roman and Crusader remains in the quarter. The Christian first seven Stations of the Cross on the Via Dolorosa are located here in the Muslim sector.

In the Christian Quarter we see the beautiful Church of the Holy Sepulchre or the Church of the Resurrection. This area is venerated on the Hill of Calvary, and is the crucifixion and burial place of Jesus. The Christian Quarter is in the Northwest corner of the Old City; from the New Gate in the North, along the West wall of the Old City, to the Jaffa Gate - Western Wall in the South. It borders on the Jewish and Armenian Quarters. It goes as far as the Damascus Gate in the East. It borders on the Muslim Quarter. There are 40 Christian holy places in the Christian quarter.

The Armenian Quarter comprises the Cathedral of St. James or Saint Jacob Armenian Cathedral. Which is a 12th century church in Old Jerusalem, near the quarter's entry gate. The cathedral is dedicated to Christian Saints: James, one of the Twelve Apostles of Jesus and James, the brother of Jesus. It is the principal church of the Armenian Patriarch, which remains under the authority of the Catholicos of the Armenian Apostolic Church.

"We must protect the Holy Lands. I have been escorted into the Muslim sites by my Muslim friends from Bethlehem, into the Christian sites by my Christian friends from Nazareth, and I have prayed at the Temple Wall with my Jewish friends from Jerusalem. I do not have enough prayers inside of me to begin to understand the daily gratitude and drama of living in such a Holy City. Both of Sharon's sons live in Israel. We parents just want peace." I say with concern.

Sometimes we parents find ourselves fearful for our children, I encourage you to say, "God's Word declares that the seed of the righteous shall be delivered" Proverbs 11:21

The Israeli strikes on the Gaza Strip in November 2012, confronted Egyptian President Mohamed Morsi with a test of loyalties to Hamas and to Egypt's landmark peace treaty with Israel. Aware of his divided loyalties, Hamas, the Islamist Palestinian offshoot of Egypt's Muslim Brotherhood are pushing for support from ideological big brother, Morsi. On the other side is Israel's hawkish leadership, who are tired of their people running to bomb shelters every time Iran sends Hamas new weapons. Israel is pushing President Morsi to commit to the peace treaty.

Imagining life under those circumstances. I understand why Israel's Iron Dome is so important and why the US spent so much money helping to build it.

To lighten the tension of this land, I picture the characters of my book in a Broadway play having dinner on the stage. I'm picturing a roundtable discussion. Please sit at the table yourself, and remember the rest of this chapter is supposition. Join us. Let us open our vivid imaginations and go back in time, could this be how the Egyptians and Hebrews ran a business meeting?

Visualize many, many decades ago, the Egyptian Pantheon of Gods had a brain storming conference deciding the people of Egypt have been suppressed, which was against the laws of the heavenly fathers, Great Company of Gods. The God Thoth decided to call upon the Lord God of the Universe and ask what can be done to bring a mass reform in the global energy structure of the world. The Great Company Gods gathered at the global round table in the western sector of the heavens causing an energy field so powerful it created a total eclipse of the sun.

At the table sat the great Ra, to his right was Ma'at, the Goddess of Truth, to her right was her husband Thoth, the God of Wisdom, to his right Jesus, the true God of Wisdom, to his right Abraham and his two sons, Ishmael and Isaac.

(Ishmael was born of Abraham. Hagar was the Egyptian servant of Abraham's wife Sarah, who was barren at the time. Hagar acted as a surrogate bearing Abraham a son named Ishmael. It was through Ishmael that the prophet Muhammad came and thus the Muslim religion. Hagar acted patronizing, superior and was sent away.)

Later (Isaac was born of Abraham. Abraham and his wife Sarah conceived a son together named Isaac. It is through the linage of Isaac that the Hebrew religion and Christian religion were formed.)

These are the religious forces of Egypt and Israel.

Jesus poured a rare aged wine, Ma'at joined him, dabbing her long hair on his feet as an ancient sign of respect to wipe away the dust, they laughed heartily together. "Be careful, I do not want get excited and multiply this pitcher of wine ten fold."

"Abraham enjoy some of this wine and some for your children, I have plenty."

"For my father, Abraham, yes, he loves the taste of the grapes," said Isaac, but for me, I prefer the barley drink. It has less fermentation, it is good for us and Isaac poured himself a mug of the barley sweetened with the nectar of the bees.

Jesus agreed, "It is okay, Muhammad, it is a healthy drink when the fermentation content is so very low, Isaac is right. "Ishmael, I understand you do not believe the fermented grape and grain is good for us. I personally do like wine."

Ishmael speaks, " We know the sin of the grape and the grain is greater than their benefit. I wrote it in the Quran 2:219"

The table agreed, everyone smiled and talked about the good times they had when they gathered people with the pure light, they each agreed how they missed pouring pure light into the hearts of the beloved ones. "There are so many people today, such crowding of the sacred space. Remember the days of pure air? I give them the clean air, the lush gardens, as I do today in Maui, Hawaii, I even send rainbows. Rainbows the sign of the covenant I made never to flood the earth again. Let the complainers make a rainbow! Where is the passion, where is the appreciation, I need to hear more praising and less complaining. If they do not want to talk to their family, they could talk to the ocean, the trees, the flowers or to me! They have lost that loving feeling. I want the agape love. Where is all that unconditional love?" Jesus may have said.

"Remember the day when people would 'be' rather than 'do' and they understood this important life lesson," Thoth said. "It is one of the greatest lesson of all. Mindless materialism leaves them empty; materialism alone means that they do not know the value of time. They are afraid of time, as well as meaning and value. It is the very reason they turn to materialism, they are afraid of time, they want to be young. They fill themselves with toys because they are afraid to face the meaning of their lives and what contributions they are making to it. He who dies with the most toys does not win. Wisdom wins, knowing the love of God wins, to be full of God is to come to a place in life where you have peace in your soul, knowing the journey was a preparation for your joyous visit with our Lord."

"I understand the Aten principle, show me the sun, the Sun God, everyone could see the sun, everybody loved the sun and feared the darkness, and were grateful when the sun would rise. Each day that cycle occurred, seeing the sun and feeling the warmth of the sun, then darkness for rest and you know they prayed for their friend the sun to come again, and the gratitude would fill their heart each morning when they would look to the East to watch the sun rise. Where is the gratitude today? The 'go forth and multiply words' were meant in a way to spread love, now there are so many people on the planet with so many opinions, it seems that nobody knows a love direction, each feels their religion is correct, and they forget respect, kindness and praise are essential to the path of peace."

Ma'at continued, "I even heard a man say, 'If you do not love the way I love, I will kill you. Hostility is the opposite of love. Contempt is the opposite of respect. Hostility and contempt never soften the spirit of another person. Never!"

"Where did you hear such a thing?" Asks Abraham. "The are all my children, I am embarrassed."

"I heard a Christ follower and say, "I will die for my faith." And I heard a Hebrew man say, "I will die for my faith." Then I heard an Islamic terrorist say, "You will die for my faith."

"That is light years away from love. People are all formed the same, born of blood, they have the same needs of hunger, protection for their young, for food and shelter, for love and respect. When my people suffer, I suffer," said Jesus. "Men and women serve and die for honor, yet, when they return from war they are not given proper respect from the governments that called them into action. Men and women soldiers need to be respected."

The God Thoth stood, "I miss the pure light so much and I missed each of you my dear friends. I called this meeting because I need help, I no longer have any power, I am so heart sick the world has been so damaged by the anger and the jealous nature of the people. I personally know each one of you, I know the love and sacrifice that each of you has put forth in creating this magnificent universe. I did not think myself to be old, yet I do not seem to have the energy or power to stop corruption. These are our children, and as parents we have failed them. They are suffering. I propose a united power for the people, for our youth, for our children. I propose an energy field similar to what we did with the pyramids, but much larger, a world energy field and energy that can be transmitted to each dwelling, a net work that can transmit energy information that will connect each of our people."

"An internal network, an internetwork, an internet. Let us cast the net, not for fish, but for the communication of men and women, for fathers and sons, mothers and daughters to stay in touch when they relocate to another town or country. It shall be used for good."

Ma'at spoke up, "If it is used for evil, the God Ammit will see those predators on the other side."

It will be a social network with a voice for the weak, a tiny chirp or tweet.

How would the world be different if we think Social Media is the technological calling of God to spread the words of love? No gossip, no negativity. To connect families and loved ones, to report a wedding, a birth or a death, to make business connections and yes, it can be used for peaceful demonstrations. Imagine sharing love and joy all over in the world.

The word spread like the wind as if Ramesses II, the war Pharaoh was instigating a revolt. The Pharaoh called his people to action, on Ramesses Street, Cairo.

"You, the rulers of Egypt have humiliated the laws of the Pharaohs, cried the people, the great Pharaohs gave purpose. There are quarries to be cut, roads to build, slums to reconstruct.

"Feed my people!" the great voice of the Pharaoh Ramesses declared.

"In my day men built greatness."

"Ishmael you have a question?" Abraham asked.

"Father, a code was placed in the pyramid, 2012 inches to equal each year after Christ, to tell of the end of darkness, just as the Mayans believed, the end of the dark period, it tells of a new year, a new day, a new dawning for all men to work together for peace. Egypt will have a new constitution and Morsi will lead us in peace, this is my prayer today. He is a 60 year old United States trained engineer, a graduate of the Cairo University and USC.

He will be developing Egypt into a country whose citizens enjoy equal rights regardless of religion, race or social class and achieving economic development based on a free economy that puts social justice as its priority within a state of institutions and rule of law.

"The party calls for a new constitution which guarantees freedom of religion and the right to apply laws governing personal affairs according to one's religious belief." Ishmael stated.

God speaks, "I remember what I said to you Abraham. 'And as for Ishmael, I have heard you: Behold, I have blessed him and will make him fruitful, and will multiply him exceedingly; twelve princes shall he beget, and I will make him a great nation."

"We must learn peace, it must come from within our souls. We must form a people's council of respect. No murdering, no burning flags to place fear in the hearts of our fellow man, we are adults and we can discuss our religion to explain our ways without violence." Thoth declares. "I am going to implant the idea of an invisible shield over my people in Jerusalem. Missiles will not be able to penetrate this air space."

The God Thoth speaks, this is a good meeting. All words shall be yours Heavenly Father. I have tried my best but, I did not have proper understanding then. "I invented the Hieroglyphs, Hiero meaning 'holy' and Glyphs meaning 'words,' they were 'Words of the Gods.' I am the scribe or secretary in the Great Company of the Gods, I keep the celestial register of the words and deeds of men, I am regarded as the Recording Angel. I became heavily associated with the arbitration of godly disputes, the system of writing, the development of science, and the judgment of the dead. I am asking how we can heal the groaning of the peoples of the earth? My toughest question is, how did people fall away from the holy words? They do not respect the very first words written? The very first. Where is the love, they still worship idols!

"I, Thoth, am the recorder of deeds. At the 'Weighing of the Heart' ceremony, I am the one who writes all the information. The scale or balance used to weigh the heart on one side and the feather of Ma'at on the other. If the heart is light like the feather, the heart went to the afterlife for everlasting life. If your heart is heavy with lies and corruption it will be heavier than the feather, then your heart will be eaten by the demon Ammit. Ammit is Satan. He would devourer the evil hearts."

Pharaoh Khufu could be heard in the wind of the heavens, "When I was Pharaoh men and women were given the same wages, the same privileges, the same respect. Sometimes you will see a statue of a queen with her arm around the king's shoulder, 'I am equal to you. It is my blood that feeds the growth of our babies inside my body.' Respect this, the hand that rocks the cradle rules the world. Infancy's the tender fountain, grow on for good or evil, sunshine streamed or evil hurled, the hand that rocks the cradle is the hand that rules the world. Mothers teach your children kindness and show them what love should be, write the things that you love about your children and place the notes on their pillows at night, as if they are messages from the angels. Be the preeminent force for change in the world, embrace our similarities and respect our differences.

"This pyramid is not a Biblical prayer, just a prayer during the demonstrations. I am simply trying to raise respect for all of our fellow men and women. I am not an all knowing person, just a girl who went to Cairo and wanted to write a book because I am tired of all the abuse. I want people to find peace." Louise

A
prayer
for peace.
~ Once upon a
time in the year 2012,
men, women and children
came to Tahrir Square. A public
square now known as the Liberation
Square designed by the former great King
Khedive Ismail the Magnificent. The center of
Cairo, his, 'Paris on the Nile River.' The revolution
was won by votes. Egyptians shouted to everyone who
loves Egypt, come rebuild Egypt. Lift your head up high for
you are an Egyptian. The vote favored the pro-democracy party
the Muslim Brotherhood and defeated the incumbent ruler Mubarak.
The x & y generations, the educated and self taught very creative internet
generations waited for weeks and they tweeted, texted and downloaded their
photos to show their struggle to the world. The power of the people is greater than
the people in power. Weary Egyptian democrats armed only with their camera phones
created the dawning of a new era of peaceful demonstrations to be an example to the world.
Let us pray that each country in our world will please give understanding and peace a chance.

How Did We Get From
Cleopatra to Christianity?

The light is hazy as I dress, a new and lovely morning, when a knock comes to the door. I look through the peep hole, and there before my eyes a huge bouquet of lotus blossoms covering the bellman from head to waist. I open the door with a sheepish grin, "Thank you kind sir, what a wonderful arrangement, they are lovely."

"They are special in Egypt, for you lady."

"I am proud to receive them, good sir, they will add even more beauty to my elegant room. Please, let me get you a tip," I desire to give him something, but he shakes his head.

"No Missy, a large tip was paid to me, by Doctor Amir," the gracious man replies.

"I thank you so much." Where to set the aromatic flowers? On the coffee table in front of the Chinese sofa? How did he know the oriental vase went with my decor? The flowers enhance my amazing view of the pyramid, filling the area with a fragrance so beautiful it is a delight to my eyes and my sense of peace. Lotus blossoms in front of the pyramid, this calls for a special note. I write a delightful thank you to give the concierge to forward to Doctor Amir. I rush to meet the others in the exquisitely decorated hotel breakfast room. I am beaming; intrigue, pyramids, flowers and an opulent buffet of Qatayef, Baklava, Polvoron, fresh exotic fruits and wonderful Turkish tea, a deliciously tasty morning. We are filled with excitement, adjusting to a land so foreign, our eyes are open wide enchanted by the lure of exotic aromas. We each look at our class lists, trying to decide which event to choose.

The morning tent is full of students many I have not seen before, the conference is so large with people staying in hotels all over Cairo. There is standing room only. We are all full of curiosity.

"My name is Professor Christopher, I am your teacher this afternoon. I have my information on the sheet I am passing out to you. The key points are for you and I, it keeps me on track. So, you do not have to listen to me repeating myself. At my age, it is a problem. This will be my last year of teaching, I am retiring to my home in the south of England." He smiles as many of the British students nod their heads. "I am an Egyptian man with an English wife, two beautiful children, two grandchildren and one Ibizan hound. He laughs. "If you missed my first class about Jesus of Egypt, please ask Todd. Stand young man. He is a Roman history scholar and will answer any questions you may have. Thank you."

Todd smiles ear to ear as he gives the class a wave. "Yes, please have a discussion with me anytime. My pleasure."

"Let me cut to the chase of the lecture. Feel free to write on notes that I outlined for you, this is fast moving and gets a bit complicated. First the Egyptian power was fading and the Greek and Roman customs copied the religions of the Egyptian deities. The Greek powers of Alexander the Great, and the Ptolemy Dynasty had ruled for 300 years. The Egyptian Gods now had Greek names then Roman names, depending on the conquering nation. The professor discloses.

"Queen Cleopatra Vll lived from 69 BC to 30 BC. She spoke Egyptian and represented herself as the reincarnation of the Egyptian Goddess, Isis the Goddess of Magic. Born in Alexandria, Cleopatra was the last Queen of Egypt, Rome controlled Egypt after her death. She ascended to the Egyptian throne at age of seventeen after her father died and following the terms of the father's will, to keep the power in the family, she and her brother Ptolemy Xlll married."

"I don't know if I would want to marry my sibling," comments one of the students. "Although, I trust my sister."

"I agree, but we have to be open to their time in history. I believe they did such things for protection of their family's wealth. Please stand. What is your name, young man?" Asks the professor.

"My name is Daniel, sir."

"You are now, for argument sake, King Daniel, you have a son and a daughter. You have worked hard maintaining Egypt's stability, it is time for your son to be co-ruler with you and time to find him a suitable wife. Everyone wants to take your power, do you marry your children to keep the ruling of Egypt in your family's control? It is a tough question asked down through the ages. Rule with your head, and love a secondary wife with your heart? Simply ponder the question. Remember, how would the lawyers handle the property settlement in a divorce? Does she get Upper Egypt, blocking the Nile traffic? Who would pay the taxes? Would you choose another Queen? Would she want half of your remaining Lower Egypt? What if the ex-wives get together, joining forces? Together they could own more than the King. These are just some questions to contemplate. Yes, Daniel, it does seam odd, yet they had their reasons. Thank you for your concern, I completely understand.

"Cleopatra's brother intended to become sole ruler, and managed to force his older sister/wife to flee to Syria, but, she soon organized her own army and a civil war began in Egypt. Their other sister, Arsinoe IV started to claim the throne. Enters Julius Caesar who came ready to sign an agreement with Ptolemy. He was gifted a magnificent hand woven red carpet, as he unrolled the rug an enchanting 18 year old Cleopatra, returning from Syria, emerged from the rug. She soon beguiled Caesar with the prospect of the riches of Egypt and of India.

"Their union gave victory to Caesar and Cleopatra, forcing Ptolemy and Arsinoe to flee the city. Ptolemy XIII reportedly died like a drowned rat in the Nile after being chased by soldiers. Queen Cleopatra remained the unchallenged ruler of Egypt, she named their younger brother Ptolemy XIV her new co-ruler.

"Still married to his Roman wife, Caesar returns to Rome with Cleopatra, wanting to make himself Emperor and Cleopatra his empress. On the 15th or Ides of March as it is called in the Roman calendar, a festival day dedicated to the Roman God Mars, Caesar attempted to tell his intentions to the Senate, but they disapproved of his behavior and two dozen members in the Roman Senate stabbed him to death.

"Intermission, second act."

"General Mark Antony was bankrupt from gambling debts, he looks to the wealth of Egypt and calls for Cleopatra. In 41 BC the Queen sails to the city of Tarsus in Turkey, the scene of the first meeting. Mark Anthony and his Roman army helped Herod the Great, siege Jerusalem in 37 BC. King Herod and the Cleopatra owned a monopoly for the extraction of asphalt from the Dead Sea, which was used in ship building. Mark Anthony wanted to build a large navy. She agreed to pay off all his debts and as part of the pact Mark Antony agreed to murder Cleopatra's sister, Princess Arsinoe.

"Antony was under her spell, he sent orders to his generals, but, his close friend Enobarbus informed him that the army deserted him out of loyalty to Rome. Enobarbus suggests killing Cleopatra and gaining back the control of Rome, but Anthony refuses, therefor Anthony's young nephew Octavian and his soldiers capture Egypt. Antony believed that she has deserted him for his nephew, he then stabs himself. She returns heartbroken to find Anthony dying, they reconcile their love, he perished, she knows she will be captured, paraded in shame, at age 39, she killed herself with a poisonous snake."

Todd stands as if ready to recite a verse he learned from the great playwright. *"With thy sharp teeth this knot intrinsic ate. Of life at once untie: poor venomous fool. Be angry and dispatch. Cleopatra, scene II act V by William Shakespeare."*

"I know it well, thank you. Some say she drank a poison, we like the dramatic influence of Shakespeare." Professor Christopher says.

"What year was that," asks another student. "Also, would you please explain what BC means?"

"The time line is designed around the importance of Christ's birth. If we draw a line and place the number zero in the center with a one on each side, every number on either side of that one rises. The left side is Before Christ, BC or Before Christian Era, BCE. The right side is the year of the Lord, in Latin, Anno Domini, AD. Therefore Cleopatra died in 30 BC, or 30 years Before Christ in the Roman calender. The word Christ is from the Greek, Khristos, the anointed one." Doctor Christopher takes his time explaining the importance of the birth of the Lord. "Yet, most scholars believe Jesus was born between 7 and 4 BCE."

The Copernicus tables where constructed for the motion of the planets based on the Egyptian year, because of its mathematical regularity. The Egyptians had an excellent calendar, but, the Romans wanted to set a standard in history after Jesus was born. This occurred later on, when the Romans realized the importance of Jesus. Before Christ, BC and after Christ, AD.

"Cleopatra's son by Caesar was named Caesarion. After Alexandria fell to Octavian, her son Caesarion was captured and killed.

"Cleopatra and Mark Anthony had two sons named Alexander Helios and Ptolemy Philadelphus. They were taken to Rome after their parents death. They disappeared in their youth. Were they kidnapped and brought back to Egypt by Cleopatra's secret service? Young Ptolemy would be in his late thirties when Jesus came to Cairo. They would have been the next heirs to her throne if the Romans were forced to leave Egypt.

Now we talk about Christianity

"Rome decided to raise taxes therefore they ordered a census count for all the Roman territory. The head of the household had to return to the town of their birth to sign the census form. Joseph had to return to Bethlehem with his wife Mary.

"Because they did not make reservations, they took refuge in a stable or cave, where their baby Jesus was born. The Magi or 'wise men' from the East visited King Herod to inquire about the child having

been born 'king of the Jews.' They had seen a new and spectacularly bright star in the Eastern sky and knew, because they heard the words of Micah, who prophesied in 700 BC. Which means Micah told people 700 years before the birth of Christ, the event will come to pass."

"Bethlehem, though you are small among the clans of Judah, out of you will come for me one who will be ruler over Israel, whose origins are from ancient times." Micah 5:2.

"Herod, as King of the Jews, was jealous. He assembled the chief priests and scribes asking them where the Christ, 'Anointed One' was to be born?"

The answer was, "In the little town of Bethlehem, a small community not far from Jerusalem. Herod sent the 'wise men' to Bethlehem, to find the child and report back to him, so he could also worship. After they found Jesus, the Magi had a dream telling them not to report back to Herod. Joseph was also warned in a dream that Herod intended to kill Jesus. Mary and Joseph took Jesus and fled the Roman ruler, secretly slipping into Egypt for protection. When the Magi did not return, Herod gave orders to kill all boys of the age of two and under in Bethlehem and its vicinity, but Jesus had left and was safely on Egyptian soil." The Egyptian professor continues.

"Joseph has taken Jesus and his family to Egypt to flee the wrath of King Herod. 'And was there until the death of Herod: that it might be fulfilled which was spoken of the Lord by the prophet, saying, Out of Egypt have I called my son.' Matthew 2:15 KJV."

"Jesus was born during the darkest time in Israel's history. Israel was under the tyrannical rule of the Romans. Yes, my beloved, Jesus will come to you in the darkest period of your life. Egyptian Monasteries celebrate both the Nativity and Baptism together on the seventh of January. This date corresponds to the 29th day of the Coptic month, Kahk." Doctor Christopher says.

"Joseph and his family stayed in Egypt until Herod's death, then moved to Nazareth in Galilee. Do you know that Jesus and John the Baptist were cousins? Yes, their mothers, Mary and Elizabeth, were cousins therefore the boys would be second cousins. Jesus was raised in Nazareth and John was born and raised in Hebron about 100 miles away." Our teacher beams.

Both men were killed for love of God. "Who knows how old?"

"Jesus was about 30 to 33 years old," declares James. "John was the forerunner of Jesus and was about 28 when he died."

"Correct. The Christian religion was a target of persecution; feedings to the lions in the Coliseum or being nailed to crosses, just a terrible period, until the time of King Constantine the Great. He became Saint Constantine, he was the first Roman Emperor known for becoming a Christian. In about 333 AD he declared Christianity the State Church of the Roman Empire.

"Then there were the Crusades, where the Christians decided to kill and of course the famous witch hunts that killed about 60,000 women, an insane time in Europe and the East coast of America. Yet, I remain a Christian who works on forgiveness on a daily basis."

"Yes?"

"My name is Ginger. In Maui, Hawaii, I saw an awe inspiring rainbow and I understand there is a biblical connection. Is this true?"

"This is one of my favorite things, a rainbow from God, the promise to Noah. The old Genesis quote, 'I will set My rainbow in the clouds and it will be the sign of My covenant between Me and the earth."

God promises to not destroy all the people of earth again. God directs Noah's attention to a rainbow actually existing at the time in the sky, and presents the patriarch the assurance.

"Where did Noah's ark land?" She stands wanting more information.

"Ginger here is the quick story. For 40 days and 40 nights it rained so hard everyone in the whole world perished, except Noah, his family and the animals resting safely in the ark. They floated about for 150 days finally resting on the mountain of Ararat in Turkey. 'Ararat' in Hebrew means 'the curse is reversed.' Mt Ararat, Uratu, in Eastern Turkey is one of the tallest volcano areas in the Middle East. But, I do not know the true answer. Durupinar, also in Turkey or Al Judi, also called Mount Cudi, in southeastern Turkey. Maybe even Ireland or Ethiopia. Sometimes it is written that it happened on the 7th month the 17th day the Feast of First Fruits. The exact date that Jesus rose from the dead 4,000 years later.

Only Noah knows the date. Good question, Noah worked on that ark for 120 years. The ark was 450' x 75' x 45'. The ancient cargo ship held 16,000 animals, no fish, they were swimming in the waters. The ark floor space would equal a 100,000 square foot home or 600 railway cars. God walked with Enoch and Noah, therefore some Egyptians compare Noah's building gifts to Thoth the guide of the pyramid builders. It is difficult to comprehend such tasks, as the ark and pyramids.

"Yes?"

"Daniel, question is did Egypt contain Noah's children?

"In Biblical traditions, it is agreed the population of the Earth was destroyed during the great flood and Noah and his family were the sole eight survivors to continue the human race, thus all humans are descendants of Noah's family. Noah's son Ham, had a son named Kush, which was the name of Nubia, Kush is also associated with the Sumerian City in Mesopotamia. Good question, I do not know, you need to ask a Hebrew scholar.

"Yes, Sacia?"

"Have they found Cleopatra VII tomb? And, was her mother Cleopatra also?"

"Her mother was Cleopatra V of Egypt and her father was a Greek man named Ptolemy XII Aueletes of Alexandria.

"Their have been searches for the tomb of Cleopatra and Mark Antony. Even Doctor Zahi Hawass has excavated, using radar at the temple of Taposiris Magna, and its surrounding area, west of Alexandria. They have not found Cleopatra, yet. The key word is yet!" The professor smirks.

Alexander the Great took Egypt from the Persians in 332 BC and made it a part of the Greek Empire. For the next 300 years, the Ptolemaic dynasty ruled Egypt, mingling Hellenic traditions with the mighty legacy of the Pharaohs. It was under the Ptolemaic Dynasty that Alexandria became the cultural and economic center of the ancient world. Egypt was ruled by Ptolemy's descendants from Alexandria until the death of Cleopatra VII.

"Cleopatra was a brilliant queen devoted to her country. She was a quick witted woman fluent in nine languages. She was a clever mathematician.

She respected Caesar for his intelligence. She was a born leader and an ambitious monarch who deserved better than suicide for fear of disgrace. She fought for her country, even when Antony showed lack common sense.

"On behalf of the Egyptians, Cyrus of Alexandria sued for peace, when the Muslims entered his city, 600 years after the death of Christ. Cyrus did not want his magnificent Mediterranean kingdom destroyed. The Arabs bragged about the conquest stating they conquered Alexandria, the city of 4,000 palaces and untold wealth." The professor reveals.

"Yes, young man."

"My name is Jason, question is do you believe the Ancient Egyptians considered the God Thoth, the God of Wisdom, the great mind that called in the universe. Was Thoth a messenger between man and the Universal God?"

"Many believed the fact that there is One Supreme God, and He sent a part of himself to guide the people. Here in Egypt we believed that special god was sent through the stars known as the God Thoth. He was like a middle man to communicate with the Pharaohs, and through the Pharaohs to the people. Later came the Ennead of gods consisting of, Amun Ra who had children Shu and Tefnut, their children Nut and Geb, and their children Osiris, Isis, Nephthys and Seth. Then Horus was born to Osiris and Isis. These were the names they gave the sun, air, earth, wind, moisture etc, it was the mythology they believed in at the time. That is the story of the beginning of Egypt."

"Todd, last question?"

"I love the picture of Thoth, Jesus and Enoch rising up to God, under the capstone raising to the glory and magnificence of the heavens. Jesus is my corner stone and my capstone. Enoch was also known to the Egyptians as the God Thoth, because he was pure and did not have a mortal death, the Supreme God called him back to the heavens, right?"

"Todd, is that a statement question?" The class laughs. "How many of you know the story of Enoch? Four, plus Todd, that is okay, most people do not know him, he is in the early section of the Torah and old testament. Todd is correct, Enoch is in the very beginning of the bible, page 8 in my Bible. Genesis 5:21, When he was 65 he became the father of Methuselah.

Enoch walked with God 300 years and had other sons and daughters. He lived 365 years and he was no more, because God called him away. He was the great grandfather of Noah. In Egypt we believe there is a Thoth/Enoch connection, supposably they knew the secret of how we might become pure as gods.

"That is all I know folks, remember to Love your neighbor as yourself," thank you, and good night."

The class gave a standing ovation to the teacher, so delighted that humor and wit of the elderly gentleman make the history outrageously fun.

He smiles saying, "thank you very much and may I please add that it is Christ like to treat people with dignity and listen to them with respect, and I applaud You."

"Todd? You still have a question?"

"Yes, I think the pyramid could be a triangle; the father, son and holy spirit. An energy calling to lift the glory of Jesus of Egypt through a spirit blessing? Jesus was in spirit before his human birth in the new testament. Am I right?"

"Yes, I believe as you do. Remember when Joshua finished the work of Moses and lead his people across the Jordan River to the promised land. The priests carried the ark of the covenant which stopped the flow of the river, so all the people could cross. God then commanded the new generation to be circumcised, to have a new spiritual relationship inside and out. Picture the circumcision. 600,000 sons of the Exodus Hebrew men healing together, forming a strong bond. The second generation of the Exodus people became a band of blood brothers in God's army.

"God then sent Joshua a visitor, and Joshua asked, 'Are you against me or for me?' Joshua was commanded to remove his sandals because he was now on Holy ground. Joshua threw himself face down on the ground, humbled by his vision of a pre-incarnate of the Jesus. He was the commander of the army of the Lord. He accompanied Joshua and his band of brothers into the battle of Jericho, . . . and, the walls came tumbling down. The ground was made holy by the divine presence. Who can be against you if God is for you?

"Jesus did reveal himself many times before His human birth in the new testament," the professors explains.

Have I not commanded you? Be strong and courageous. Do not be frightened, and do not be dismayed, for the Lord your God is with you wherever you go. Joshua 1:9

"Do you know there are over 24,000 manuscripts on Jesus? First written on Egyptian papyrus, then, like the dead sea scrolls, manuscripts were written on animal skins. If you seek after the truth, you will always be led to Jesus." Todd says.

Speak what you believe about God's word and believe what you speak.

"Many of you are not speaking out what you believe about God's Word. Instead you are speaking out what you see, and experience. Others suffer in silence. Not saying anything, because you have resigned yourselves to your negative situations. I am an accurate historian, the Bible is truth." Todd declares.

"I agree," the professor says. "All strength comes from truth. Be a Christian apologetic, the classical Greek term meaning. "I make my defense." The Holy Spirit is the spirit of truth, which gives us courage. Do you want to be free? Know the truth. Unless you love the truth, how can you know it?

The 10 commandments are God's rudder to guide each person and every nation. You can trust your conscience when God is your Savior and your Lord. The Word of God is the basis of your conduct. Sin and lostness run in our blood. Sin always makes us it's slave. It is the cycle of sin; it takes us farther than we want to go, and deeper that we expect. Every decision we make comes with consequences.

"Jason, question?"
"I want to know about the Rosetta Stone?"
"Another tribute to the Ptolemaic dynasty. King Ptolemy V, about 200 years before Christ ordered a decree to be written on an Egyptian

stele. A stele was used to publish laws, to commemorate military victories, to record exploits and honors, and to mark boundaries, like the stelae of young Tut's father, Akhenaton when they built the city of Amarna." Doctor Christopher continues.

"The Rosetta Stelae was a black granite stone issued at Memphis. The stele was erected after the king's coronation and was inscribed with a decree that established him as new ruler. The interesting thing about this stele is that King Ptolemy V spoke Greek and had the decree written in Greek, and Egyptian hieroglyphics and also in the Demotic script. Demotic was a very ancient Greek and Egyptian language. Demotic Egyptian first appeared in 650 BC and was as a spoken language until the fifth century AD."

The writing of the stelae in all three scripts, gave the clue to translating hieroglyphs. The Rosetta Stone was discovered in 1799 during Napoleon's conquest of Egypt.

"I thank you very much, and to you a good night." The professor smiles knowing he gave us a full plate of information.

Trust in the Lord with all your heart;
and lean not unto your own
understanding.
Proverbs 3:5

Ankh - Eternal Life

Egyptian Gods and Goddesses

Imagine young Moses being raised in a Royal Pharaoh's Egyptian household. He was found as a baby in the papyrus reeds of the Nile River, and was rescued by an Egyptian Princess. He was born in the land of Goshen; described as the best land in Egypt, suitable for both crops and livestock. Joseph received the land because he translated his pharaoh's dreams and filled the storehouses with grain during the 7 years of abundance to survive the 7 years of famine. The land was his reward.

Moses was adopted by Pharaoh's daughter. Some say his name is the last syllable of an Egyptian Pharaoh, Tuth-mose. He was cared for by a his nurse, who was his Hebrew mother. Moses enjoyed the privileges of royalty, and he learned the protocols of Egyptian court. God chose the perfect man to speak on behalf of the slaves of Goshen.

We gather in the conference room with our homework assignments about the mythological characters that Moses knew so well, the Egyptian pantheon of deities.

Black Elk speaks, "We Indians take names of great animals, my name is Elk and my friend's name is Bear. The Egyptian gods combined the animal strength with the intellectual power of the human. My people revere the sacredness of the animals. The Eagle is

seen as a messenger from my ancestors in heaven. The gift of an Eagle feather is a very great honor, it is a favorable message from the spirits commanding the receiver to action." The chief continues.

"Today we rely on five senses; sight, taste, smell, hearing and touch. We know animals have receptors to intake and interpret sensory stimuli in very different ways then we do. Some species are able to detect currents, water pressure, electrical and magnetic fields. The Ancient Egyptians believed they had the wisdom of animals and their people had over 300 different senses. When we multitask, we lose our sensory, auditory, mind, and body awareness. We have reduced our great power of concentration."

Black Elk abruptly stands with a grin so bright, I need my shades. "**I am the Sun God, Amun Ra.**" He says. "I am the most powerful God. I have a head of the mighty falcon wearing a solar disk. I am the creative power in Egyptian history. I am regarded as the source of all life and sustenance.

"My center is in Heliopolis in the Cairo area in Lower Egypt. It is one of the oldest cities of ancient Egypt. Lunu was its name before the Greeks invaded. Heliopolis, is Greek and means, the City of the Sun or the City of Helios, the Eye of the Sun.

"This is the home of the Ennead, the powerful nine deities. These deities are the greatest gods, they are my family. The Ennead consists of Shu, Geb, Nut, Tefnut, Osiris, Seth, Isis, and Nephthys. It is I who appointed Thoth, 'scribe of the Ennead.' Then I retreated from the Earth, knowing Thoth's wisdom would allow him to serve as teacher and guardian for all humanity.

"In My culture, all power is derived from Me. Myself and Nut, the Goddess of the Stars, we created the pharaohs and of all the lesser gods in the beyond.

"My Egyptian mythology tells this story, every night when I sail to the West, My people could not see Me. They thought I died during My night voyage through the Underworld. Thoth, My secretary and counselor, along with his wife Ma'at, Goddess of Truth, stood next to Me in My boat, to protect Me, on My nightly voyage across the sky. The night boat would carry Me through the underworld and back towards the East in preparation for My rebirth."

Jheri says, "I am **Ma'at, the Goddess of Truth and Justice**. I am the goddess that regulates the stars, the seasons and the actions of mortals and deities.

"I am at the 'Weighing of the Heart' ceremony. The God Thoth records all the information. The scale or balance, is used to weigh the heart on one side and my 'feather of truth' on the other. If your heart is light like the feather, your heart goes to the afterlife. As a goddess of the Egyptian pantheon, I am paired with a male aspect, My masculine counterpart is Thoth and our attributes are the same.

"I Ma'at, am a young woman, I hold a scepter, the symbol of power in one hand, and an ankh, symbol of eternal life in the other. I am depicted with wings on each arm and I have an ostrich feather on My head."

I am the **Great Hathor, "Mistress of the West,"** I welcome the dead into the next life. I am the goddess of beauty, equal to the Greek Aphrodite, and the Roman, Venus. Sacia declares, "I am the daughter of the Great Sun God Amun Ra. I am the goddess who personifies the principles of love, beauty, music, motherhood and joy.

"I am also, **Sekhmet, Goddess of War, Eye of Ra,** wanting to destroy man kind. I am a woman with two opposing sides to My personality.

"One day, My father Ra was angry with the people who do not obey his authority. He sent Me, Sekhmet to Earth. I began killing men and drinking their blood. Father Ra becomes scared, he wants to punish man, not destroy them. Ra poured blood-colored beer on the ground, tricking Me. I thought it was blood, and drank it. The darker the color of the beer, the higher the alcohol content. Soon I am very relaxed. I stop the slaughter, and become loving, and kind. I am My old sweet self, Hathor."

Egyptians know the Sun that brings life to the desert is the same Sun causing draught. The dualistically of the Sun. "Sekhmet, the Eye of Ra, the destructive Sun Goddess and Hathor, the beautiful Love Goddess."

Sharon spins like a whirling dervishes. "**Nut, the Goddess of the Sky** is My name. At night you see My starry body, arching from horizon to horizon, over Geb's strong earthly body.

"Though sky and earth are apart during the day, every evening, I come down to meet Geb. We have a problem. I ask Thoth, God of Wisdom, to please give Me with the answers. During the 360 days of the year, I am unable to have children. Thoth gambles with Khonsu to win 5 extra days for Me, which extends My year to 365 days. During these 5 days, I am pleased to say, I give birth to Osiris, Set, Isis, and Nepthys.

"I, Nut, protect the dead when they enter the afterlife. During the day, the heavenly bodies, sun and moon make their way across My sky. At dusk, I swallow them, they pass through My belly during the night, and are reborn at dawn.

Jason steps forward, "I am **Geb, the God of the Earth**. I lay beneath Nut, the beautiful Sky Goddess, separated only by the air we breathe. I, too, am a member of the Ennead of Heliopolis. It is My laughter that creates the earthquakes. It is I that allow the crops to grow, I am the great Earth under your feet.

"In the Ennead, our group, the of nine of us Gods were created in the beginning by the Sun God Ra. He is the father of the first divine couple, Shu and Tefnut. He is the grandfather of Nut and Myself. I, the Earth God, lover to Nut the Sky Goddess, am the father of Osiris, Seth, Isis, and Nephthys.

"My oldest representation is a fragmentary relief of Myself, is an anthropomorphic being accompanied by My name, Geb. It dates from King Djoser's reign, 3rd Dynasty, and was found in Heliopolis. King Djoser built the first step pyramid in Saqqara, Egypt."

Daniel takes a bow, and flings his arm to the floor. "I, am the great **Osiris, the God of the Underworld.** I sit on the throne with My wife, Isis, watching the weighing of the hearts. I am not only a merciful judge of the dead in the afterlife, but I am, also, judge the 'underworld agency' that grants all life. That includes the sprouting of the vegetation and the fertile flooding of the Nile River.

"I am the guardian of sacred grain, barley, wheat and emmer. The Egyptians believe that grain has sprung spontaneously from My mummy, as a gift to man, a symbol of life after My death. I am the first to drink wine from My grapes and have taught men how to plant the vine in Egypt. The grape and grain must not be combined or the thunder of Seth will strike the temples of the brain and pound unmercifully the next day.

"I am being tricked by an alluring woman god, Seth's wife, who appears to have magically taken on the appearance of Isis. She gives birth to Anubis. Who later invents embalming, so he can embalm me for the afterlife.

"Seth has a vendetta against Me, because mother likes Me best. I inherit the throne. Devious Seth plans a big party to deceive Me. Seth makes a beautiful coffin with My measurements. He tells the guests that he would give the coffin as a gift to anyone who fit inside perfectly. Guess who fit inside perfectly? Me, Osiris!

"Seth, the dirty rat, quickly closes the lid, seals it and throws Me into the Nile River. Later I climb a ladder to Nut, My sweet Sky mother, for safety in her arms."

James lets out a hearty laugh, that bellows through the room, "I am **Seth, brother of Osiris, God of the Desert**, the maker of violence and sandstorms. I am a God of Evil. I am the master of the dysfunctional family unit. I am the God of Darkness, and Chaos. Dryness is the enemy of the fertile, prosperous valley of the Nile. My evil is a powerful force! I can create devastating draughts that can destroy My nation.

"I have an animal's head with a long curved pointed snout, slanting eyes, and square-tipped ears. Sometimes I have a forked tail. I am a combination of an aardvark, antelope, long-snouted mouse, pig, camel, giraffe, greyhound, and jackal.

"Living in this dysfunctional household, I have conflict with My nephew Horus, brother Osiris, and My sister Isis.

"I am terrified. Isis might be able to bring Osiris back from the dead, since she is a great magician. So I find where she hid her husband's body and I cut it into pieces, and I scatter them up and down the Nile River."

Meagan smiles graciously and proudly takes center stage, "I am **Isis, the mother of Horus**, the great ruler of Egypt. I am a healer and magician! I wear a throne on My head and I have a sun disk and horns. I am worshipped as the ideal mother and wife. I am the matron of nature and magic. I am the friend of slaves, sinners, artists, and the downtrodden. I listen to the prayers of the wealthy, maidens, aristocrats, and rulers. I am the Goddess of Magic, Motherhood and Fertility.

"Horus and I wear the same headdress. I am the first daughter of Nut, Goddess of the Sky, and Geb. the God of the Earth. My magical skills restore My husband to life. With the help of Thoth, I ask for magical powers from his religious Book of the Dead, to bring her husband back to life. Thoth worked his great magic and brought Osiris back from the dead. Osiris and I then have baby Horus. I am the Goddess of Children from whom all beginnings rise."

Todd, with his bravado, swaggers to the center of the room, he bows graciously. "I am the great **Shu, God of the Air**. My father is Amun Ra and my twin sister, Tefnut, is the Goddess of Moisture. I am sometimes depicted as a man wearing a headdress with a tall ostrich feather. As the God of Air and Wind, I have a cool and calming influence.

"Without Me, there would be no life on the planet. I am one of the great Gods of the Ennead of Heliopolis. My sister, Goddess of Moisture moves to warmer temperatures in Nubia. This caused great problems for My Egypt. I call the peacemaker Thoth, who wooed her to return to her people. She was entertained with baboons, Nubian musicians, and dancers as they went from city to city bring back moisture and water until all the land rejoiced. Being thankful to Thoth for moisture in My air, I vowed to carry an ankh the symbol of life." Todd bows again and proudly returns to his position on the side of the room.

Ginger, smiles sweetly, "I am the **Tefnut, Goddess of Moisture**, of dew and rain. I am the daughter of Amun Ra. I am sister and consort of Shu, the God of Air. I am the great mother of Nut, the sky and Geb, the earth. My grandchildren are Isis, Osiris, Nephthys and Seth.

"I have the head of a lion, yet I am a human. I wear wigs and a serpent and a solar disk. Sometimes I become a lion headed serpent. I am different from Sekhmet because my ears are pointed, it gives me a much cuter look. I am, also, the Eye of Ra. I escaped to Nubia because of a rage with my brother, Shu. Thoth, the Wisdom God, told me the land would dry without me, my importance was needed and he brought me back home to Egypt. I am part of the powerful nine members of the Great Ennead of Heliopolis. In Karnak, the pharaohs to call Me during their prayers for health and for the wellness in this dry land.

"I, **Anubis, Lord of the Underworld**, only usurped by Osiris," says Anastasia, "I am the Jackal, who takes care of the dead and their funeral arrangements. I am seen on the edge of the desert where the Egyptians are buried, we jackals guard the souls of the deceased.

"I am the Guardian of the Scales. The Ancient Egyptians believed that when you died, you travelled to the Hall of the Dead. I, Anubis would weigh your heart against the feather of Ma'at. The Goddess of Justice, Ma'at, sits on top of the scales to make sure that the weighing is carried out properly. You can see Me steadying the scales to make the weighing fair.

"Deciding the weight of truth by weighing your Heart against the ostrich feather Ma'at. Heart light as the feather, you go to the afterlife, heart heavy with sin, the demon Ammit the Devourer, and Bone Eater will greet you." Anastasia says as she scowls and starts kakling like a hyena, walking around the room trying to scare us.

"I am **Thoth, God of Magic and Wisdom**. Egyptian history starts in the waters of chaos. One day an island rose. I, Thoth, as the divine Ibis, decide to hatch the cosmic egg. Ra, the Sun God is born. And, the world began. I, speak order into existence and create the greatest God of Egyptian mythology, the Sun God Ra. The sound of My voice is so pleasant it created a snake goddess and four frog gods, who continued My song, helping the sun to make its journey across the sky.

"I am the secretary and counselor of Ra and with Ma'at, my Goddess of Truth and Order, I stand next to Ra on the nightly voyage across the sky. I maintained the universe.

"I am prominent in the Osiris myth, being of great aid to Isis. After Isis gathers the pieces of Osiris' dismembered body, it is I, who give her the words to resurrect him, so she could be impregnated and bring forth Horus. When Horus is slain, it is I, who gives the magic to resurrect him.

"I am the recorder of deeds and the inventor of Hieroglyphs. I am the scribe in the Great Company of the Gods, I keep the celestial register of the words and deeds of men, I am the Recording Angel. As the inventor of physical and moral law, the Companies of the Gods of Heaven, and Earth, and the Other World appoint Me to 'weigh the words and deeds' of men. My verdicts are unalterable. I am more powerful in the Other World than Osiris himself. Osiris owes his triumph over Seth in the Great Judgment Hall of the Gods entirely to the skill of My words as an advocate. My advocacy is needed to secure acquittal on the Day of Judgment.

"I am considered to be the heart and tongue of the Sun God Ra. I translate Ra's will into speech. I am related to the Logos of Plato and the mind of God. In the later history of ancient Egypt, I became heavily associated with the arbitration of godly disputes, the arts of magic, the system of writing, the development of science. I civilized and educated men; teaching civics, religious practices, medicine, art and music. I kept a great library of scrolls. I created the universe 13.7 billion years ago. I made many new galaxies so far away their light is just now arriving at the Earth.

"I am the author of over 40 books assisting the living, yet, I am remembered most for my books assisting the dead on their journey to the afterlife. The deceased person would be judged by a panel of 42 assessors of the dead, which corresponded with the 42 administrative areas, from this originates of the legend of the 42 Books of Thoth.

"I shall read from my Book of the Dead, one of my spells, Spell 101. Please replace the letter N with the deceased's name.
    "O, you who emerge from the waters, who escape from the flood and climb on to the stern of your bark. You have included N, a worthy spirit in your crew.
    "O Re in this the name of Re, if you pass the dead who are upside down, you shall cause N the worthy spirit to stand up on his feet; if you hale, he will hale.
    "O Re in this your name if the mysteries of the Netherland are opened to you in order to guide the hearts of your Ennead, you shall give N's heart to him; if you hale, he will hale.
    "Your body, O Re, is everlasting by reason of the spirit."

"This is to be recited over a strip of royal linen on which this spell has been written in dried myrrh; to be placed on the throat of the blessed dead on the day of the burial." I say as I take my seat and join Black Elk at the conference table.

"What is that paper you have?" The chief asks.
"I have another spell. A judgement spell." I respond.

"Let's have a show of hands. How many want to hear a bit more about the words from the Book of the Dead?" The chief asks the group, knowing he wants to listen.

"This is the last chance in Egypt to hear Toth read the words of Thoth." Daniel declares. "Tell us, Louise, make us feel like we are the mourners, we feel the pain of great loss of a dear loved, explain what you would do. Make it be you, what do you see in your tomb. Take a deep breath, and be yourself."

'They are so serious. I remember directing a play in college, I will direct myself.' I thought. 'For some reason my heart is pounding, yet, I am not afraid of dying. I am not sure why I am being hesitant? They all like me, why can't I open my mouth. I am having a self dialogue. If I stand here any longer it will become embarrassing. My throat is choking. My first acting role and I play myself dead. I over analyze.'

All of a sudden a calmness comes over me, I smile and graciously say, "Thoth's Ancient Bible contained a selection of magical and religious texts called spells to protect the dead from harm. Each person would prepare, hoping for an easy transition to the afterlife. If I would have been living 5,000 years ago in Egypt, I would replace the letter N with my name. Try it tonight. Read the powerful words of the Spell 30B out loud. When you do, you will have a greater understanding of the importance of caring for the truth in your soul. Thoth wanted us to have an afterlife of bliss in the Field of Reeds, the Egyptian heaven. Of the 189 spells, this is the text I would have chosen to be carved on the wall in my tomb. I would practice Thoth's bible for judgement day. Once I would be declared dead, my heart would be removed and weighed on the scales of balance against the feather of righteousness. Remember, this was the first bible, according to the very Ancient Egyptians. Their old beliefs were rarely discarded, new ideas and concepts were added. These spells are meant to help the dead progress in the Duat, a vast area under the Earth, connected to Nun, the waters of the primordial abyss. It is the region through which the Sun God Ra travels from west to east. It is where Ra battled Apep, the evil god, the deification of the devil.

"The Judgement of the Dead. Spell 30B,

"O my heart which I had from my mother! O my heart of my different ages! Do not stand up as a witness against me, do not be opposed to me in the tribunal, do not be hostile to me in the presence of the Keeper of the Balance, for you are my Ka, my soul which was in my body, the protector who made my members hale. Go forth to the happy place where to we speed: do not make my name stink to the Entourage who make men. Do not tell lies about me in the presence of the god; it is indeed well that you should hear!

"*Thus says* Thoth, Judge of Truth, to the Great Ennead which is in the presence of Osiris: Hear this word of truth. I have judged the heart of the deceased, and his soul stands as a witness to him. His deeds are righteous in the balance, and no sin has been found in him. He did not diminish the offerings in the temples, he did not destroy what had been made, he did not go about with deceitful speech while he was on earth.

"*Thus says* the Great Ennead to Thoth who is in Hermopolis: This utterance of yours is true. The vindicated Osiris Louise is straightforward, he has no sin, there is no accusation against him before us, Ammit shall not be permitted to have power over him. Let there be given to him the offerings which are issued in the presence of Osiris, and may a grant of land be established in the Field of Offerings as for the Followers of Horus.

"*Thus says* Horus, son of Isis: I come to you, O Wennefer, and I bring Louise to you. His heart is true, having gone forth from the balance, and he has not sinned against any god or any goddess. Thoth has judged him in writing which has been told to the Ennead, and Maat, the great witness. Let there be given to him bread and beer which have been issued in the presence of Osiris, and he will be forever like the Followers of Horus.

"*Thus says* Louise: here I am in your presence, O Lord of the West. There is no wrong doing in my body, I have not wittingly told lies, there has been no second fault. Grant that I may be like the favored ones who are in your suite, O Osiris, one greatly favored by the good god, one loved of the Lord of the Two lands, Louise, vindicated before Osiris.

"I left the words as 'He' thinking I may get faster passage if I were a man. Modern Egyptians changed the word bible to the 'book of the dead.'

I did not read these words before I came to Egypt, because I was told I was not a Christian, if I read such things. I was also told that the ancient hieroglyphics were 'demonic.' I wish people knew facts before they made judgements. The word is 'demotic,' a name for 'cursive' hieroglyphics. The manuscript hieroglyphics are the most common to us. The Rosetta Stone has both.

"The only way I could travel safely through the underworld to the afterlife was if you knew Thoth's ancient bible. There was one gate for each hour of the night. I must pass through all 12 gates. Pure spirit and Thoth's knowledge was required to get to the afterlife. The Book of Gates states when a king dies; he unites with the sun and becomes one person with Ra. The king's death parallels the path the sun takes each night. For 12 hours he battles demons, in the third gate he faces the Lake of Fire. The fire of damnation. How did Thoth know about the ring of fire? Later the king must conquer the snake, which represents Satan. Getting to the afterlife was quite an ordeal, because the snake, Satan comes back at the 10th gate, wanting new information. I had to study to outsmart the devil. Osiris was the god of the underworld, he expected me to know truth. It was he, who made the decision if I should have a wonderful afterlife. Or not.

"How would Thoth know about the journey? Believing the heart was the seat of wisdom, he speaks of the importance of truth, of knowledge and of judgement. The Egyptian religion influenced their descendants faiths and cultures, including the Abrahamic religions." I smile, feeling confident and grateful I had this experience. "We rarely talk of death, it is liberating, and curious at the same time.

The chief puts his arm around me, "Thank you, I enjoyed that."

"Some of the spells in the Book of the Dead originate in the Pyramid Texts, found in the chamber of Pharaoh Wenis, the last ruler of the Fifth dynasty, 2345 BC. Some spells have words common to the earlier Predynastic Period, before 3100 BC. The Pyramid Texts were to help the Pharaoh overcome the hostile forces and powers in the Underworld. They reflect a belief in an astral afterlife among the circumpolar stars. This predates the ideas of the pyramid builders, who believed in a solar afterlife spent in the company of the Sun God, Ra."

Moon Bear reads. "Conflicting information, astral verses solar. I do not know about this, I feel our meeting best come to a close. Who wants to summarize?" He asks.

Todd stands, "Fast forward. Moses showed the pharaoh his gods are weak and useless compared to the great universal God, the God Yahweh. I want to pose this question. Is it that the Israelites disobeyed God, therefore He sent them for protection (by being held together as one family) in captivity by the Egyptians. Or was it they were sent by God so He could "introduce" Himself to the Egyptians? The power of the Egyptian gods was lost when Moses commanded the pharaoh of Egypt to 'Let my people go.'

Ten plagues swept through Egypt. Exodus 7:14

1. **The waters turned to blood.**
2. **Frogs emerged everywhere.**
3. **Dust turned into gnats.**
4. **Flies covered the land.**
5. **Live stock died.**
6. **Boils appeared on the people and pets.**
7. **Hail rained from the sky.**
8. **Locusts descended on the crops.**
9. **Darkness fell on the land.**
10. **God sent the Angel of Death to kill the first born.**

During the night the king sent for Moses and Aaron and told them, "Get your people out of my country and leave us alone! Go and worship your Lord, as you have asked." Exodus 12:31

"The Hebrew people living in Goshen were held together as a large family unit and they were protected from the plagues. What is God saying to the Egyptians by this act of protection? He shows He is the great God, the only Yahweh. Moses then began his exodus, leading the 600,000 Hebrew men out of Egypt." Todd states informing us of his wisdom.

Exodus 14:19. "All this time God's angel went ahead of Israel's army, but now he moved behind them. A large cloud had also gone

ahead of them, but now it moved between the Egyptians and the Israelites. The cloud gave light to the Israelites, but made it dark for the Egyptians, and during the night they could not come any closer."

Daniel adds, "The exact pharaoh of the Exodus was never named in the Torah. It could be Dudimose, Ahmose l, Thutmose, Horemheb, Ramesses l, or Ramesses ll. Why would the name of the king that endured the plagues and drove the Hebrews into the Red Sea not be written in bold text. Moses you are credited with this information, you told the story about exodus. Why is the pharaoh still a mystery and not exact history?"

"There are many questions." Moon Bear answers as we all shook our heads in agreement.

"I say this prayer when I pray over people," I responded. The prayer God told Moses to say to the Israelites. It comforts my voice to say it, and my ears to hear these words of peace."

"The Lord bless you and keep you; the Lord make his face shine upon you and be gracious to you; the Lord turn His face toward you and give you peace." Numbers 6:24

Todd stands, wanting to end with these words, "The illustration of the Ankh is a design also used in the habits worn by friars and monks. You can visualize them wearing this design. The ankh is the Ansata Crux meaning handled cross. The Egyptian academics at the University of Cairo tell us the ankh is representative of the role of the Nile River in Africa. The oval head represents the Nile delta with the vertical marks representing the path of the river, the East and West arms represent the two sides of the Egyptian country and their unification."

The ankh, is the Egyptian symbol for eternal life. The belief that God had chosen Egypt as a safe place for Jesus to hide him from Herod was a great source of pride to the Egyptian Christians. The transition onto the ideas of Christianity were already familiar to the Egyptians, because their ancient religion believed in death and resurrection of a god, the idea of the judgement of souls and a paradisiacal abode of the righteous souls, an afterlife for the faithful.

While their Roman counterparts worshipped in catacombs and underground vaults, the Egyptian Christians built their churches openly. Each person the Empire struck down, another would be converted by the example of the martyr. Romans persecuted Christ followers, many Christians decided to leave their land rather than face imprisonment for non-payment of debt due to high taxes. Finding peace and a religious fulfillment in the rural country side became appealing to many Egyptians. Thousands flocked to a communal life style at the St. Simeon Coptic monastery, which is an ancient, abandoned fortress monastery located near Aswan.

A great number of Christian monasteries are scattered about the East, from the 300 built in Constantinople, to St. Catherine's Monastery which houses Moses' Burning Bush at Mount Sinai. To St. Antony's Monastery, which lies at the foot of Al-Qalzam Mountain near Al Zaafarana, in Egypt, one of the oldest active monasteries in the world.

Saint Anthony is the Father of Christian Monks. (Picture him wearing the ankh type robe.) He is credited along with Egyptian born Pachomius, with founding Monasticism, (word origin, Greek) a religious life renouncing worldly pursuits, devoting one's self to spiritual work. Both monks and nuns are considered monastics. Roman Catholicism, monks and nuns are called brother or sister, while in Orthodox Christianity, were called father or mother. From the word monasticism in Christianity, originates the words of monk and monastery. Many Coptic popes came from the Monastery of St. Macarius in Wadi Al Natrun. The Christian monk embraces the monastic life as a vocation for God.

There are classical tours to visit many of the ancient monasteries. Such as the White Monastery, the Deir el Abyad and the Red Monastery, the Deir Amba Bishoi.

There are 260 chapels or shrines located in the Necropolis, which is a large burial ground called 'city of the dead.' On the northern edge, a church dating back to the 5th century AD, is regarded as one of the oldest churches in Egypt. The Christian remains of the Necropolis of Al Bagawat in the Kharga Oasis predate Christianity. The Chapel of the Exodus is situated behind the group of chapels located on the central ridge. It may be considered one of the oldest Christian chapels in the Necropolis, with paintings from the first half of the fourth century. There are paintings of Moses leading the Israelites from Egypt, Moses in the Sinai, the Egyptian King and his army, Noah's Ark, Adam and Eve, Daniel in the lion's den, Sadrach, Mishach, and Abednego in the furnace; the sacrifices of Abraham, Jonah in the whale, Jonah out of the whale, Rebeca at the well, and the Garden of Eden.

Another outstanding contribution was Pantaenus, at the Didascalia, the famous catechetical school in Alexandria where early Christian scholars proved that reason and revelation, philosophy and theology were not only compatible, but essential for the wholeness of a persons character. This was the first Catechetical School in the world built in 180 AD.

Inside the Luxor Temple, five churches were built during the Byzantine period. None of these churches exist today, but, within the temple, there are a number of statues and column bases with dedications which date to the Christian period prior to the legalization of the religion. In the Temple of Karnak, an ancient 4th century Christian church as established in the Great Festival Hall of Tuthmoses III. There are paintings of saints on six of the columns.

"Can you understand the mysteries surrounding God? They are higher than the heavens and deeper than the grave. So what can you do when you know so little, and these mysteries outreach the earth and the ocean?" Job 11:7

LouiseToth.com

The Cairo Museum

I have dreamed of the Cairo Museum since I was a young girl and fell in love with the first Indiana Jones movie. Indiana's father was a professor and had a speaking engagement in Cairo and took the whole family to Egypt, young Indy was about ten. His father brought his own former tutor to teach Indiana and travel with them experiencing the mysterious city. What better place to learn the city's history than in its museum. Now I have the chance of a lifetime. As I enter the door I meet my very own personal museum curator, my private tutor.

I look around like a kid in a candy store, all this history, I understand why Amir is so concerned, if a bomb goes off in here it would end these artifacts forever. The central Cairo Museum houses the greatest collection of ancient Egyptian art and antiquities.

The museum was built in 1902 and contains the largest collection of Pharaonic artifacts in the world.

The properly appointed structure holds innumerable masterpieces including the death mask and tomb treasures of Tut, experimental art of the age of Tut's father, Akhenaten and many profoundly moving sculpted portraits, mummies and wall paintings. The golden relief of Tut's family. Tut deep in loving conversation with his wife, Ankhesenam. King Tutankhamun's golden artifacts under the museum's light blazed like the sun's powerful energy. Tut's royal cartouche carved in gold, befitted his kingly status. Tut's golden mask is so detailed and the inlaid precious jewels honors the craftsmanship of the era. For the next three hours I listen carefully to my guide, gathering his information into my heart. So much exotic energy, for my eyes and senses to take in, completely a spiritual experience to see such powerful lives lying before me. Everything in the Egyptian Museum is extraordinary. It is one of the most magical collections on Earth. The greatest ancient treasures, including those from Tutankhamun's tomb, which take up nearly half of the second floor. Thousands of people every day are mesmerized by Tut's exquisite golden death mask, displayed in a special room along with two of his three golden coffins and other pharaonic jewelry. There are stone statues of pharaohs and ancient Egyptian gods that reach heights of 20 feet, intricately painted sarcophagi, papyri, delicate glass objects and household objects made of wood and clay. The Palette of Narmer, a 5,000 year old stone carving, contains one of the oldest known hieroglyphic inscriptions depicts the unification of upper and lower Egypt under the Pharaoh Narmer of the First Dynasty.

The secrets were lost until the discovery of the Rosetta Stone. The stone was carved in Egyptian and Ancient Greek. The hieroglyphs were translated by comparisons to the Greek text and the mysteries of Egypt were revealed. The Rosetta Stone gave Egypt's history life again. The Stone is housed in the Egyptian collection of the London Museum.

Abdul Aleem, my guide, "Have you met our great archaeologist, Doctor Zahi Hawass? He was in the museum earlier."

"Yes, I have met him, he was one of the speakers at the conference, he went to school where I grew up, small world, isn't it?"

"I am fascinated and pleased to have such a receptive student. My name means 'Servant of the Omniscient' you can call me Abdul." He says with his charming British accent. "You know you have a revered Egyptian name."

"Look at this case, these are scarabs. Do you know they are the strongest animal in the world per weight. They were thought to have the power of Ra, the beetle can roll up to 50 times their weight. Male Onthophagus taurus beetles can pull 1,140 times their own body weight. Imagine that, I cannot even pull two times my body weight. The scarab was seen as an earthly symbol of Ra's heavenly cycle and were popular amulets and are still used in jewelry today."

"I use them in jewelry making, with other ancient beads and gemstones of turquoise and carnelian," I mention very proudly. "Scarabs are stones of the God Thoth, the God of Wisdom. The backs of the scarabs appear to represent both sides of the brain. The dynamic creative powers of the right side of the brain and the hard working executive powers of the left side."

"You must know that Thoth was a holy sage and the heart and voice of Amon Ra." Feeling receptive to his knowledge, it is a joy to have all these energy forces running through my body. "Ra," he says proudly, "was the Golden One who represented the physical aspects of the sun, the light and the heat. Thoth was the moon energy, the energy that represents the emotions." We gaze upon them each day in the sky, enjoying their light. Let me tell you a cute story.

"At one time the sun and moon were equal in brightness, but the Goddess of the Sky, Nut was in trouble and went to Thoth for help. Thoth gave some of his moonlight to Nut to make five extra days. Now the sun is much brighter than the moon. Egyptology, numerology, astronomy and astrology are so fascinating, don't you think?"

"I do not believe in astrology." I laugh.

Do you know that on your birthday the sun returns to the exact position in the sky as it was on the day you were born? It is called the solar return. "Lady Thoth, do you know what constellation you were born under?" asks Abdul.

"I have six planets in Leo, my sun and moon are both in Leo."

"The Great Lion, you are a Christian girl, how fitting to have so many lions around you to protect you. The Essene's say when Jesus was a child in Egypt, the lions walked with him through the desert to protect him. You are like the great lion, very protective of the people that you love. I am right, yes?"

"Very protective."

Our mythology believed that Ra ruled the Sun; you have six astrological planets in Leo ruled by the sun, means they are ruled by Ra." Abdul laughs, "Six Leos is rare, you look like a gift of the sun, hair the color of the sun's light, eyes the color of the sky, skin beautiful, and a heart for giving the light."

I adore the complimentary romantic way he speaks. "In the Chinese calendar I am a sheep. I love the tenderness of that. When Jesus told his disciples, "I am the good shepherd," he was assuring us that we are always safe, completely protected and under His watchful eyes."

"The lion lies down with the sheep, and there is peace. I love it also."

"Do you know that since Napoleon's invasion of Egypt, many have tried to get Egyptian treasure. We are working on plans for a new facility, the Grand Egyptian Museum intends to hold many of the collection's highlights, including Tut's treasure near the Pyramids at Giza," says Abdul as we step into the next room. "We will be heavy with alarm systems."

He continues, "I pray to God, the lion will lay down with the sheep and we will be safe. The plans God has for you are plans to bless you." We speak about being close to God, the heavens, the stars, the keys to wisdom and I feel his respect for Egypt.

Grand Egyptian Museum (GEM) will be one of the largest museums in the world, and it opens in 2014. Expect an IMAX theater.

Abdul loves the stars, he tells me he grew up looking at the heavens, the Orion belt and how he developed an understanding for astronomy and the Star Map. Astronomy was the language of intelligence. Galileo was put under house arrest when investigated by the Roman Inquisition in 1615. He believed in heliocentrism, the astronomical model in which the Earth and planets revolve around the Sun which is at the center of our universe. The word comes from the Greek helios 'sun' centered, opposing geocentrism view which placed the Earth at the center. Galileo believed as the ancient Egyptians believed and countered the Roman information as incorrect. The Romans suppressed so much knowledge, they pushed it underground.

I am disappointed that the Romans were more interested in barbaric gladiators fights than the wisdom of the heavens.

The heat in Cairo can be stifling, whole families will go up to the roof top to sleep outdoors under the stars that are billions of years old. Just imagine! Growing up lying under the sky each night, breathing in the fresh air, talking about the constellations, the world axis, the shooting stars, the wondrous delights of the milky way, all of heaven's beauty. He tells about the Orion theory based on the exact correlation of the three pyramids at

Giza with the three stars forming Orion's Belt, in the relative positions occupied by these stars in 10,500 BC. The geographic relationship of the Nile, Sphinx, and Giza pyramids which he believed directly corresponds with Leo, Orion and the Milky Way.

"Do you know a galaxy contains hundreds of billions of stars, and there are more than 100 billion galaxies in the universe with a star count estimate of 300 sextillion in our great universe. Imagine that. Sometimes when I meet people with big egos, I tell them that fact, and think, 'get over yourself, who do you think you are, who made you God.' He twitters, "Then I laugh inside at the ridiculousness of mortal man."

"Do you know the oldest accurate star chart of 1534 BC is Egyptian?" He says his family would talk about the Moon's influence upon tides and rivers, and the Egyptian calendar. "Our Coptic year is the extension of the ancient Egyptian civil year, three seasons, four months each. This calendar is still in use all over Egypt by farmers to keep track of the various agricultural seasons. Our Coptic calendar has 13 months, our countries agricultural needs are met by their increasing knowledge of the constellations, whose appearances change with the seasons, allowing the rising of particular star groups to herald annual floods or seasonal activities.

"We watch the rhythms of the heavens, and make connections between the patterns in the night sky and the effects of the moon, planets, and stars on our bodies, the oceans, and on our gardens. During an ascending moon, sap is drawn up, so moon gardeners will be looking to graft, and to harvest non-root plants. The rhythms of nature are the rhythms of life. We Egyptians were very much involved with astronomy; lining up the pyramids with the stars. The Ancient Egyptians technological genius! To be able to build a temple and have interior columns leading to one of the temple sculptures, and have the sun's rising timed perfectly to wash the statues with the dawn's early glow. That was and still is brilliant!"

I have always been in love with the variance of the unique color pallet that God uses to paint the sky each evening, listening to Abdul is so relaxing, we both are in love with God's masterpiece of heavenly stars. Tonight I will dream of tap dancing on the Milky way, and feeling free.

"Do you know Thoth was an Atlantean Priest-King who founded a colony in ancient Egypt? He wrote the Emerald Tablet in his native Atlantean language?" Abdul tells me. "Maybe?"

"The Emerald Tablet is beyond the belief of many scientists, yet if they grew up looking at the stars every evening for generations, they would be more open to the possibility. When I look at the milky way, I say to myself, how could you not believe there is more going on in the universe then we know? Thoth's information may date back 36,000 years BC. They believed in star and moon cycles. I do not know the answers." He whispers.

"Everything has its season. God has set up seasons in our lives. It is frustrating when our dreams are not on our timetable, but every season is not harvest season. There are plowing seasons, planting seasons, watering seasons. We would love for every season to be a time of increase. Yet without the other seasons, we would not be prepared. It is during the plowing seasons that God brings issues to light that we need to deal with." I reply.

"I say to people, if you do not believe in the moon's cycles, remember only one thing. Never open a bee's hive during a full moon!" He let out a hardy laugh, "They tend to swarm more. Luna means moon, and the bees act like lunatics at this time. That is why the moon calendar is essential for the bee keeper. Do you know there are 20,000 species of bees? In ancient times the bee was seen to symbolize the lands of Northern Egypt. Mass amounts of bees were needed to produce the honey to ferment the barley to sweeten their beer. I can taste it now," he grins. Egyptians love their nectar, savor the flavor, sweet beer, crisp glazed duck, and honey dripping onto homemade bread. Bees are more gentle on fruit or fire days and they give more nectar. Bees may become endangered, our ecosystem depends on them. Try honey on the Holy bread, called Qurban, the bread is round, decorated with a cross in the middle, surrounded by twelve dots representing the twelve disciples of Jesus." He suggests.

"Honey bread sounds perfect, let's get some and sit under the stars, to be so close to God's love, and the infinite depth and glory of His sky," I agree with a smile and a nod, I am getting hungry.

We agree if we are connected to God, we become so close to others with the same love, Abdul's graciousness and gentle spirit remind me of a man with a peaceful soul. We say good bye, appreciating our lovely time together.

While writing in my journal, keeping excellent notes for my book, the phone rings. "Hello Louise," speaks the gentleman on the other end of the line, "how is my friend today?"

"Your museum is awesome!" I declare.

"I am so proud of you learning with a trained instructor, we have an incredible museum, top in its field. I must fly to Abu Dhabi tomorrow, I will be at the Emirate Palace, if you need to contact me." He waits a moment in silence. "Are you still there?"

"Yes, it just made me think of someone. I have a friend who owns a business at the Emirate Palace, the Barakat Gallery."

"Louise, what is the chance you know someone who has a gallery there? Really, what is the chance?"

"I met his parents and family when I was in Jerusalem, they invited me to have a dinner at their family home. It was so enjoyable, especially the little children, they called me the pied piper, the young children were looking at my eyes the whole evening following me around. Their mother told me they never saw azure colored eyes, this was a real education, they even drew a picture of me, they were so sweet. The one little boy came really close to me, then he whispered to his mother, 'mama, she has eyes the color of the sea,' his mother translated to me. Since then I use that expression to honor our moment together. I can still picture their little faces, their big brown eyes wide with the sense of eagerness, their hearts open allowing their love to pour my way. For a moment I thought, 'this is what it must have been like when Jesus had all the little children around him, admiring Him and desiring to learn from Him. Children are so pure still very connected to God and still holding on to the hands of the angels." I say with sweet fondness of that memory.

"I had the funniest experience with one of the brothers. He took me to a villager outside of Bethlehem to look at some local artifacts, thinking I may want one. I looked at the one unusual little clay type doll and said no. He told me I could have it at his price and triple my money easily if I took it to his brother's store in Beverly Hills. I said I was a Christian and could not have an idol. He told me I could make a great return. I laughed and said that would be two strikes against me, one for making money on it and two for being responsible for putting an idol in someone else's house. I was quite impressed with the response. Both fellows sat up straight, chests high, smiling and said they were proud to know me, they valued my principles. I felt strong for standing my ground, we all felt good about the moments. I am sounding like a gypsy."

"Like a gypsy Queen," he says pleasingly.

"I will put that line in my book. Maybe you could give it to my friend at the Emirate Palace?"

"You are writing a book? I am finding out wonderful things about you, we will both give the book to him, I want to take you to Abu Dhabi, I want you to meet my friends. I am so pleased, I am proud to know you also.

"I will take you for a real treat when I return. You will enjoy it, it will be one of your most loved events, I have seen similar situations and it was exciting, you will think about it for your whole life. You will have done something none of your other friends have done."

"I don't know how to do this, I am an open spirit, yet I have had experiences where women have bonded against me saying things that were not true. It was so hurtful to my soul. For me to say I have done something that others have not arouses meanness in some people." I respond.

For if you forgive men when they sin against you, your heavenly Father will also forgive you. But, if you do not forgive men their sins, your Father will not forgive your sins. Mathhew 6:14

The number one regret people have at the end of life is that they wish they had been true to who they were and did not live their life to meet the expectations of others.

"Get over being so generous. Anyone that says bad things about you needs to get their head examined. You are with people here on your same level, but at home you have jealous people around you that are not up to your standards. By that I mean they are not Holy Spirit centered, if they were they would not say words like 'you are not welcome here' when you walk in the room. Do not put up with their humiliation, stop trying to let others have their way at your expense." Amir could sense a deep wound.

"Remember everything they are trying to do to you, has already been done to them. Think about it. Control freaks are easy to recognize because they always want to lay guilt. Everybody does something to them, they do not take responsibility for the damage their words do to others. You are a healthy girl, feel sorry for them. Your mental and physical health is one of your blessings, it all comes because of your open heart. Do something to bless them." He says.

A man's heart determines his speech.

"The ego is a false sense of self, the selfish side of our humanity. You do not have the burden of negativity here at the conference. Their erroneous judging perpetuates negativity. I know about these things, I have seen it, people that act like they are better than others. Amir says. Humanity creates negativity, it never comes from God."

Remember you are experiencing everything for God. The earth is a tough school house. The more trauma that comes your way the faster you evolve, it tests your strength and endurance. I believe competition is what is damaging to the soul.

"If you cannot speak your hurts trying to show respect to jealous women, you are not allowing yourself to grow. Do those women appreciate that you backed away? I can tell by your silence they did not show kindness, and when someone screams at you or tells lies, baby, you have my permission to stop acting like a lady!" Amir continues.

"You do not have to try to like everyone. Jesus did not like everyone, some of the Sanhedrin, some of the Pharisees, and some of the heads of the Roman government told lies about him.

"The people that hurt you, I bet they never walked where Jesus walked or had a meditation in the ancient pyramid with a respected Indian Chief? I am proud of you. You have worked so hard on your spiritual path, you are a seeker of the knowledge for and about God, that is the reason for our existence. I applaud you for all that you have accomplished in this lifetime. It is all about the spiritual path to God." Amir whispers.

"I like to give the golden rule. When I walk into a room I know I have contentment, to humiliate anyone they way they do to me is the opposite of my life of empowering. Humiliating someone is the worse thing a person can do to the human soul. So, I decided to make free four page websites for them, so I could be done with the hurt and move on." I reply in an understanding way.

"You do live your life with an open heart." He says.

"If we look to the Word of God, we see God's definition of love. First Corinthians 13 tells us 'Love is patient and kind. It does not envy, nor boast. It is not proud. It is not rude. It does not seek its own way, is not easily angered, and keeps no record of wrongs. Love does not rejoice in evil, but rejoices in the truth. Love believes, hopes and endures. Love never fails.' This is how God responds to us, and this is how we should respond to the people in our lives, with patience, kindness, hope, humility and love. Scripture tells us that God is love, and His character never changes!

"I get upset when mediocrity challenges excellence. It takes ten good words to make up for the one negative word. Louise, I respect myself and my opinion and I happen to have a very high opinion of you. Write your next book about bullying." Amir states.

"Thank you, my friend. Because it is not just the words, it is the condescending voice they use to crush my heart. It is done with full intention and done quite well, they accomplish their purpose. I am going to choose my thoughts each day more carefully."

"You are a softie on the inside, and I like that about you. Bulling is an epidemic, I am very sincere about your next book, you will give strength to other women who go through the same thing. Ask if they would like to be a chapter in your book about abuse? You could learn a lot from them. Why do they want to hurt, why do they lie, what do they get out of it? People do not become manipulators over night.

"God gives us 86,400 seconds a day. When your time is limited you do not have to respond to every critic. Some people like to find fault. Do not waste your gift of life on plans that are not God given. God has a divine appointment for you, Louise, and God has the right people to celebrate you. You are a beautiful woman inside and out." Amir says defending me.

Happiness is a choice. Yesterday you let your thoughts push you around, today you push your thoughts around!

"There is a difference between worldly Christians that are self centered and world class Christians who are fully alive with joy, confidence and enthusiasm that is contagious, because they know they are making a difference. We are supposed to encourage one another and give strength, not suck the life out of each other. They probably wanted some of your life.

"Just get out of their way, because it is not about you, they have issues from their past and are projecting. Remember people are as sick as their secrets, and it will affect their health. I am so sorry you had to deal with their abuse. You were smart to say nothing back, they would have blasted you to raise their dopamine and they would have felt great and you would have felt like a truck ran over you. Just get out of the way." He says.

"Everybody's perception of their truth is different from someone else. I may see things my way, my truth, because it is what my brain knows from my life. You may run into people who do not even think the same way, their truth come from their life, and who they are and what they experience. Your truth comes from your life and you may see a completely different view. Fortunately, you and I, are on the same page due to our listening skills. I delight in the way you sit and listen, without reacting, without ego." Amir does admire my respect.

"Yes, I have spent years being patient. I believe I may have an advanced doctorate degree in patience," I say reflecting on my life. "People do need to learn each others truths, it would take the stress out of most situations."

"To have a feeling of freedom and independence, we each need to empty the trash that separates us from the truth. If our body stands at point A, the truth may be at point C. We have collected years of false judgements that keep us from the belly of truth. When we clean out the garbage in our storage closet we get closer to the truth." I say.

"Louise, I respect you. You need to know that verbal abuse is abuse in the form of words. Words injure sometimes even more than physical wounds because it damages the soul and lowers the immune system. Maybe they were raised by wolves." He laughs. "When people come at me with their abusive attitudes, their I am better than you attitudes, I silently pray over them, it makes me feel better.

My secret is ~

"Close the mouth and connect to God's light. Your name, Louise, means heroine. Pray these words. 'Lord please help me to be the better man and stay connected to you. You are my strength, you are my rock, please send two of your strongest angels to stand beside me, and a third angel to put their hand over my mouth.' You will start to smile and they will be bewitched, bothered and bewildered."

I have a quick exercise to relieve stress. I stand and put an imaginary string at the top of my head connecting it the heavens. The angels pull up on the string and my neck gets longer, my shoulders looser, I wiggle the stress out of my spine and hips, knees, ankles and toes. Soon my arms and hands move around like a puppet and I am smiling. My magic string making me feel lighter, connecting me to a higher energy that lifts up and fills my brain with a childhood memory of joy.

"Amir, you are funny. I grew up in a home where we better not complain or ever talk back. If we kids fought or were misbehaving in the house my parents would take my brothers and I to visit a center that cared for handicapped children. We quickly learned that life can change in an instant. We learned to stop being selfish and to develop an attitude of gratitude, for we had no reason to complain or be negative. Compassion took over my heart at a young age. We were not in wheelchairs, we could hop, skip, run, jump, we could reach the ice cream in the freezer, our hands and feet were straight. Through this compassion, I found glory in everything and rarely notice bitterness and manipulation until it is right in my face. It completely throws me off, so I outwardly pretend I do not hear it. I use all my energy to rise above the coldness to a place where the air is clean and I can breathe again. Also, I grew up in a neighborhood of all boys, I am used to directness not jealousy. If there is a problem, boys call you on it and try to solve the problem."

When you look back over a lifetime, you will know that love is the answer to everything. Your parents taught you a great and valuable lesson.

May God hold you in his arms as you sleep, may He wipe away all fears and tears and fill your heart with an indescribable love.

"If we shoot for the moon and miss we may still land on the stars. So attach your string!" He chuckles.

Ancient Egyptian Beauty Worshipers

I woke to a knock at the door, "Come on Louise, brunch. Sunday brunch," Jheri calls, "you do not want to miss Sunday brunch at the Mena House, it is a five star feast. I will save a seat for you at our table in the dining room."

I stroll into a room fit for a king's party, magnificent ice sculptures in the shape of King Tut at the pastry table, ice swans at the duck and pheasant table, Ramesses the Great at the beef table, and an ice carving of Neptune at the seafood table, a very interesting combination to please everyone. There are waffles, organic vegetables, green eggs and ham, cheese bars, lobsters, large trays of shrimp, petit filet mignons, lamb with mint, large carving stations, pastas of every kind and shape, hot entree stations, cold entree stations, chocolates galore, Turkish coffee and teas. It is the first time the whole group is completely quiet tasting everything in sight.

"Todd what is that you are putting on your food?" I am curious.

"Turmeric, it boosts the immune system. There was a study at the Al Azhar University here in Cairo finding it has an effect, also, in lowering cholesterol. It has anti oxidant properties, it is a spice that makes the food a bit yellowish, but it is fine on the scrambled eggs. One of those Egyptian secrets. Todd came up for air, pulling out the class listings, "Are you going to choose one from column A?" The Cambridge grad has a very English dry sense of humor.

"I believe the class is titled, "Beauty Secrets" I really doubt if they are going to reveal the coveted secrets of the ancient ladies, but I am game."

"I am going to be there, just in case," laughs Todd, "just cannot get enough secrets, you know, he smirks with a cute ingenuous grin."

I declare with a southern drawl. "You are a gentleman and a scholar."

Upon entering the lecture tent we notice a very sweet fragrance, and a new young good looking professor wearing an upside down cone on her head, "My name is Elizabeth, I am from the British University, here in Cairo. Notice I am wearing an Egyptian black wig. Do you notice anything else?" she asks as we take our seats.

"You have an unusual cone on top of the wig, a bit like the fascinator hats that are so popular again, but yours does not have feathers," Todd replies trying to capture her attention.

The class giggles at his antics.

"When you look at pictures of the ancient Egyptian women, you will note a cone on their head tied with a string. The cone is made of hard fat, impregnated with perfumed oils, and worn on the head. Imagine during the warm evenings the fat melting, drenching into the wig with the pungent fragrance," Elizabeth hints with a curious grin.

Pointing, Todd asks? "Is that a picture of three young maidens wearing perfumed fat cones on their heads? It sounds a bit gross and primitive, the ladies would be dripping with the oil from the fat cone. My mind is thinking the fat acted like massage oils."

"Thank you for changing your point of view, yes, you are correct," Elizabeth encourages the eager young man. "The ladies wigs were woven in a vertical design therefore the oil did run down her wig and I am sure on to her shoulders."

Female wigs were woven longitudinally; even then women wanted to look longer, slimmer and taller. They made long hair a sign of beauty.

"Under the desert heat, hairlessness was also a sign of health and beauty. The Egyptians shaved themselves all over. Bronze razors were found in the tombs dating back over 5,000 years. The Pharaohs appeared sometimes with a clean head, other times wearing the wigs that they invented. They loved their wigs, males and females alike. They used human hair, and invented artificial hair, from the divided leaf of date palm fronds, and the less expensive wigs were made of soaked straw, or rattan for the working class. The long hair protected their necks from the sun.

"Notice when you see an image of an Egyptian king, the male wig pattern on King Tut and the female wig on his wife, Ankhesenamun are different. The masculine wig is woven with a horizontal pattern and the feminine wig is woven with a vertical design. As I say those words I must say sometimes they switched their wigs just for fun, when you are king, you can set any fashion you like. It is good to be king." She laughs.

Every Egyptian's motto. "You, too, can say, I am yesterday, today and tomorrow. I have the power to be born a second time," the professor states.

"No one knew the human body like the Egyptians, to the Egyptian, the body was as critical as the spirit. They needed the body to be preserved after death for the spirit to reenter. They were students and well trained doctors preserving a human being for the afterlife, with many experienced cosmetologists decorating their bodies for their journey. The Egyptian God Thoth and his forty two sacred books, had given to humankind contained a fountainhead of all knowledge, much of it was devoted to medicine. He was most important healing divinity. Thoth became a patron god of physicians, a source of medical knowledge. Thoth was incorporated into the Greek god Hermes and the Book of the Dead collection became the Hermetic Collection." The professor continues.

"Here is a test for future mothers, the Egyptians had an interesting method for diagnosing pregnancy. The barley and wheat was not just for making beer and bread, it was a key component to discovering if the lady was with child. Do not dismiss Thoth's ideas. This ritual had some success. The hormonal content of urine is a factor in urine examination for pregnancy today. What do the women do with the pregnancy stick today? In Ancient Egyptian times, the wife would urinate on to a mixture of wheat, barley seeds, dates and sand. If grains sprouted, the woman was to give birth. If only the wheat grew, the baby would be a boy; if only the barley grew, the baby would be a girl."

"I like her, she gets right to the point," Todd chuckles.

"Oils were a base of every Egyptian's beauty tool kit, they were the first to document the wearing of make up applied with carved ivory tools. They had every cosmetic invention that we have today; blushes, lip gloss, eye shadow and eye liner," the English professor tells us as she walks about.

"I admire the way the Egyptians adorned themselves with cosmetics, grinding a powder of gold, turquoise, carnelian, and lapis, starting a multi billion dollar beauty business that was not just for the women. Egyptians had equal rights, the men loved jewels and oils and cosmetics as much as their women. Even young King Tutankhamun's solid gold burial mask was embellished with enhanced eyebrows and eye liner, to protect his eyes. They believed in beauty for the afterlife, and were buried with their cosmetic cases near their bodies," I said to Todd.

Egyptian eye make up was not only used to cut down glare, (as used by the football players of today.) It was also used to as an insect repellent to keep the flies away. The Egyptians needed to be using their hands for creating, not for swatting.

"The Egyptian pharmacopoeia used metals and minerals, including copper, salt, alum, carbon from charred wood, and iron from meteorites found in the desert, and antimony a silvery, lustrous gray metal. Eye paints were probably in antimony, an important pharmacologic substance used later in the Renaissance Era. Black eyelid linings were produced by a composition of antimony and lead. The green color in eye makeup came from copper salts. These natural substances are antiseptic, especially copper in fighting eye blindness and prevent eye infections. Imagine working in the sun without sun glasses.

"One serious beauty secret still used today is moisturized sun screen. A little juniper oil was necessary in the desert heat. It is documented that the workers had a strike because there was a shortage of oils to make a type of sunblock for them to wear while working on the job." The teacher says, "Ma'at, who stood for balance, order, morality and justice, expected proper wages, it was a religious duty. In 1170 BC, the laborers had the first sit down strike in recorded history. Letters were written to the Vizier complaining about the lack of oil and wheat rations. They refused to return to work until their grievances were addressed."

"They needed sunblock, it had to be difficult to work in the sun and heat," Todd replies, "An alternative would be to do like other cultures and siesta during the noon hour to avoid the direct sun."

"Very much so, hence the old quote, 'only mad dogs and Englishman go out in the noon day sun." Elizabeth delights, "Lyrics by Noel Coward, and Sir Noel was an Englishman."

"The Egyptians invented perfumes from their fragrant flower blossoms. Do you know it takes 10,000 pounds of flowers to produce one pound of flower oil? Imagine the flower gardens and the fragrances as the wind gently moves over the land.

"Today, rose oil is used in over 70 percent of all perfumes."

"That is why they have the beautiful perfume bottles in the bazaar," Todd pipes in feeling proud he caught her attention.

"That is very true the bottles are much more advanced than the fat cones infused with perfume," she chuckles thinking of what he had said, about the melted fat being used as massage oils.

Beauty has proved to be a strong ally helping women cement their power and prestige. As we know with the legendary, mysterious appeal of Cleopatra. She was not born a beauty, she nurtured a soft skin as well as a soft voice. A positive personality and positive intelligent discussions embellished with an artistic flair captured the hearts of two of Rome's most powerful men. Her success was attributed to her confidence and breathtaking demeanor.

Her beauty was more than skin deep. Cleopatra's legacy, originates in the ancient Egyptian Queen's world of beauty secrets, number one, hydrate, hydrate, hydrate. Who says water and oil don't mix. They are the most important beauty secrets for a healthy, soft glowing skin, inside and out. Born in Alexandria, she grew up on a Mediterranean diet high in olive oil consumption. Remember, she grew up with the Greek Ptolemy family and married Italian men. She enjoyed the pleasures of the typical crops of the region including grapes, oranges and tangerines. Life by the sea was excellent for her skin, the ozone, fresh breezes, clean air, and abundant sea life. It is good to be queen. Cleopatra was credited with writing beauty secrets, an art she was universally acknowledged as mastering.

Ancient Egyptians went to great lengths to nurture and enhance their hair, it symbolized wealth, status, beauty, motherhood and fertility. To maintain natural hair growth and strength of their hair, Egyptians were pioneers in using castor oil to strengthening hair follicles. To get the full benefit of this treatment, hot oil wraps are infused with the oil and massaged into the scalp to ensure the deep penetration of Vitamin E and fatty acids in the concentrated oil.

It was one of the world's oldest health resorts used by King Herod the great was the Dead Sea. Egyptians prized the products, from balms used in early Egyptian Mummification to the minerals for makeup. The salts are known to combat stress and aging. Also, they are full of pigments, such as zinc oxide and titanium dioxide which is found in almost every sunscreen. It has a physical blocker due of its high refractive index. Vestiges of the ancient Egyptians' concerns with beauty and body care linger even today. We use titanium dioxide and zinc oxide in our make up because they have anti-inflammatory properties, mineral makeups have a calming effect on the skin especially for ladies who suffer from rosacea. Zinc oxide is also anti-microbial, therefore these mineral makeups were necessary for Cleopatra's acne.

After a salt scrub to the exfoliation of the body, Cleopatra would enjoy a lengthy soak in milk and honey. Milk contains lactic acid; a form of alpha hydroxy acid, which removes dead skin cells, causing the younger layer of skin to emerge. The Queen of the Nile added whole milk and honey to her bathwater. Goat's milk which contains capric-capryllic triglyceride is helpful to moisturize, while natron or baking soda softens the skin and honey locks in moisture for the skin. Archeologists have uncovered tombs of three ladies of the court of Tuthmosis III. They found jars containing cleansing cream of oil and lime.

Cleopatra drank, an aloe vera drink for a vibrant youthful glow. She revered this old therapeutic herb renowned as a healing plant as one of her best beauty secrets. Aloe Vera has been known for its 200 active nutrients, which heal the skin with anti-inflammatory properties. This ancient Egyptian herb of the past has burn healing capabilities and ability to decrease the effects of scars and wounds

Egypt's gold therapy on the skin for its curative and antibacterial properties and energy revitalization was applied all over her skin. All this pampering, no wonder we would see so many pictures of Cleopatra lounging on her Nile boats.

"Let us end with this thought, Egyptians invented circle hand mirrors made from polished bronze, round like the Sun God Ra, so when they looked at their reflections, they felt as if they were gazing at the face of a god or goddess." Elizabeth is enjoying her attentive student.

The following day Todd told me he took Elizabeth out for drinks.

"Yes?"

"She wants to talk to Amir."

"Tell her to call him."

"It is not as simple as that, she knows things."

"Are you with the CIA now. What things?"

"She won't tell me. She wants to meet with you, and have you ask Amir. Top secret and all that jazz. I am to ask if you will please meet with her. Please do it and put in a good word for me. She is cute, and all this espionage is turning me on."

"Todd, you are so darn cute, that headful of curls and big flashing smile."

"Don't forget my wildly amazing greenish eyes. I can bring her to you today. She agreed we could meet in my room."

"I have not been to your room are they all alike?"

"No, yours is bigger, you have a suite."

"What time shall I be there?"

"Noon."

I walk to Todd's room at noon sharp, knocking on his door, Elizabeth opens the door slowly, invites me inside and apologises that Todd was called away for awhile. "Please sit down," Elizabeth instructs. "I would like to ask you a favor. I realize Amir is your Security Concierge."

"Yes," I say, knowing something serious was about to be asked.

"This is my dilemma, A young man came to me with some antiquities wanting to get some money for them. I do not know if they are valuable. If I go to the authorities the antiquities will be confiscated, and I will be questioned. Maybe Amir could help them return the items for a price, he could buy them and donate them to the museum. I just hate to see them leave the country. If I go to him myself, I will be uncomfortable for the rest of my life, that is why I am asking you to do it for me."

I thought for a minute, I am afraid to act without asking Amir, but, I realize it is important to get the items returned. "You want him to buy the items back for a small price and return or donate them to the museum without a word said about this again? Do you have a price in mind? Ask them to write a list of what they are willing to trade. Amir will give the price that he feels is fair, this way it will be in their handwriting not yours, then you are covered, no one can say you took the antiquities. I will ask Amir," I feel cornered and unhappy that she put me in the middle.

"I love you, thank you so much, I know Amir will listen to you. At that moment Todd opens the door, "All finished girls?"

"Yes, I am going to leave you two alone, enjoy the afternoon," I say with a pounding headache. I go to my suite and immediately make the dreaded phone call.

Amir's line is busy, I leave a detailed message for him with instructions to call me back.

Twenty minutes later the phone rings.

The connection is so bad I am not sure if it is Amir calling or Todd playing with me, "I cannot hear you I am going to hang up the phone." The phone rings again, "Louise, we were disconnected. I am sorry they came to you. Tell me again."

"Amir, someone asked me today if you would consider buying some artifacts which you could donate to the museum, the person who asked me does not want them to leave the country. They may or may not be valuable. Apparently it is a young man who has them, and just needs some money. I am sure he tried to sell them, but apparently got low offers."

"Does this person have photos?"

"Yes."

"They could be junk, but you are right in asking me, I will buy them even if they are junk. Where did the kid get them? Never mind, he will not admit that. Who asked you to call me?"

"The person said they would feel uncomfortable asking you."

"I wish people had more courage, I hate games."

"I feel the same way." I blurt out my frustration, "it is cowardly."

"So, this person does not want to feel uncomfortable, yet, they do not care how uncomfortable it is making us feel." Amir says.

"I am so uncomfortable playing the middle man, do you want the truth?"

"Always." Amir replies.

"Elizabeth."

"Okay, I know what guy she is talking about. I am sorry she made it a hush, hush matter, thank you. I will take care of it with her, do not worry, I want you to enjoy your time in Cairo and not have to be put in stupid situations. You handled it well, I am proud of you. I will talk tomorrow."

"Good idea."

"I will call you around lunch time tomorrow. Again, I am sorry about this. Bye." Amir says feeling tired of always cleaning up other peoples messes. "I want you to relax and enjoy yourself. Elizabeth over reacted and should never put you in a position of knowing secrets and using you. She put a burden on you. Louise, you are blessed to grow up in a country with a freedom of speech. For you, your world is a world where truth is strengthened. Truth seeking and trust building seem to be your motto. Know that lying is a cooperative act. People that lay secrets on you are going to manipulate you through guilt. Never let people set you up. I am a little disappointed in her behavior. I am glad we had this talk."

Relaxation Day

"Why are you calling me at 8 am?" I miffed at Todd as I sat up in bed.

"I want to know if you want to go the Khan today, Elisabeth and I going about nine, and she asked if you would like to join us?" he replies.

"Perfect, I need to get some dancing outfits."

"Are you going to be a whirling dervish?" Todd retorts with his English accent.

We fall into a laughing attack, "no silly, a belly dancing outfit. You have a dry ridiculous humor." I reply.

"You are silly, too"

"9 am in the lobby." I say, still laughing.

"Cover up your body."

"The tradition is to cover the body, yet there are belly dancers. I am confused?" I banter with him.

"It is an odd male custom. Remember the controversy, the belly button could not be shown on the television hit show, "I Dream of Genie."

"I bet you saw that on Nickelodeon, I liked that show."

"I like that show, also." I say trying to stall until I decide if I really want to go to the Khan Bazaar. 'I will be down in 50 minutes, I want to order some Danish and coffee."

"I have already eaten and had a run around the pool." Todd brags.

"Okay, superman, I will be down in 45." I respond.

"Do you want help?"

"43 minutes."

"I will get the coffee, and have the kitchen make a boxed breakfast for you."

"I like the way you were raised, your consideration, goes a long way."

"It is the golden rule, my friend."

"Thank you, Todd, thank you." Now I can take my time, 43 minutes is plenty of time to shower and dress and take that long walk through the lobby. I found a beautiful Egyptian batik top in the gift shop. I used to make this design with wax resist dyeing techniques. I picked it for its color combination of browns and blues, perfect with my turquoise beads. Hair in a pony tail and I am ready to go. I was constantly admiring the artistic elements of this African culture, the vivid dye baths of their fabrics, raw colors woven next to each other in harmony, all the colors getting along, muting and blending into each other. I want everyone to get along, what a wonderful world that would be. I guess that would be heaven. The art of imagination, these were the words of the famous physicist Albert Einstein, "Knowledge is limited. Imagination encircles the world." Egypt is imagination, the great minds of the people and their endless supply of imagination.

Todd and Elizabeth are relaxing on the sofa in the lobby. "Louise, which day did you decide to take the trip down the Nile, there are two different groups available to choose from, I want us on the same boat for friendship and entertainment." Todd asks with a gleam in his eye.

"You mean you want to tease me." I reply enjoying his manner.

"I agree, it is fun, I wish I would have a sister like you, I am an only child."

"I am not an only child, and I wish I had brothers like you, you tease me in a silly way," I start laughing as the words came out of my mouth. My life would have been different, you are humorous and you allow me to just be myself with you. That is a blessing. My brother would tickle me until I would cry, I could hardly breathe, it was not fun for me at all. He would hide behind the shower curtain at night waiting to scare me, and jump out at me or hid under my bed and grab my ankles in the dark. I was terrified of the dark." I said remembering.

"I would not have done that, my parents would never have allowed such behavior, it is not acceptable. You would have been a great sister, you are hysterically funny, have a quick wit, plus, we are uplifting and see humor in things." Todd says as he gets up to put his arm around me as if he were being the big brother I needed.

Just then my cell phone ran, "Are you in Cairo, I am in the lobby with Elizabeth and Todd right now." I say with a smile on my face.

"I took care of things for Elizabeth, she can relax. Where are you going now?" Amir inquires full of curiosity.

"To the bazaar to get a friend a belly dancing outfit."

"I have work to do, but, I will send my driver to take you three to the bazaar and he will wait for you. Please do this for me, I do not want to spend my day worrying about your safety. He will be there in 25 minutes, and he will take you anywhere else you wish to go. Todd can be the extra body guard, he looks like he was a soccer player, fast on his feet."

"Can I tell him what you said?"

"You can always repeat whatever I say unless, I tell you it is confidential, and nothing is really confidential except government documents which I will not tell you, and my Swiss bank account numbers," Amir says in his gracious serious manner.

"You make me feel strong. I know exactly where I stand, with both feet planted firmly on the ground. We will wait here for your car. May I call your driver, David, like you do?"

"You may call him anything you want, he likes you. I will call you when you are at the bazaar, to see how you are doing. May God be with you, my friend."

"With you too, Amir."

"I take it we are going to be spoiled today," Todd beams.

"He said you are a great body guard for us ladies. He said you look like a soccer player, fast on your feet, you could protect us."

"He is observant, I noticed when he stands next to you he does not just focus on you, like I do when I talk to you, he stands strong paying accurate attention to you and quietly looks around the room watching people's eyes and mouths, as if he were trained to be a body guard for one of the presidents or high officials." Todd reveals to me.

"I agree, when I was in Jerusalem at the King David Hotel, I enjoyed dinner with one of King Juan Carlos' body guards, he said he was thinking the same thing of myself, that I do that."

"You are like that, a bit aloof, watching and waiting to see where someone needs you. I saw you walk right up to that young girl no one would talk with in the hotel the other evening, you just made your way over to her and complimented her on the colors of her blouse. You have a generous gift of knowing what people need, great compassion, I can see you are happiest helping others. Jesus would have called you friend."

"You are the perfect brother. I cannot remember being complimented when I grew up, not just me, I never heard compliments to my mother, either. I believe that is why I am an encourager, I give what I wanted for myself and I get to hear the words each time I give them away to someone else," I am enjoying my self analysis.

David arrives at the hotel to take us to the Khan Al Khalili bazaar.

"We are looking for dancing outfits." We all say together.

"May I make a suggestion?" David asks politely, I have a sister that works in the Marriott Hotel gift store, she makes the most inticate dancing outfits, she has books of photographs of the work that she has done. May I suggest a private time with her as opposed to walking through the bazaar, up and down the streets. She will give you the best price when I tell her are a friend of Amir."

Todd sat back and reached his long arms around both of us girls, sitting like a king with his queens, "Thank you David, you just made my day. A cool hotel with your sister sounds like heaven to my ears. I can sit and have a drink. King for a day. Only, if you join us David. I could use some male company while the ladies are shopping."

David was wearing a handsome grin, "I would love to, sir, I would love to. The Cairo Marriott is on Zamalek Island surrounded by magnificent gardens, you will like it sir."

"Call me Todd, please."

"Thank you Todd, would you like me to tell you some history of the hotel?" The king that built your hotel is the very same King Khedive Ismail the Magnificent. The same year he built his hunting lodge, the Mana House in 1869, he was the ruler of Egypt, he prepared a great festival for the opening of the Suez Canal, the highway to India. He established a group of palaces on the Cairo Nile. El Gezera Hotel was one before it was bought by the Marriott Omar Khayyam Hotel in 1982." David is proud of his knowledge and pleased to inform us.

"I wrote a paper on the turmoil of the Suez Canal. Ten years in the making and thousands died of heat and bad conditions. Egypt was finally connected to the Mediterranean Sea and the Red Sea allowing water transportation between Europe and Asia without navigation around the Cape of Good Hope at the south end of the African continent." Todd says.

Todd is a wonderful story teller, we are listening so intently we did not realize that David has parked the car and is sitting quietly listening to his new friend.

"I have to call Amir, before we get carried away in the fantastic hotel, his mother lives close by, would you all mind if I ask her to join us?"

"Please do, we would love to meet her," Todd and Elizabeth say together.

"Hello Louise, how is the bazaar," Amir asks in a clear voice.

"Do you know David has a sister who designs and makes dancing outfits?"

"Yes, I forgot about that, she works at the Marriott. I hope he took you there instead of the bazaar."

"Yes, we are about to enter the hotel and I am wondering if you and your mother could join us for lunch."

"I will give you mother's number, she will be thrilled if you ask her directly. Tell her I will be joining you there about one o'clock. Thank you, that is very thoughtful of you."

I dial the number. "Hello Alexandria, it is Louise calling you with an invitation to join us for lunch at the Cairo Marriott today about one o'clock."

"Oh, you precious child, I would love to join you, I live very close, it will be such a pleasure."

"I am here now with Todd and Elizabeth and your son's driver David. Your son will be here at one." I am happy to report.

"I shall be there at one also, my sweet child, habibi."

"Habibi, I have a special affection for you in every way, you are a sacred soul, you are a sweet beautiful soul, I mean that from the bottom of my heart," I say sincerely.

"I am so pleased, you will love the hotel, my dear, the original Gezirah Palace was constructed to resemble Versailles where Empress Eugenie and her husband the French Emperor Napoleon stayed. The king that built your hotel wanted them to feel comfortable when he invited them for the opening of the Suez Canal so he built a place that would suit them. The French love it, a very impressive hotel, I will see you at one o'clock."

"I love that she knows history and shares it with us. Have you been to Versailles?" Todd inquires of me.

"Yes, I took some classes at the Sorbonne, both are located in Paris. I have always very been interested in history and architecture, from the pyramids to the building of Versailles. I am in awe of all the details it takes to create such master pieces." I reflect remembering my studies.

"God is in the details." We all seem to say at the exact same time.

Todd stretches his arms to the East and to the West as if he were to fly saying, "God is in the details." When I pay attention to the details I am truly in the moment. You are so present to the moment, I have watched you look at the details of a flower, as if you are studying the great works of the Creator.

I smile lovingly, I feel I have the best new brother in the world.

What a hotel. David told us the hotel has 6 acres of palace gardens and is a 20 minute walk to the Egyptian Museum. The roof of the palace is an open air theatre which faces the Nile, how cool is that to watch a movie under the stars.

"How about the Omar Khayyam Casino?" David interjects.

We are going to stop into the ladies lounge, guiding Elizabeth into the door. "You look worried, let me hold you and pray over you. God, I am lifting up your precious daughter to you, precious Elizabeth, I am asking you to keep your strongest angels around her. Bless her and comfort her, continue encouraging her and strengthening her in all your ways. Thank you God, amen."

"Thank you, Louise, I needed that, Amir talked to me and took care of everything. Thank you so much." Elizabeth discloses with a big sigh.

Stop focusing on the negative, say, "God's Word tells me that my God shall supply all my needs according to His riches in glory by Christ Jesus." Philippians 4:19

"When you came to me, you had a troubled heart. The way God teaches is through anointing within. It is continuous anointing. In any situation He is teaching us by the presence or absence of peace. When I told Amir, he had peace when he took it out of my hands."

When we saw Todd waiting for us, we both kiss him on a cheek, took his arm and walk to find the others.

"Whatever just happened? I love your energy, what a delightful shift, you are both lighter."

The three of us are so pleased to be sharing a special moment. The three new friends.

David is waiting to introduce us to his sister, Sophia. What a delightful woman, stylish, gentle and creative. She shows us what she has for sale and decides she wants to design and make a complete outfit for each of us. She measures every inch, placing the charms, little coins and the proper fabrics to reveal and conceal. She knew exactly what she was doing, and we are getting excited to learn to dance from a real Egyptian dance class.

Todd meanwhile picks up a brochure from the concierge desk asking about the casino. He mentions he is at the Mena House, the concierge smiles, "When you have a Sphinx and the Great Pyramid in your back yard, do you really need a casino, Sir?"

YAHWEH
LORD OF LORDS

GREAT I AM
HEALER
COUNSELOR

ELOHIM
ANCIENT OF DAYS
ADONAI

ANOINTED
THE LIGHT
KING OF KINGS

EL SHADDAI
FATHER ABBA

MESSIAH

JEHOVAH
SHEPHERD

HEARER OF PRAYER
SAVIOUR

DELIVERER

LAMB OF GOD
REFUGE
ALPHA AND OMEGA
PROVIDER
PRINCE OF PEACE
JESUS
COMFORTER
CREATOR GOD

Lunch with Amir's Mother

"Louise, I must tell you, I am an older lady and some people simply treat me as if I am invisible, but you bring such interesting people and conversations into my life. You want everyone to be knowledgable, you are a natural teacher. I love who you are and how you include all ages into the circle," Alexandria beams.

"You are easy to love. I did not grow up with discussions, we always had to be quiet at dinner, therefor conversation was a rare occurrence. Your kindness feels like love to me. I enjoy people who are kind inside, who do not carry judgements." I reveal to her as she is hugging me close, "You are a dear generous mother."

I say a little prayer to help me with that. "Lord, forgive me for reacting in unloving and disrespectful ways. Help me to understand the key to motivating another person is to meet their deepest need. As an energizer I know my respect motivates love and love motivates respect. Open my heart and mind to what You intend for us to discover from your Word on how to reclaim love and respect in this world," She tells me.

"David suggested that you are going to be on the Nile this week. Is that correct?" Alexandria asks with intent interest.

"Yes, we are going to the Valley of the Kings, Luxor and Karnak."

"How about this idea, I want to talk to you in private. I have a small plane that seats very comfortably the pilot and six passengers. I also have a lovely flat in Luxor near the Winter Palace Hotel, which is a five star hotel on the banks of the Nile River just south of the Luxor temple. I would be more comfortable if my son would travel with you. My son is well connected, he would be told of unusual events about to happen. Please think about my offer.

Amir and David come strolling out of the casino to join the rest of our group. "We got lucky, we are up $15 each."

Changing the subject since his mother was there, I put my arm around her as we stroll into the restaurant, "I love this hotel, the gardens, the adjoining Gezira Sporting Club, the architecture and construction of the palace reflect the Khedive's passion for the Neo classical style so popular in Europe. I studied some architecture. I understand this hotel accommodated the first performance of Verdi's Opera Aida. I saw that opera in the ancient Roman Baths of Caracalla, I was impressed with the singing and the horses riding through the Roman ruins. I believe it was my very first opera." I delight in my memories.

You started at the very top, how exciting in the ruins of the great old baths of Roma, sitting outside under the stars, sipping your cappuccino. We love the same things," Alexandria says proudly, "to think I have so much in common with an American girl."

"What a wonderful lunch, I really enjoy the coffee here. I hope they have the same in Luxor. Our itinerary takes us to the Valley of the Kings." Todd expresses as we are finishing our meal.

"Oh Louise, when are you thinking about this trip?" Amir asks sitting back in his chair looking at me inquisitively.

Todd speaks up, "Some of the group are going tomorrow."

"That soon, no, I cannot have you do that. Give me a day to sort things out and I will take you myself. That would be Todd, Liz, you Louise, myself, and mother would you like to come?" Amir asks with an attitude of graciousness.

"I will have to give it thought." Alexandria responds wondering if she would be a bother to the younger group.

"How long did you want to stay? We have a boat there and mother has a large flat near a wonderful old hotel, it could be a really exciting time for all of us. I will take you, I do not want to worry, I will have no peace, you will have a delightful, well-protected time. Since our home is located in Luxor, we are very respected, you will be treated to the best, everyone will be watching out for you. If mother decides to come, David would you please also join us, to be a companion to mother?"

"Yes, I will wait for instructions," David is excited. This is a special day, bringing his boss and friends to meet his sister and now receiving an invitation to Luxor, a very good day indeed.

"I have to get back to work, I need to finish my projects tonight and tomorrow, then we have three days plus the weekend to relax and enjoy the beauty of the ancient cities of Karnak and Luxor, the old Thebes area."

"David, please drive mother home and walk her to her door, then come back here, either spending the day here or taking Louise where she wants to go." Amir states.

"I will drop Elizabeth back at the university, she has a class to teach, and then I will take both of you to the Mena House."

David tries to entertain us up on the drive with his broken English.

"Do you know what one act on American soil bankrupted the country of Egypt?"

"Serious trivia something on American soil caused Egypt to go bankrupt?" Todd replies. "I have 20 bucks left, let's play for money," knowing he had no idea of the answer. "What one act? Bootlegging, that is it, bootlegging!"

David laughs in a deep hardy way. "It is more complicated, I will take your 20 dollars. When the Civil War ended it led to a bankrupted Egypt, which led to the occupation of the British on Egyptian soil in 1882. That is the year the Gezira Club was built for the British soldiers, which is where you, Louise, dined with Alexandria."

Six degrees of separation.

"Say what, you are teasing my brain," Todd is being silly. We laugh and play with him, but, had no clue of the answer, no clue at all.

"Cotton was first cultivated in the Old World about 7,000 years ago, mostly in India. Cotton has been spun, woven, and dyed since prehistoric times. It clothed the people of ancient India, Egypt, and China. Our Egyptian agriculture was transformed by the introduction in 1820 of long staple cotton." David tells us.

"I love your Egyptian sheets, that is how you get a high thread count, it is a longer type of cotton so the thread could be spun thinner and finer without breaking the threads, interesting, I was wondering how it is accomplished. I am being serious. Cotton bankrupted Egypt?" I question.

"During the American Civil War, British and French traders invested heavily in cotton plantations in the southern parts of the United States. The Egyptian government headed by Viceroy King Khedive Ismail the Magnificent took out substantial loans from European bankers. After the American Civil War ended in 1865, British and French traders abandoned the more expensive Egyptian cotton and returned to cheap American exports.

"This one act sent Egypt into a deficit spiral that led to the country declaring bankruptcy eleven years later in 1876, and it is a key factor behind Egypt's annexation by the British Empire six years later in 1882. We owed them money, they moved in and set up rules to organize us back from chaos. We have Egyptians speaking with English accents and many attractive offspring resulted through the decades." David explains.

"I am glad I did not bet more, I never would have guessed that answer in a million years, you could have won my house, my car, my dog," Todd teasingly complains in a southern British accent.

"Well, here we are at the former Royal Lodge of the King that should have stayed out of American investments. He had it all. Glad I am not a king, the Pharaohs stayed in their own back yard, well as I say that, they expanded greatly south through Sudan, east through Turkey. Have a great evening, I enjoyed myself, Todd, you are a man's man and a ladies man. Excellent breeding," David took a liking to Todd, his charm is undeniable.

"Todd, sometimes you sound like a country western song," I trip over my tongue laughing before the words got out of my mouth, we both catch the wave of giggles and fall against the wall in exhaustion.

"I have heard that many times, but I never thought I would hear it from you."

"Todd, it is so out of context, you are a graduate of one of the most distinguished British schools in the world, and you put on the country voice, the vulnerable folksy country voice and it wins the hearts of everyone. Vulnerable like a fox in a hen house," I start to laugh again. The hens want to grab those curls. Get a hair cut and stop torturing me."

"You like it."

"Yes, I sometimes wish I had a head full of curls, I have straight hair." I say with a bit of silliness.

"We would have beautiful babies, beyond beautiful."

"Maybe you really are from the country? Where brothers and sisters marry?" I could not get the words out and we are laughing again.

We schlepp our bags of gifts through the lobby, trying to compose ourselves to act properly in this very sophisticated hotel.

Sharon comes running after us. "We are leaving at 7 am tomorrow, are you packed?"

"We will meet you there, we are going a day later, long story, see you in Luxor. Are you sad to leave this hotel?" I ask Sharon.

"Yes, when can I have a pyramid off my patio? I will always remember this experience. Amon may join the group if there is room on the Nile Cruiser." She replies.

"Would he like my room on the boat for free? I doubt they will give my money back this late, I will be staying in Luxor at Alexandria's flat. Enjoy, we will see you there, you have my cell." I tell Sharon.

"Come in, for a minute, it is clean the maids were here, chocolate on the bed, fruit on the table, clean sheets each day, just like home." Todd is always a gentleman. He opens the door to his room.

He turns on the television, a news program reports an event of terrorism. I sit watching the photos of one of our US Embassy being bombed. "It just makes me sick, it is really scary, that is where we go when we are in a foreign country for help, we do not expect to be blown up." I walk into the bathroom and become sick and dizzy. "Todd, I do not know why this is effecting me so much. Maybe because I travel alone sometimes and it is hard to feel safe. I feel so dizzy."

"Lay down on the bed, I will make you a cup of tea in my magic tea pot." He says trying to comfort me noticing how pale I look.

"Please, if you have mint tea it will settle my stomach, thank you."

"You sure are sensitive."

"I get scared for myself and for innocent people. The population has doubled since I graduated from college, to think we felt safe hitching a ride, not now."

"No way, never." Todd says emphatically. "Never."

"People drank and did drugs when I was in school, but it seems different now."

"Did you do drugs?"

"No, but I drank beer."

"I bet you were fun, and a real beauty."

"The opposite of how I feel at the moment."

"Put your head on the pillow and rest for a few minutes, getting sick is no fun, I can still remember holding on to the toilet bowl like you just did, not fun at all. Mine was better because it was the result of a party, not a result of compassion."

"I feel safe with you, Todd, thank you, I am just going to rest for a few minutes," I close my eyes and fall sound asleep.

Todd calls Amir, to let him know I fell asleep in his room, so he did not feel concern if he rings my suite.

"Hello Todd, how is everything going, I am finishing up a meeting. How are you?"

"I am fine but, Louise got sick and is resting in my room, I just want to let you know."

"How did that happen?"

"She was watching the news and there was a bombing at a US Embassy, she did not feel well and immediately got sick."

"She was going to stop in the Embassy here, that is why it probably upset her. She is very vulnerable."

"I hate terrorists," Todd rages, knowing his anger is more frustration.

"Usually terrorists are on drugs and their brains are damaged. It is why I hate illegal drugs so much, every illegal drug is a benefit to terrorism. Afghanistan has been the greatest illicit opium producer in the entire world. The Senlis Council, which is an international think tank that focuses on conflict zones like Iraq, Somalia and Afghanistan, have proposed legalizing opium production for medical purposes. Opium can be manufactured into morphine and codeine, legal pain killers. That will solve the problem of illicit opium production in Afghanistan, and it will lower the price of prescription drugs worldwide, making healthcare more affordable for those requiring morphine

or codeine. Drugs eat away at our brains and the neurotransmitters cannot connect. We must protect women from violence, and drugs. In Louise's country 10,000 babies are born addicted to drugs each year because the mothers were taking drugs, sometimes it is through the father's sperm at conception, if he was an user. Drugs are chemicals that put the mothers and their babies in harms way, and makes life more difficult." Amir says with true concern.

"Did she tell you she grew up an hour from the Amish in Pennsylvania. She went to Kutztown University on the border of the Amish organic farmland, watching the horse drawn carriages pass her window each morning. She is a very receptive girl."

"Todd, that's an aware thought. I did not know that about her, it makes perfect sense. That is why she would be more conscious, growing up without pollution, a wholesome body would be more receptive. Drugs are chemicals designed to block pain, they would make a person less sensitive to that split second of energy. You are on to something, Todd. I only knew she lived near the Philadelphia area, she told me she took her students on field trips to see the Liberty Bell and to see the Declaration of Independence. What is your room number, I will be there in thirty minutes?" Amir responds quickly.

Todd picks up the book on the dresser, the English version of the hotel Bible. The book falls open to Psalm 110, Praise of God for His Goodness. Todd starts to read. How many hotel rooms has he been in and saw the book, but this time he feels he seriously needs to open it and read some passages from the ancient Torah or old testament section.

"I will give thanks to the Lord with all my heart in the company and assembly of the just. Great are the works of the Lord, exquisite in all their delights. Majesty and glory are his work, and his justice endures forever. He has won renown for his wondrous deeds; gracious and merciful is the Lord. He has given food to those who fear him; he will forever be mindful of his covenant. He has made known to his people the power of his works, giving them the inheritance of the nations. The works of his hands are faithful and just; sure are all his precepts. Reliable forever and ever, wrought in truth and equity. He has sent deliverance to his people; he has ratified his covenant forever; holy and awesome is his name. The fear of the Lord is the beginning of wisdom; prudent are all who live by it. His praise endures forever."

The door starts to open, and Amir stands watching Todd sitting on the chair with the Bible in his lap, gazing at the words.

"Thank you so much, thank you for reading Biblical words over her."

I sat up feeling better. "I am sorry, I fell asleep, I am so distressed. Bombing, shootings, killings, what is going on? Where are we safe? I remember the massacre in Queen Hatshepsut's Temple. Remember the Islamic terrorists Al-Gama'a used machine guns and machetes killing all 62 visitors including their kids. They killed four Japanese couples on their honeymoons. Imagine being on your honeymoon. The BBC stated a note praising Islam was found inside one disemboweled body. The terrorists disguised themselves as members of the security forces, so they could lock the unsuspecting tourists in the temple. If there is no god, there is no morality. I want to go to my room and order something for my tummy and go to sleep. Could I ask a favor, could we leave Thursday for Luxor, I think I need to just lie by the pool and relax, I feel wasted."

"The mummy of Queen Hatshput, the female Pharaoh who ruled in the 15th century, was only found recently and confirmed by DNA tests." Todd mentions to me. As if the finding of a mummy will cheer me up after the news report.

Both Todd and Amir walked me to my room. As I opened the door the most beautiful white bird was flying about my suite, "I thought I closed my patio door, this is not like me to leave it opened." We all walked outside to admire the beauty of the great pyramid in front of our eyes; the night is dark, the grass has a clean scent, the garden palms sway, the sounds of the wind whistles through the branches and the ancient pyramid lit for depth and majesty. Breathtaking.

Holy Spirit protect me today so I can do your will. Cover me with your protective shield impenetrable by evil. May the light of God surround me, may the love of God enfold me, may the power of God protect me, may the presence of God watch over me, wherever I go. God is with me.

"Relax tomorrow, I want you to clear all bad events from your head and fill the space with the fun we will all have at my mother's home in Luxor. You will feel it to be a very special place. I had a good upbringing and I have many pictures to show you. I grew up as you did in a wholesome environment, in our other house we had a large garden." Amir spoke words to comfort me.

"You probably had an organic vegetable garden?" He says smiling.

"Yes."

"Your mother was a stay at home mom, cooked dinner, canned fruits and vegetables, and taught you to sew your own clothes?"

"Yes."

"Similar to my life. Except my mother hated when I wanted to make my own clothes."

We started to laugh. "Sometimes you have that little boy charm, your mother is a very lucky woman, and like all little boys, you must have been in love with her, very protective. I may see photos of you at about four years of age, I will ask Alexandria. I bet she has some in her flat in Luxor." I say. "I can picture them on the piano."

"You will see them on the piano." He says proudly.

"You are going to take me to the home where you grew up, a home filled with childhood memories, so precious. I hope your mother can come because I can learn all about you from the time I spend with her. Do you know what a rare opportunity this is for me. The essence of your childhood will still be in the house."

"Yes."

"I am going to plan something very nice for your mother for being so generous to me, you will also enjoy my surprise. I will enjoy it, too. I am very excited to travel to Luxor as soon as my tummy feels good enough to board a small plane." I say with a giggle.

The next day, no classes for me, I sleep most of the day, then I put on my bathing suit wanting to relax by the pool. I pick a chair with the vision of the Giza Pyramid behind the swaying palms, what a sight. As I relax on the lounge chair, I am thinking I need a cigarette in one of those long holders like the old silent movie stars.

Todd joins in, sitting right next to me, "Amir told me to check up on you, are you relaxing?"

"Yes, I would like a cigarette, and I do not smoke."

"Do you know Gianaclis?"

"Who?"

"Nestor Gianaclis was a Greek who arrived in Cairo before the British, he founded the Egyptian cigarette industry and shipped them to Europe and the United States. What brand do you think the Americans copied? You will know the motif." Todd is always testing my mind.

"Of course, it would have to be Camels." I say, thinking how much information Todd has in that handsome head of his.

"Cute and smart, yes, the Camel company copied the Egyptian motifs: the camel, the palm tree and the pyramid. You are a clever girl."

"Let's order Turkish sweet tea. Is it okay if we leave for Luxor the day after tomorrow?" I inquire hoping for a yes.

"Excellent, I have work to do and I can get my reading done out here at the pool with the Sun God Ra casting his glorious face upon mine, peaking from behind the Great Pyramid, I truly want to savor these moments, these are what the big memories are made of, being in the shadows of the greats." Todd replies with his excellent scope of words.

"Professor Christopher mentioned the nave of the hanging church in Coptic Cairo. When you studied churches at the Academia del Roma." Todd says politely. "Which nave did you like the best?" Todd teases, thinking he is clever.

"Saint Peter's Basilica, in Vatican City." I reply.

"Named for whom?"

"Who are you, Groucho Marks? Who is sleeping in Grant's tomb?" I laugh, "I bet you watch the old reruns of Groucho."

"I do watch them. So, who was sleeping in Saint Peter's tomb? He asks.

"Todd, you are silly. The basilica was named for Saint Peter, one of the twelve apostles of Jesus and first bishop of Rome," I giggle to myself, "remember I grew up Catholic, need I say more? We did not study the Bible, we studied saints. You know it has tallest dome in the world, it is the wondrous work of Michelangelo and a dramatic reminder of God's many talented artisans beaming in the Roman skyline. The Romans persecuted the Christians for 300 years, and now they own the most splendid central head quarters ever know to the heads of a Roman empire." I respond lovingly.

"The Sistine Chapel, with the Creation of Adam painted on the ceiling." He grins, "Michelangelo and his band of artists. Did you see the Vatican Library?" He inquires wanting more conversation.

"I stood in awe of the magnificence. I never knew anything of that magnitude."

I agree, Todd proclaims, "The library holds some 75,000 manuscripts and over a million printed books, plus the oldest preserved Bible in history."

"Do you have a computer in that brain?" I smirk.

"How about in Germany? I know you took a class at the Heidelberg University. Sharon told me. Last question, I promise."

"Todd, I truly think it is impossible for you to have a last question. That answer would be the Cologne Cathedral. The nave is about 200 feet, and as with most Gothic cathedrals, the plans were laid out in the shape of a Roman Cross. It has two aisles on either side. It is thee highest Gothic vaulting in the world. They used flying buttresses, like the Notre Dame de Paris Cathedral." I say with fond memories.

"That cathedral suffered terribly during the French Revolution. The robbery of its religious artifacts and useless destruction. Whenever there is revolt, beauty is destroyed," Todd says with a heart sick voice, "I pray this will not happen here in Cairo."

"Amen to that." I reply thinking of how difficult peoples lives really are. All the text in the Roman Vatican Library preserved perfectly, yet all the manuscripts in the Alexandria library burned when the Romans invaded Egypt.

The heart is the center of wisdom and compassion.

"I must tell you I grew up next to a German professor. His family liked to read excluding television from their home. At night he would read the Bible to his wife, in German. I have the big old 1879 book at my place now, although I do not understand a word because it is German. For me it is very consoling to hear someone read privately to me old manuscripts of history including Biblical history. I feel it would be comforting to people to turn off the television and read to each other." I say feeling better.

"I do not have a television. It wastes so much time, I used to start to watch a great program, then I kept watching whatever came on, finally I gave the TV away. I love reading instead, it is better for me. Amir and I had an interesting chat. I told him that you grew up with all boys in the neighborhood and you were a tomboy. He wanted to know if you knew about the osprey?"

"My father's side is all boys, mother's side is all boys, husband's side was all boys, and I have two sons. Someday when I have a grandchild, I bet the baby will be a boy. I love boys and I do love the osprey design."

"Then you know about boys and their toys." Todd looks curiously at me.

"Yes, I do. There was a hostage issue years ago at an American Embassy which prompted the invention of the Osprey fighting machine. The pilot's logo was designed after the God Thoth, a strong body with the head of a bird. It is a fascinating tilt rotor aircraft for Marines. I bet you and Amir would love one. You could transport food to the starving kids in Africa. It is about 20 million above my budget now, it is a kid's transformer toy built for real men and women of the proud Marine Corp."

"Neither of us knew about the logo. I told him you would add a fact we did not think of, and you succeeded. The God Thoth Logo, a man with the head of a bird (osprey). I am going to miss our conversations. I ordered light food for us before I sat down." Todd says with charming consideration.

The waiter brings us a handsomely carved papaya fruit stuffed with quail salad and date nut bread, each selection laid out on strips of palm, garnished with the local figs. Then he brings floating candles in a large clear container filled with exotic flowers as I lie back in the chair to admire the arrangement, a young lady comes to me to gently rub oil on my feet.

"You will like, it gets very dry here, this oil is light and very good for your feet," the maiden informs me as she pulls her little stool to my feet.

"This must be heaven, I just need someone fanning me with a big palm fronds," and Todd claps his hands.

"Yes, the palm branch, the symbol of triumph and victory, the reward of champions and celebrated military successes."

"Go to sleep Todd." I lay my head back, looking at the light blue sky filled with pure white clouds, in contrast to the darker blue of the pool water, the color deepened by the sapphire colored pool tiles, the rich hues, soon I fall in and out of a light sweet sleep on the lounge chair.

The sign of a gracious hotel, "Is there anything I can get you, would you enjoy a light mist?

All I have to say is, "Yes, please."

Life as it should be. My body and soul truly appreciate the pampering, so healing, such a dramatic contrast from the night before. As I am drifting I am picturing the most joyous place where the beauty is indescribable, the colors so magnificent, the depth and richness of the flowers, the sky, the softness of the grass, the lush plains, the vistas of beauty far greater than my mind can hold. The spirit of angelic voices, vibrating through out the heavens saying, "God is good."

Do You Record Your Full Moons?

The next morning I am poolside when Amir's phone rings. What a joy to have a cell with a local number. He had set up my ring tone to sing the Maurice Chevalier song, 'Louise.' Each time the phone rings the French people near me start to sing, "Every little breeze seems to whisper, Louise . . ."

"Hello, Louise, it is Alexandria, I am wondering if I could come to the hotel and meet you for tea, I have a question I need to discuss with you."

"Of course." I reply with inquisitiveness.

"About 3?"

"I will meet you in the lobby, I am excited to see you, is everything okay?"

"Yes, Louise, thank you for asking."

"See you at three."

I wore a long Egyptian blouse and black slacks, waving as her driver opens the car door. "Hello Alexandria, I love when you come to see me." Let's sit in the lounge and have Turkish tea. "I love the sweet tea."

"Louise, my dear, I must discuss this with you in person, I feel like a third wheel. I am debating with myself about going to Luxor, I do not want to interfere with you young people."

"You must go, I have a wonderful event planned for us, and you will have a heart filled with love for the rest of your life." I insist. "Plus it is your house. None of us are couples, we are all friends and age has nothing to do with friendship. Please, I enjoy you." I plead with her.

"I will come with you then. What is it, I am excited?" She asks.

"I want you to meet the most amazing Indian Chief Black Elk and his friend Moon Bear, they are in Karnak now. How many Indian Shamans do you know?" I am curious.

"None, my dear." She replies.

"They will be deprived of the pleasure of meeting you if you are not there. I guarantee it will be as rewarding to them as it will be to you. Chief Black Elk has the most fascinating life with a linage of history that will keep you on the edge of your seat."

"I will invite them to lunch at the Winter Palace Hotel and show them my Luxor. Oh, now I am so excited. You made my day. We will leave tomorrow morning. I will have Amir organize us. Thank you my dear, I am full of dream energy, I have Indian dream catchers in my home, I will show them my collections. I have much work to do. See you tomorrow," Alexandria says eagerly as she walks back to the car. "I must go now, I have to meet with Sofia, David's daughter." She says as she waves goodbye.

Amir calls me about seven o'clock, asking if I would like to see him, as he was knocking on my hotel door.

"I stopped at mother's house before coming here, I walked in the living room, stood in shock at the shopping bags and these words came flying out of my mouth, 'What have you done with my mother?' We laughed so hard we fell on the sofa in tears. Louise, my mother and I never laugh, it was so much fun. She looks adorable, she was wearing tights and a lounge tunic top. My mother always wears skirts and sensible shoes. She had flats on. Sofia took her shopping and to a different beauty parlor, her hair is dark, in a Liza short style and she looks ten years younger." He is hysterical, "I came to tell you I took care of your bill here for the extra days you had to stay waiting for me to be free. We have a small plane, so put your main clothes in storage here at the hotel, they will keep it for you until you return back to Cairo. It is all arranged for you. See you tomorrow." He says as he walks back to the lobby.

I am still laughing as I start to pack, 'I need only a carry on bag, and purse, I will leave my big suitcase in the hotel storage. Amir says the plane is a Cessna 206, a small plane, the less taken the better, they have shops in

Luxor if I need anything extra. I am not crazy about small planes,' I will get over the fear.

I dial the concierge for a wake up call, set the alarm for extra time. I think about sailing on the Nile with Amir and Alexandria, letting the river take us for the ride of a lifetime, dreaming about the places and moments of the past, as we glide along the amazing Nile River with all its history. The baby Moses, his basket hidden in the Nile reeds, the bewitching Cleopatra, the powerful Julius Caesar extending the Roman empire across the Mediterranean. Her scandalous relationship with the married Roman dictator. The chiseled good looks of Mark Anthony, romance, love, conspiracies, murders pacts, remembering Shakespeare's tragedy, so many stories of intrigue on the fertile Nile.

I know I will be there for magnificent moonbeams over the Nile River. I write about the golden color of the moon's reflection each month listing where I am located when I look to the sky for the full moon. I always write it down in my gratitude journal along with three things that I love about the day, it changes my life, I enjoy reading about my past adventures when the moon was full.

I sit glancing at some of my entries; full moon over St Thomas, US Virgin Islands, full moon sailing on the Delaware River, full moon over Laguna Beach, full moon over the water off my boat dock, full moon above the setting sun in Cabo San Lucas, Baja. The Baja moon over the setting sun is a very rare, breathtaking event, the moon and sun were so orange both the moon and the sun looked like suns. Full moon over Maui, full moon over Monaco, full moon over Palma, Mallorca, full moon over Crans, Switzerland high in the French Alps, full moon over Jerusalem after meeting Premier Shimon Peres, the Israeli Prime Minister, who later became President. Peres won the Nobel Peace Prize together with Rabin and Yasser Arafat. Full moon over Bethlehem, Israel, and full moons over my former home in Bethlehem, Pennsylvania.

With my list, I think to myself what a fantastic life the good Lord gave me. When I get low, I pull out the moon list and smile at the wonderment of the human experience on this planet. I ask people to do the same, knowing each time when they look at a full moon, I will be watching the same moon, and saying a blessing to connect everyone who is looking at the moon at the same moment. I close my journal and fall into a comforting sound asleep.

This is the day that the Lord has made. Let us rejoice and be glad today.

Waking full of zest, showering and dressing in a flash, I decide to wear my sneakers, my heaviest and bulkiest shoes, zipping my little shoes in the carry bag, I feel happy knowing that would please the pilot.

Todd knocks at the door at 6:30, "What type of plane does Amir have?"

"Cessna 206."

"Guess I will wear my sneakers, also. All you have is that little carry on?" He looks around the room. "Where are the rest of your things?"

"I already checked out and put them in storage."

"I have a question? What are those little baggies of powder you put in your water?" He asks.

"I mix my favorite hemp seed protein, pumpkin seed powder, sprouted brown rice, Chia seed powder, with green vegetable powders and a fruit powder. It is very tasty. I mix it in water or juice when I travel for the extra healthy energy.

"When I was a missionary at the Optimum Health Institute, I learned valuable lessons. I heard about wheatgrass juice and how it cleanses the cells and purifies the blood. When we cleanse our bodies, we quiet our mind. Only when we quiet our mind, can we find peace. Our bodies are self healing. I believed in it so much, I took my sons there.

"At home, I walk up the street to PCH to the Nekter Juice Bar to get my wheat grass. I am so thankful Steve and Alexis opened a store that is natural, raw and vegan. I know I need to eat more raw vegetables, that is a fact. Juicing the veggies is the easiest way to get the vitamins and alkalizing greens into my body. Our American food, and your English food, Todd, is basically an acidic diet. That is why people have heartburn. Instead of taking antacids, drink green juice with apples. Balance the acid with alkalizing fruits and veggies. I believe it is mandatory for people like me who love desserts. Sometimes, I buy a large green drink and bring half home to add protein powder. I also make my oatmeal with almonds that I soak over night, put into my vita mix with a bit of water and agave and whip up a fresh fluffy almond milk. Nekter has an almond drink flavored with vanilla beans. I make my oatmeal with that also when I am lazy." I say laughingly. "My grandma used to say, 'If you want nice hands, keep your liver clean.' She was right, the greens detoxify the liver."

I believe in the Bible as my guide, and I love Biblical food. Genesis 1:11. "Let the land produce vegetation, seed bearing plants and trees that bear fruit."

"I do eat the Ezekiel sprouted breads." Todd tells me.
"How about the Manna breads?" I ask.
"What are they like?"
"A sprouted bread also, moist and heavier with protein and fiber. My favorite has raisons, you will like it. I do use butter and honey. Manna is from heaven, according to the Bible. The Lord rained manna for the Israelites to eat when they left Egypt." I say sounding like a teacher.

"I am picturing the Garden of Eden with all the beauty, the green plants and trees, close your eyes for a minute and do it with me, the colors of the flowers, the water falls, the pure air and imagine lying down with a lion." Todd smiles, "Thank you so much," he says. "I really enjoy the lush garden ideas it put in my mind. Very relaxing."

Delight yourself in the Lord, and He shall give you the desires of your heart. Psalms 37:3

I take a deep breath, "That is a lovely vision, now please go make sure Elizabeth has arrived."
Seven sharp we are in the lobby when David pulls up, "Amir and Alexandria are at the airport getting things ready, I am excited to be joining you." David says with a sense of pride.

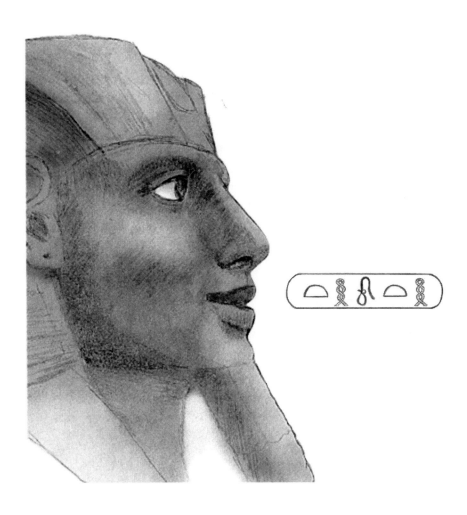

Flying to Thebes

Soon after the Sun God Ra rose in the East, we ascend into the skies of Cairo, looking down at the Alabaster Mosques that are punctuating the city like a Muslim explanation point! The city of a thousand minarets!

The plane is turning south between the desert lands and the fertile Nile Valley. The Nile appears like a shimmering snake winding through the desert sands, kept in place by long rows of swaying palm trees. We could see Beni Hasan, an ancient cemetery site where Howard Carter went as a teenager to use his artistic creative talents copying tomb decoration. The West Bank is more of an archaeological paradise than the East Bank. The intriguing string of pharaonic mortuary temples and richly decorated tombs of the nobles and the workmen's village of Deir el-Medineh is the gateway to the amazing Valley of the Kings and Queens.

"When you go to the Valley of the Kings, my dear, think of our fellow Christians who hid in some of the caves and tomb areas. That is an adventure I never want to experience." Alexandria explains.

"I beseech thee, Jesus Christ, my Lord, suffer me not to follow after my desire; let not my thoughts have dominion over me, let me not die in my sins, but accept Thy servant for good."
Coptic graffito in the Tomb of Ramesses IV.

Following the Nile River we fly over the ruins of the Temple of Karnak and the Temple of Luxor with the famous Hypostyle Hall at Karnak, the open air museum with its array of statuary and reconstructed temple structures. What an adventure, we do not want to land.

"Imagine what a spectacular, spectacular event it would be in a hot air balloon," Todd beams like a kid with his first kite, thinking where it could take him, up and away through the air currents landing on a magic carpet to travel even farther.

"You are on, your wish is my command, tomorrow a hot air balloon ride or we could do it tonight, how about a sunset ride? Take a vote," Amir suggests. "Okay, tomorrow wins."

Adventurous people in an adventurous land.

"Let's get the white jackets and English hats like Howard Carter," I suggest, "Todd you may want a high quality hand carved meerschaum pipe, you would look smashing. I bet you have a collection, Amir, and I bet you look dashing, smashing and flabbergashing." I laugh.

"Do you know, my dear, the hotel is near my house. You cannot get lost, simply ask for the Winter Palace. It was built in 1886 during Queen Victoria's reign. You will love it, it is well appointed and Howard Carter, on November 4, 1922, announced his discovery of King Tut's tomb in that very hotel, putting daily notes on the bulletin board in the lobby. The Egyptologist was staying at the hotel when he discovered the tomb."

Alexandria proudly continues, "George Edward Herbert, the 5th Earl of Carnarvon was an English aristocrat best known as the financial backer for the excavation. He was married to the prominent Rothchild banking family of England. He started the work in 1914, later closing the project, because there was a war that lasted for three years, then he resumed the project, and low and behold, Carter fortunately found the hidden mysterious doorway to the tomb. It was in 1922, just picture it, they were exhausted and frustrated, financially devastated, and imagine the relief when they found the doorway, and opened the tomb of young Tutankhamun. Have you been to the Valley of the Kings? Dry sand, and more dry sand, sand dust and more sand dust, then, the biggest discovery in Egyptian history. King Tut. Digging for years, then just months after the discovery, the financier gets a bad bite. George dies from an infected mosquito bite, how is that for a heartbreak? At least he saw the treasure. Do you know it took Carter's team ten years to remove and catalog all the items in the tomb? Ten years."

"Amir, you have the most delightful mother, she is the reason you are who you are. I admire you, Alexandria." I express with the conviction of adoring child.

"We are landing, I love my sweet Luxor," Alexandria sings with pleasure. "Let's walk on the Al Sahaby Lane, it is a real pleasure, a colorful Egyptian market in Luxor, we can have lunch and get groceries for the house, it is next door to the Nefertiti Hotel. I am giving you hotel names in case you get confused, it is easiest and safest to meet at a landmark hotel."

After lunch we take a carriage to Alexandria's home in an old building opening to a lush atrium courtyard, a paradise of plants and birds behind closed doors. A few steps to the huge hand carved wooden doors which open to Moroccan tiles, lanterns, pottery, carved buffets and cabinets unparalleled artisanship and elaborate motifs. The exquisite craftsmanship is breathtakingly beautiful in its details.

"Who wants to take a ride with me, I may go to the Pharaoh's Stables. Let's unpack, set a time and all of us go for a donkey or horse ride through the villages on the West bank," Elizabeth recommends.

"Three o'clock?" Todd checks the time looking at his watch.

We all leave for the Pharaoh's Stables by following signs to the Amon Hotel. It is a short walk from the ferry terminal. We pick the healthy looking horses and have an amazing experience riding through the villages on the West bank, receiving adoring smiles and waves, especially from the children. We pass the temples on horseback deciding to return during the week at sunset, the evening ride is an experience not to be missed.

We vow to fiercely hold onto life, and love life with a forcefulness that is absolutely awe inspiring. Why? Because life has an expiration date! Life is a temporary assignment!

We are happy to get back to the house, for a shower and a drink at the hotel. I stay back to enjoy the old photos Alexandria has around her home. Some of Amir's pictures remind me of a young Indiana Jones. I day dream of Amir playing down the street at the Winter Palace Hotel, walking around in his three piece cream colored suit at eight years old. What a handsome child. Growing up in a mythical atmosphere on the banks of the Nile in a tropical garden. A magical experience of history and luxury peering into the lives of royalties that the hotel hosted throughout the years. It is my type of hotel, the 86 rooms appeal to a dream deep in my heart, calling on the allure of colonial charm, the distinction of fine woods, elegant materials and harmonious decor, perfect for my imagination of events swirling around the discovery of King Tut.

When Alexandria and I walk into the hotel to meet the others, we see them laughing and singing at the piano bar having themselves a grand ole time.

"Let's relax on the porch. It is a perfect place to have fellowship." She suggests as she puts her arm in mine.

"Fellowship, fellows on the same ship." I agree, new friends on the same ship of life. "Let's take the rocking chairs, and people watch." I love being in her company.

We sit on the hotel porch, taking in the spectacular view, unwinding after a day of adventure. A young Alexandria has so many stories inside her, so much I desire to know. We sit together rocking comfortably thinking of life's adventures, smiling contently, two different generations with the same desires, the same spirit. We were truly suitable companions rocking to the same beat.

American Indians

"I have my surprise for you today, I am bringing my two gentleman friends to meet with you at the Winter Palace and I will invite them here for the lunch I will prepare. You all can simply relax and enjoy their company. I saw your Indian doll collection and the Indian dream catchers in your bedroom, I know you will enjoy showing your home to these spiritual medicine men. I bet if you meet them at noon, they will still be here after dinner. All you have to do is smile, I bought all the food needed to feed our tribe, if I have your permission we will make your home a comfortable retreat for an ancestral meeting. I believe your people both hunted with bow and arrows, the Ancient Egyptians have much the same feeling for hunting as the Ancient American Indians. You built pyramids as offerings to your gods, both spiritual, earthy tribes, both invaded by people with different ideas, who lied and cheated you and stole your precious treasures, the Indians treasure, precious valuable land. I feel calmness in their presence and I want to share their wisdom with each of you," I proclaim.

"What can I do?" Amir asks.

"Let's find velvety blankets, sweet tobacco, artistic pipes, and we will transform comfort into an art form."

"Do you want the finest meerschaum pipes? I have enough for all of us and some smooth tobacco. I will lay out the finest ones from Turkey and let them pick an ivory pipe, one for each of them. How about if I gift the pipe to them for good luck? That way, whenever they smoke it will remind them of our friendship." Amir is a pleaser, excellent upbringing.

"Candles, I have boxes of mint scented candles. We will provide the perfect setting for relaxing." Alexandria is glowing.

The house is prepared and well cleaned, yet David decides to give a quick cleaning to the carpets, he always refers to them as Amir's magic Persian carpets, and he knows the shamans would be aware of the work. How many hours the women spent, sitting side by side, working each day on the huge frame, the small hands weaving the crimson and magenta threads, looming the elaborate and extensive rug. This is an important meeting and it requires an exceptional venue. The chickens are in the oven, stuffed and excited to give their tasty bodies for the white man/Indian tradition of giving thanks or Thanksgiving. I had to buy chickens, I could not find a turkey in Luxor. The long table is set with bowls of fruit, berries, nuts, local figs, corn bread and bottles of wine gracing the decor. Cobalt blue glasses for water, beautifully carved crystal with large decanters are conveniently placed. Pillows, big and small carnelian pillows everywhere.

"They are not going to want to leave." Todd says sweetly.

"Good, then I can have private teachers, my mind is always hungry for interesting conversation and I bet their ancestors are an open history book." Alexandria agrees as she is thinking how she would keep them with her.

"Liz and I are going for flowers, bundles of flowers. This is fun."

"We will see you all at noon, the house is perfectly set, this will be a pleasurable day." David declares, "I am proud to be here."

"Amir is at the hotel early, to be a good host, he is sitting in the lounge ordering Turkish coffee. He immediately recognizes the gentlemen as they walk in the hotel door. Alexandria walking in behind them, Amir stands up with a proud grin, "Mother, I would like you to meet Chief Wallace Black Elk and Moon Bear."

I am standing in the doorway leaning against the wooden frame, enjoying the expressions on the faces of the people I love. I decide to walk around the grounds until they feel comfortable. As I stroll in the Royal Garden I peek inside the Horus Room through the lush garden of ruby flowers, swaying palms around an enormous aqua color swimming pool. I sit on the bench to appreciate the botanical beauty when a sleek black feline with emerald eyes jumps on the bench across from me, watching, facing me as if to say welcome to my world. We sit there in silence, smiling as if the cat thinks she is a black panther knowing how magnificently beautiful she appears.

"I bet your name is Bastet, protectress of cats, daughter of Ra. Let's walk together" slowly we follow the path, soon we are strolling into the lobby, both of us beaming with contentment. Amir knows I want to give him privacy to be with his dear mother, reminiscent of the days when his father was with the family.

"Thank you, I see you met Bastet," he smiles at the cat.

"Come, we have the house prepared for you, if you would like to follow Alexandria she will show you the way." I wink at the chief.

"I was going to treat everyone to lunch, I get paid quite well for this conference," Black Elk grins, if you insist, I do prefer the privacy of an intimate home."

We walk down the street to the old building. The chief had been to parts of Spain that had the same type of old building conversions with luxurious space awaiting. Amir opens the door to the beauty of their lush atrium courtyard, their paradise behind closed doors, the fragrance of the lemon trees and a French lavender lilac tree, that so generously gave up its flowers to be the centerpieces in Alexandria's parlor and bathrooms. The gilded cage of young chirping yellow and greenish blue canaries hangs on the branch of the old Sycamore tree. A few steps to the huge hand carved wooden doors opening to Moroccan splendor.

"Our people are very much alike, my Native American people love ritual and ceremony. We still hunt with the bow and arrow as did your famous King Rameses in his battle at Kadesh." The chief is pleased with the earthy nature of the garden.

"Thank you for the hospitality." As we enter the great room, Moon Bear relaxes into the large stuffed chair in the corner and lit the pipe Amir offers to him. "What an unexpected pleasure. I saw a sign at the hotel that the Winter Palace was built in 1886, it was about that time Black Elk's grandfather joined the Wild West Show."

"Really," Alexandria takes a deep breath. "A wild west show with real cowboys and indians?"

"Yes, as Sitting Bull had done the year before. Grandfather was baptized Nicholas in order to join the show, you had to be a Christian to be in a Quaker show."

"Please tell us more," Alexandria says as I hand him a drink.

"The Bill Cody's family were Quakers, Louise knows, the town next to hers in the East is Quakertown, outside of Philadelphia. William Penn, the founder of Pennsylvania wanted to setup a state that would be run on Quaker principles, that were opposed to slavery. When Bill Cody's father gave an antislavery speech at the local trading post in the West, a group of proslavery men stabbed him. Bill was without a father at eleven years old.

"The boy learned he was good with horses, roping, riding and shooting. Later he was hired by the stage coach companies, he became a scout to hunt and kill bison to supply the Army and the Kansas Pacific Railroad. As a well known scout he often led rich men from the East and royalty from Europe on hunting trips, he was the scout for the Grand Duke Alexi Alexandrovich of Russia. He developed his reputation for bravery as a master buffalo hunter.

"Then, guess what?" An author, Ned Buntline wrote dime novels about 'Buffalo Bill, the King of Border Men' which turned into a theatrical production. Cody got the idea for Buffalo Bill's Wild West Show in Omaha, Nebraska. Do you think it would be entertaining? Over 10,000,000 spectators came within the first two years." Black Elk speaks.

We all sit quietly listening.

"The very next year in 1887, Queen Victoria requested the presence of Buffalo Bill's Wild West Show at her Golden Jubilee at Windsor Castle. That was the year my grandfather Black Elk joined the show. He first played at Madison Square Garden in New York. Imagine playing Madison Square Garden? Want to know the names of the other star shooters? Annie Oakley, Calamity Jane, Geronimo and Wild Bill Hickok.

"The parade was an affair involving the Congress of Rough Riders, they were top marksman from around the world. They opened the show with a parade on horseback. Guess who it included? It included the future President Theodore Roosevelt, who stayed in our Mena House Hotel. My grandfather met the greats! Pope Leo Xlll, King Edward Vll, Kaiser Wilhelm ll, and King George V." It was an exciting time.

"Do you know they needed two ships to cross the Atlantic? It was a huge troop, including 200 passengers, plus almost 100 Native Indians, 180 horses, 18 buffalo, many donkeys, and Texas steers. They toured England for the next six months and each year after that Europe was booked until 1892. The show continued without Black Elk, he went to fight at Wounded Knee in 1890 on the Lakota Pine Ridge Indian Reservation in South Dakota." Moon Bear declares with great pride.

Alexandria is mesmerized. "I am so fascinated by your history. Louise told me you were unbelievable, and I am speechless. Let me get you some more wine. Please continue."

"My grandfather married Katie War Bonnet. They had three children, Benjamin, John and Lucy Looks Twice. They were baptized into the Catholic religion, because grandmother was Catholic." Black Elk says.

"Many people living in Europe thought the Wild West Show represented America. The cowboy became an American icon of the romantic west. Do you know that Buffalo Bill Cody became the most recognizable celebrity? He was known as the greatest showman on the face of the earth." Black Elk continues the story. "Imagine that."

"This is how my conversation started with Louise, she walked up to me after class, looking carefully at me and her eyes shinning like the light of the angel, saying, "I saw your ancestor in a photo in Cody, Wyoming at the Bill Cody Museum. It was a photo of him with the Queen, cowboys and other young Indians." We stood there for a minute, because I did not mention anything about the Wild West Show in my presentation." He smiles looking right at me, looking right into my heart.

Alexandria calls everyone to the table, "the feast is ready."

We all are being teased by the aroma of the toasted birds and are anxious to enjoy the meal with Indians.

Chief Black Elk put his arm around me and says, "Louise has a friend who has blessed mother earth, not far from my home."

I smile back at him, "Yes, Gerry and Dennis Weaver built a massive Earthship in Colorado."

"Dennis as in McCloud? Todd asks me. "I love him."

"Yes, he took an environmental problem, old tires and made a resource. His family and crew filled each tire with dirt, then they pounded and sledgehammered the mud until each tire weighed about 400 pounds. 3,000 tires were used to make their 10,000 square foot home. How is that for creativity?" I am missing Dennis's big smile.

"What did they use in the spaces between the tires? Was it cans?"

"Todd, did you see it on PBS?" I ask him.

"No, on the Discovery Channel."

"Correct, cans, then they used stucco. Their elder son Rob produced a film about the building of the earth home. Gerry told me she would tease the younger sons, Rusty and Rick, "with 3,000 tires, every six months we have to rotate the rooms." Ha ha.

"Dennis has some Indian blood, he loves the earth as we do." Moon Bear agrees with the protection of mother earth.

"Let us have the lunch that is prepared, I am so moved, I want to hear more, but I want to feed you. Chief, let me get you a plate, and Moon Bear also, I will pile it on, eat what you want." Alexandria is over the moon and could not be happier.

"I want you to experience their knowledge." I express, to her feeling immense joy.

"You have a warm and inviting home, much better than the hotel. I am impressed with the rug, I am thinking how much work goes into the weaving of a detailed design of many colors of close hues, much concentration. If I were a younger man, I would sit on the rug, but, I am enjoying this firm and comfortable chair," Black Elk is well pleased.

"Louise, you are a talented woman, you and mother are so fast and organized. You have brought love into our home in a most unusual way, Indian Shamans, who would have thought? I am sharing food with Indian Shamans in my mother's home." After lunch and drinks, we are ready to hear more. "Tell us more about the ancestor." Amir is enchanted.

"We speak from our experience. Doubt has separated us from our Creator, creating the reality we experience. We must understand the true nature of the earth. Humanity must come together in trust to bring universal telepathic language back with no time and no space. We lived in a Garden of Eden on the plains of America, it was paradise, we knew every step we took on Mother earth was a prayer. Today man abuses the mother." Moon Bear states with a sadness in his voice.

"My people had a good life. In early days we were close to nature. Native American farmers often grew cotton, hemp, tobacco, and medicinal plants. We were hunters and gatherers like the ancient Egyptians. We judged time, weather, many things by the elements, the good earth, the blue sky, the flying of geese, and the changing winds. We looked to these for guidance and answers. Our prayers and thanksgiving were said to the four winds, to the East, from whence the new day was born; like Ra rising from the East, we say the prayers to the South, which sent the warm breeze which gave a feeling of comfort; to the West, which ended the day and brought rest; and to the North, the Mother of winter whose sharp air awakened a time of preparation for the long days ahead. We lived by God's hand through nature and evaluated the changing winds to tell us or warn us of what was ahead." Black Elk affirms. The chief's voice is deep and hypnotic as he tells his story.

"All birds, even those of the same species, are not alike, and it is the same with animals and with human beings. I believe the reason God does not make two birds, animals, or human beings exactly alike is because each is placed here by God to be independent individuals. Native Americans understood the animals, they ate of the earth; fish, buffalo, deer, birds and small game, and rabbits. Meat could be cooked fresh, smoked, or dried for long journeys or winter months. They also ate plants, berries, fruits, flatbread is another common food still to this day. Like the bread and bitter herbs the Egyptian Moses ate at his passover meal, before he left Egypt for the long journey across the great desert. Everything was good until the white man came, they came like water, never stopping, they used fast rotating guns that sprayed many bullets. How smooth the language of the whites, when they can make right look like wrong, and wrong like right. They wanted to settle us on a reservation near the mountains. We did not want to settle, we loved to roam over the prairies where we feel healthy and free, when we settle down, we grow pale and we slowly die."

"My great grandfather, elder Black Elk, was a famous holy man, traditional healer, and visionary of the Oglala Lakota Sioux and cousin to Chief Crazy Horse, the Lakota resistance leader.
"Grandfather was also Black Elk, born December 1863 on the Little Powder River in Wyoming. About the age of 12 he helped at the Battle of Little Big Horn and was injured at the Wounded Knee Massacre.
"The mass grave at the Wounded Knee Massacre contained 150 men, women and children. The Indians were broken in spirit, they thought if they would wear a special Ghost Dance shirt as seen in Black Elk's vision,

the shirts had the power to repel bullets and the machine guns would leave them alone. Tragedy arose from the spraying bullets."

Alexandria says she has a prayer in the piano bench, that she would like to sing. She sits at the keyboard and sings a solo, it is called, 'Old Indian Prayer.'

> *This is my Lakota Prayer. Set your heart on things above.*
> *"Wanka Tanka, Great Spirit. Teach me how to trust my heart. May I love beyond my fear. Teach me how to trust my mind, and my intuition. May I love beyond my fear. Teach me my inner knowing, the senses of my body. May I love beyond my fear. May I understand the blessings of my spirit. May I love beyond my fear. Teach me to trust these things. May I enter my sacred space. May I love beyond my fear. Now I walk in balance with the One. And, I love without fear and appreciate each glorious sun."*

We are choking with tears in our eyes and hearts so proud of Alexandria for having the strength to carry on, singing as clearly as if she did it for a living. The Lord carries her voice through each cord and graces the notes perfectly.

We have plenty of food, drink, tobacco, smiles, and hugs. Soon Moon Bear is playing Amir's drums, Black Elk singing with Alexandria, Elizabeth playing the piano, David on the Pan Flute, Todd and I serving desserts and Amir capturing the activities in charcoal on his sketch pad.

I thought, 'nothing could be more powerful than the three hours we spent together during the ritual inside the Giza Pyramid, now to hear about the ancestors, my American history.' I am touched deeper than I can possibly express.

We know it has to end, yet we want to keep them to ourselves forever. David escorts both of the guests back to the Nile Cruiser, taking the long way through the cobble stone streets of Luxor in the ancient carriage. "I have never been on an Egyptian horse and buggy ride, I feel like a king," laughs the chief.

The three man ride through Luxor enjoying their man time together smoking their new gifts, the very handsome meerschaum pipes.

Have You Tried Hot Air Ballooning?

An early morning balloon ride over the ruins of the West Bank, when the air is cool and the shadows are short. Does life get any better than this? Amir booked the trip through the hotel the day before. We have a blast getting in the basket, leg first or head first, we laugh. We are thankful no one is taking photos of the adventure. Bottoms up! What is more fun, the laughter of getting into the basket, or the arial view? The sensation is so personal, we are in a basket, not a small plane, but an Egyptian basket. Oh, it was a proper basket, tightly woven rattan, but, still a basket. Soon we are floating on the wind currents in the oldest successful human carrying flight technology, in the oldest recorded civilization.

"The longest trip was the first nonstop trip around the world in a balloon. Leaving Switzerland and landing just 17 miles from Luxor in the Egyptian desert; breaking distance, endurance, and time records," the balloonist proclaims quite proudly.

"I love being close to the ground like this, compared to my first ride in Crans, Switzerland, situated at an altitude of 5000 feet. That part was fine, then my son and I left the plateau, the earth dropped 5,000 feet, and so did my stomach."

"What an adventurer," Amir chuckles as he holds the side of the basket tightly. "That is a very exclusive ski resort, a frozen lake to a dry desert. "What a Wonderful World!" I feel like the Louis Armstrong song."

I chime in, "and I say to myself, what a wonderful world. Oh, Yeaah." "This is why we have our own balloon," and the laughing begins. Two artistic friends in a hot air balloon floating along the Nile toward the Valley of the Kings. Is this a moment to remember? How can we not be joyful and happy and want to sing?

The West Bank is for cemeteries! We are flying over the Mortuary Temple of Ramesses III, over the Valley of the Kings, over the Tomb of Tutankhamun, over the Tomb of Thutmose III, past the Tomb of Horemheb, past the Tomb of Merneptah, and we are almost heading into the Tomb of Ramesses VI. We could have flown to heaven. With my open heart, I feel as if I hear the words of God. "Can you imagine what heaven is like?" I ask Amir.

The wind shifts and the balloon turns toward the Tutankhamun Restaurant. Smell the spices and curry? The cooking vent is sending the aroma to seduce the balloonists. The balloon made the decision for us, "We land here for food," the operator turns down the flame, and the balloon slowly descends landing perfectly on the sand. We watch the second balloon do the same, except it tips at the very end, Todd is laughing so hard he has to crawl out of the basket on his hands and knees. Alexandria took some humorous photos of the big strong athlete who could not step out of the basket without it tipping over. What a major bonding point between them? She says, "I am the one who wanted you on the trip to protect us and you are so silly." They both catch the laughing bug and he pulls her to the ground with him, they lay on the dry sand making sand angels. When is the last time you made sand angels? David and Elizabeth join them while Amir and I go inside for a cool drink.

"Amir something is bothering you," I sense his seriousness. "Do you need to get back to work?"

"Yes, I do and I need to take David with me." "I wish my life was easier, I have to much responsibility, only because so many people do not accept the responsibility to do what is right. The spiritual connection has been lost and greed and fear prevail. When we lose the Holy Spirit which connects all things, we lose our compassion." Amir says with a fed up attitude toward his work.

Just then the dusty, sandy foursome enter the building, laughing and carrying on. They are having so much fun, and are so full of sand like children without a care in the world and no shower in sight.

"We have to make sure the winds will carry us home, the sky is getting dark, please move fast," the operator suggests, "we get you to come with us now to catch the westerly current. We have to hurry, the balloon does not have an engine, we need west winds."

"I was not hungry anyway, were you?" as we grab the muffins on the way out the door. We are not a minute to soon, as we jump into the baskets, the wind catches the mylar and off we go. Todd and his group are still laughing, he picks up Alexandria and puts her in the balloon, while David and Elizabeth dive in. The current carries us back to the Luxor and the hotel van takes everyone back to the Winter Palace.

"Best my silly guests do not enter the hotel in their sandy condition. Please drop us off down the street," Amir chuckles to the driver.

The shower is so appreciated, there is nothing like warm water and shampoo to humble the soul. Thank you, God for hot water and plenty of it.

I am making lunch, laughing, opening beers, everyone is so gracious, sitting around the long table eating buffet style with a gratitude for the togetherness. It is a time etched into each one's memory, a precious moment that can be called upon whenever we need to feel the power of the stories. We each loved being still and listening so respectfully to the words of the wise ones.

"I dream of sailing the Nile in an Egyptian Felucca, from Aswan to Luxor back to Aswan," Todd repeats some information he reads from a hotel brochure. "Aswan has become a winter resort, because of the dry climate. The eastern bank of the Nile is the gate to the African continent. The city is small enough to walk around, graced with the warmth of the setting sun on the Nile. Today the pace of life is relaxing, am I correct Amir?"

"Yes, Todd, the Nile is precious at Aswan, flowing through the amber desert, granite rocks, and round emerald islands covered in palm groves and tropical plants. This was Nubia in ancient times, and you can watch the sailboats etch the sky with their tall masts or sit in floating restaurants listening to Nubian music and eating freshly caught fish."

Throughout its long history, the Nile River gave life and prosperity to the Nile Valley. It literally controlled the growth of civilization. Today, man has taken control of the river itself with the Aswan Dam. There are no more floods in the Nile Valley, no more need for the ancient scribes to survey the silt deposits but the legacy of all the events are evident in the archaeological sites still standing in Egypt.

"Todd, how about I fly us down to Aswan, it is a quick trip, if you take a sailboat it is three days and two nights, that is a six day trip, flying we can do it in the afternoon. How about early evening, maybe four o'clock would be better. We will just fly over the area, I do not want to land and get clearing to take off again in that small airport.

"Amir, you rock, it will be perfect." Todd exclaims with surprise.

"Let us finish and walk to Carter's house at the bottom of the road. We can take a carriage to the Luxor Museum it is between Luxor and Karnak Temple on the Corniche el Nil. The museum has a small but quality collection of antiquities. I will fill our water bottles, we need shoes, sun glasses, hats and our good spirits. I do not mean to keep repeating myself, but I am having a blast," Alexandria declares knowing she will miss the group when they have to go home to their families, 'meanwhile they are my family.'

The ruins of the temple complexes at Luxor and Karnak stand within the modern city of Luxor, the former site of the ancient city of Thebes. Luxor has frequently been characterized as the world's greatest open air museum. The wealth of the ancient city at its height brought merchant traders of frankincense, myrrh, fine woven linen, juniper oil and copper amulets for the mortuary industry at Karnak and great amounts of precious Nubian gold.

We heard an Egyptologist tell the story to a group in the Temple of Luxor about how the Christians hid in the temples, camped, burned fires for warmth on the cold winter nights and the smoke rose and stained the ceilings. The Romans were searching to killed Christians. They cried for help in their way, before the Romans captured them. They carved out the inside art of the pharaohs on the walls, but kept within the lines, as if to say, "We were here, and we matter. We mean no harm, we want to tell the Christian story of great sorrow before our family is fed to the lions."

The Egyptologists must be frustrated, their land was captured and ruled by so many dominating countries each obliterating the other.

The Temple of Luxor is largely the work of Amenhotep III and Ramesses II the Great, whose colossi and obelisk stand at the entrance. A 13 foot statue of the God Thoth was recently discovered in the mortuary temple of Pharaoh Amenhotep lll.

This town is a tribute to Ramesses ll, a dominating ruler, protecting the borders and accumulating great wealth. He is not one of my favorite pharaohs, he lowered his integrity by cheating the rulers before him. He decided to eternalize himself in stone and he ordered his masons to change the sculptural reliefs of previous pharaohs. Ramesses' carvings were to be deeply engraved in the stone, obliterating the words and drawings of the other pharaohs. He is still referred to as Ramesses the Great, the third Egyptian pharaoh of the nineteenth dynasty. He is often regarded as the greatest, most celebrated, and most powerful pharaoh of the Egyptian empire. His successors and later Egyptians called him the Great Ancestor. He inherited the throne from his father, Seti I, when he was a teenager. He was a strong king who ruled over Egypt for 60 years, three times the length of Tut's life.

I thought it humorous when the Egyptologists decided to fly the mummy of Rameses to Paris, France, for a mummy exam. Ramesses II was issued an Egyptian passport. The mummy was well received at Le Bourget Airport with the full military honors befitting a king. He would have been very proud. The mummy was diagnosed and treated for a mummy fungus, which was quite understandable when your bones are over 3,000 years old. Pharaoh Ramesses II now lives in the Cairo Museum.

"The carriage is waiting," calls Todd. It takes us to the small airport where Amir's pilot is waiting.

Alexandria directs her conversation to Todd, "Do you know about the Kush?

"Tell me please." Todd replies "You are so much more fun than a text book."

"Egypt reigned over Nubia, it was an Egyptian province governed by the Viceroy of Kush where the mines were filled with gold and gold rules the empire. The Nubians, or Kush, lived in Sudan and the Aswan area for 7,000 years. King Kashta, the Kushite, invaded Egypt in the 8th century BC, the Kushite Kings ruled as Pharaohs for a century. You will see their influence in Karnak."

"That I did not know. Rulers other than the Egyptian Pharaohs?"

"A century, and they lived right where we were in Karnak." Alexandria is a treasure chest of information.

As we fly closer to Aswan, we could see the majestic twin temples originally carved out of the mountainside in the 13th century. "King

Ramesses II and his Queen Nefertari built the great Abu Simbel Temple to show their dominance over the southern Egyptian area called the Sudan," Alexandria explains like a school teacher.

"Glad to have you on board, mother, I am always proud of you."

"Let me tell you this, ancient creative genius engineers and their architects studied and understood the heavens and solar phenomenas. They not only built but built according to the raising of the Sun God Ra. The axis of the temple was positioned by the Egyptian architects so perfectly that on October 22 and February 21, the two months after the Winter Solstice, the rays of the sun penetrate the sanctuary and illuminate the sculptures on the back wall. Except for the statue of the God Ptah, he was in the shadow, he was the god connected with the underworld who always remained in the dark."

"Do we have the precision to design, build and achieve this task according to the movement of the heavens? I am flattered with your knowledge." Todd affirms her with a look of adoration.

"When the Aswan Dam was built in the sixties, before you were born, my dear, the magnificent wall of statues at Abu Simbel had to be cut perfectly block by block and moved to the western bank of Lake Nasser."

"I was already in school, young lady," Todd replies smiling at her.

"Relocation of the temples was an enormous undertaking but very necessary to protect from submerging under the waters of the lake. "What happened in the nick of time?"

"I do not know, are you teasing me?" Todd loves playing with her.

"At the last minute the funds became available to engineer the massive removal of the statues. The two rock carved sandstone temples were salvaged and are now protected by the UNESCO World Heritage Site. Ramesses was commemorating his victory at the battle of Kadesh. "He was quite a promoter, he exaggerated the scene in which the Egyptian king fought against the Hittites. The famous relief shows the king on his chariot shooting arrows against his fleeing enemies, who are being taken prisoners. It was probably the largest chariot battle ever fought involving over 5,000 chariots." Alexandria has the mind of a young scholar.

"I cannot picture 5,000 chariots, that is 10,000 horses, 10,000 wheels, a driver and an arrow man. Most chariots had two wheels and two horses. I cannot think of the words, what do you call a chariot driver?" Todd continues to brain tease.

"Scared." Elizabeth chuckles.

"Really, what? Come on Alexandria, I am counting on you knowing everything?" Todd begs her.

I shall tell you young man, "A charioteer is the driver and a spearman, bowman or archer did the hunting. The chariot and horse were introduced by the Hyksos invaders in the 16th century. Our military success became dependent on them. The best examples of our chariots were the four found in Tut's tomb. Did you enjoy my private tour?" Alexandria giggles with a smirk on her face.

"I am impressed with your knowledge as well as your beauty." Todd replies in a respectful manner.

"You are such a fibber, young man, I believe I am developing a crush on you. Elizabeth, are you jealous?"

"I am jealous everyone here is so quick witted."

"I love you children, what shall I do for entertainment when you leave me?" Alexandria laughs trying to hid her longing for a big family.

"I recommend that you give private executive tours. I do believe you could lure an eligible widower into your web of intrigue, and when you take him home for tea, he will sink into the brown leather chair. Then you play the piano; sing one of your torch songs that you have hidden in the piano bench casting your cares to the wind and rose petals to the ground."

"You make me laugh so hard I may wet my lacy bloomers. Is your father anything like you, Todd?"

"No, I wish he was."

"Mother, you two are kindred spirits. I have never heard you laugh as much as when he charms you."

The pilot turns north toward Luxor. Amir is very contemplative all the way back, everyone could see he is concerned about something. The look on his face is evident of stress. He tells us he has business and will have to drop us off and take the plane on to Cairo.

Standing In King Tutankhamun's Tomb

The next day I have an appointment with my original group, we have special privileges for a private tour in Tut's tomb. I hurry to meet them at the boat; they have great accommodations on the cruiser, discovering ancient history at their doorstep, what moments we are sharing. I grab enough snacks at the Casablanca, a little restaurant with classic Egyptian food, enough for the whole group, just in case others did not make it to breakfast. Sharon is missing me, "I was so sick yesterday, I had no fun at all, everybody on the ship was sick." Tutankhamun's revenge.

The sun sets on the West bank over the Valley of the Kings and the Valley of the Queens. The West was for the afterlife, the ancient powerful cities of Thebes, now Luxor and Karnak stood on the sunrise, East bank of the Nile. Looking across the Nile River each night as the sun sets in the West over the tombs of the ancient kings and queens, was a constant reminder. The ancient Egyptians believed they had to be good to be judged graciously. Believing they could take it all with them to the afterlife, they were buried with their most sacred valuables. Egypt was their Garden of Eden, and they were certain they would return. Therefore, they were buried with their precious jewels, furniture, food and hundreds of clay containers of beer and wine. Many containers of white wine sediments were found in King Tutankhamun's tomb, this young king loved his white wine. The twelve of us are so thrilled, all lined up, ready for our private tour and meditation, ready to step foot into the most sensational archaeological find the world has ever seen!

I follow Moon Bear as we walk into the entrance of the King's tomb, I understand why the tomb caused so much difficulty for the tomb raiders to find. They thought that King Tutankhamun was too young to be of any value. The boy king was not worth risking the chance of getting caught. The sands of time blew over the desert area. The entrance was so small, and hidden by the rubble that had been heaped upon it during the building of the later tomb of Ramesses VI, which was above it. The Ramesses workers had built themselves basic huts upon the debris to stay while working. The memory of King Tut's royal burial was erased; the tomb remained safe from the ancient tomb robbers and modern plunderers and from the archaeologists who systematically explored the Valley of the Kings.

I gasp at the beauty as I enter the tomb, the carved wall on my right side seems as though it could have been painted yesterday. There is a railing for my left hand to hold as I walk down into the tomb. The paintings and treasures are unsurpassed in the history of Egypt. The guide tells us, "Tut's name has three parts, First Tut, then the second part was Ankh, then third Amun, Tut Ankh Amun." King Tutankhamun, King of Egypt, ruler of the 18th dynasty. All those centuries ago, and young Tut's tomb wasn't discovered until 1922, a fascinating fact. Imagine for 34 centuries, King Tut was concealed and preserved under the heavy desert sands. The artist's paintings on the inside walls are so glorious, the attention to detail, the intimacy, and the love.

We have all heard the expression. God is in the details. That means God is love. Artists understood. It translates to 'Love is in the details.'

We each admire the exotic eye makeup on the pictures. Elizabeth had told us at her seminar the eye makeup had a multi three fold purpose; to protect the eyes against the glaring Egyptian sun, to maintain an exotic appearance, also to act as the Eye of Ra protecting the wearer.

The walls are pure in color, bright, almost raw dyes, as if the tomb is still being completed and the artists were waiting for the paint to dry. The pigment of the dyes withstood the centuries and they still proudly wear their magnificent colors. Egyptians are revered specialists for long lasting color dyes.

Tut's father Amenhotep IV changed his name to Akenhaten, the Living Spirit of Aten, the one God. He decreed only Aten would be worshipped in Egypt, with the pharaoh as the only priest. The priests became more important than the pharaoh because of the donated wealth they held. The problem for the king was that only the priest could interpret the will of the gods and the pharaoh had to obey the god's wishes. This unsettled the king and he wanted his power back, so he closed the temples of Amun Ra, evicted the priests and set up a new capital city called Amarna. His father taught him there was only one god ruling the universe, not many gods.

King Tutankhamun was born to King Akhenaten and Queen Nefertiti. King Akhenaten inherited a wealthy peaceful kingdom. The name of the new Sun God was the last part of his name, the Aten. Young Tutankhaten, for his first nine years the last part of his name was aten, also. Tut grew up learning the worship of just one god, Aten, his father's new religion was born, called Atenism. Aten, Amun, and Ra later became combined into one god. Soon there were threats to the peaceful city, believing in one god became dangerous.

"This is one of many hymns written to the God of the Sun, Aten." Says our guide as he reads the verse to their one god, Aten.

'You arise beautiful in the horizon of heaven, O living Aten, initiator of life, when you shine forth in the eastern horizon, filling every land with your beauty.

The earth grows bright when you have risen in the horizon. The whole land performs its work. All cattle are content in their meadows. Trees and pastures flourish. The one who makes men's fluid grow in women, bringing to life the son in the body of his mother.

How various are your works. Sole God, whom there is none other. You establish every man in his place, making their sustenance. You have made their tongues different in speech, their complexions distinct, for you have differentiated country from country. You make the seasons to allow all that you have created to prosper.

There is no one else that knows you like your son. You have made him skilled in his ways and in your power.'

"Thoth, please come up here and read this. I will wait until you are ready, I want you to see this." Moon Bear calls.

"We have someone named Thoth with us in our group." Dan says.

The Egyptian guide is wide eyed, "Please come to read this, it is your name and it is from your heritage, "our guide held a copy of Thoth's book matching the verses to the inscriptions on the wall."

I stand there, thankful it is translated out of hieroglyphics, I find the English verse: Book of the Dead, verse 151. *"Your right eye is the barge of night, your left eye is the barge of day, and your eyebrows are the divine novelty. Your parting is Anubis, God of the Dead, the book of your head is Horus, son of Osiris, your fingers are Thoth, God of Wisdom, your lock of hair is Ptah-Sokar, God of the Necropolis."*

I respect our guide and his knowledge, yet it is a bit much to be reading a 4,000 year old verse over the sacred space in the king's chamber. King Tutankhamun's real mummy rests in this tomb. This is beyond powerful. A 3,300 year old mummy, before my eyes, my cells are vibrating, I am still shaking not expecting this experience. God is in every atom and molecule of everything. This mummy still has DNA. These are his bones, the bones of a nineteen year old pharaoh. They were badly damaged when Carter tried to remove them, that is why they are here in the case and not in the Cairo museum. I am feeling emotions so overwhelming I cannot make a sound, but my mind is translating my deep feelings.

'Who am I to be here in this holy place. Your sacred ground, your prayers, your space. This is your resting area. The body of a king, down to your bones, so personal, so intense. That I should be here alone with my group, looking at your wall paintings. If you were a private person, this is rude of us to be here. Am I showing you, Oh King of Egypt, the respect you deserve?'

I am thinking of the love and expense his family went through to mummify him and put him in this beautiful coffin. The royal body was found in a series of three coffins, inside each other, then in a stone sarcophagus, enclosed in four more shrines. This is the most impressive coffin ever found in the history of man. His mummy case is an artistic wonder. The craftsmanship of each piece, the inlay of lapis, turquoise, and carnelian stones. I keep thinking to myself, 'here I am standing in the chamber of this great young king.' A moment beyond words!

I have empathy for the men who worked so hard to carve the walls, knowing it never crossed their minds I would be standing on their sacred ground. Their beloved King Tutankhamun's burial chamber, their greatest and holiest room. I do not know if the workers had to stay and die here keeping Tutankhamun's resting place private. I do not know that story, but I do know it is a sacred, sacred place.

King Tutankhamun, beloved young king of Egypt; for those of us who have children, the sorrow felt of losing a child not yet 20 is heart breaking. Young Tut knew the pain. He and his wife had two stillborn children. Their little mummies were placed near him in the tomb.

Tut's beloved wife and family paid special attention to all the details, expressing their love in a 110 kb gold coffin case, the most impressive coffin in the history of the world. Beside its bullion value, which is worth a great amount more today, the craftsmanship is impeccable.

His family placed amulets to protect him during the magical passage to the afterlife. As all the layers of coffins were opened, around his neck, a green felspar figure of Thoth; at the level of the king's navel was the scarab inlaid with a heron, and a heart amulet mounted on a gold plate with the text derived from Spell 29B of Thoth's spiritual Book of the Dead.

The Amarna Letters which are written on stone, indicated that Tut's wife wrote to the Hittite King after Tut had died. She was afraid to take one of her people as husband and the king agreed, but, the son he sent was killed before reaching his new wife.

Ay married Tutankhamun's widow and became Pharaoh as a war between the two countries was fought, and Egypt was left defeated. Ay had been King Tut's advisor during his ten year reign. Tut's wife believed it was Ay, her grandfather, who murdered the young Hittite prince.

Imagine the tension for Tut's wife. You are about 23, you were four years older than Tut, to insure your families position, you marry your childhood sweetheart, young Tut. You are tired of death. You lost two husbands. Your two babies die at birth. Now you have to marry a man who you feel killed your husband. You also feel, the young son of the Hittite King, may have been murdered on his way to be with you by Ay. Marrying Ay was not a dream, but a nightmare. It insured him the throne.

Young Tut died in the winter, maybe from a hunting accident, breaking his leg in a fall from his chariot, chasing wild lions. It was his passion. Everyone knew he respected the hunter and the hunted. Why was there a dark spot at the base of her husband Tut's head? What caused that mark? Did someone want to harm him enough, knowing he would get dizzy chariot riding? Mystery, murder, intrigue, suspense.

Tut's father Akhenaten was a Pharaoh of the Eighteenth dynasty and the son of the Pharaoh Amenhotep III and Queen Tiye. Their city of Amarna became known for its devotion to the arts and music. The new art style was known as Amarna art, very different from conventional Egyptian art styles. It has a romantic movement and activity with figures having longer heads and the faces are shown exclusively in profile. The human body is portrayed differently in this style of artwork than Egyptian art. Many depictions of Akhenaten's body show a feminine side, as opposed to earlier Egyptian art which shows men with perfectly chiseled bodies.

Young Tut and his family moved back to Thebes and Tut, at age nine became co-regent on the throne with his father. The Armana tables are the correspondence of the monotheistic Egyptian Pharaoh, Ankenaten and the family's correspondence.

Tut's father died and in his third year as king, Tutankhamun reversed several changes made during his father's reign. He ended the worship of the God Aten and restored the God Amun to supremacy. The ban on the cult of Amun was lifted and traditional privileges were restored to its priesthood. The capital was moved back to Thebes, which is now called Luxor. His father, Akhetaten's beautiful city of Amarna was abandoned. Tut changed the last part of his name from aten to amun.

The golden treasures Carter had taken from the tomb of the New Kingdom Ruler Tutankhamen are testimony for the splendor of the golden era. It allowed the New Kingdom artisans to create.

The golden treasures of Tutankhamun's tomb are a testament to the "Ark of the Covenant" that housed the words of God. Within a 100 year span, after the death of Tut, the craftsmen left Egypt for the promised land. The artisans who built the Ark would have learned their trade or in

the Egyptian craft guilds prior to the Hebrew Exodus. The Seraphim on the lid of the Ark are similar to these ones from Tutankhamun's tomb.

Moon Bear asks the guide to please some up the family history.

"Let's start with Tut's great, grandfather Thutmose IV, then grandfather, Amenhotep III, which meant Amun is Satisfied. He has over 250 statues, the most surviving statues of any Egyptian pharaoh. He was loved, Egypt was powerful, with unprecedented prosperity and artistic beauty. His son had the same name, Amenhotep IV, but changed it when he worshipped the Aten, his one god. He believed god was the light, the sun was the light, therefore the sun was god. It seemed to follow the rule of logic. If the premise is true, God is light, the sun is light, therefore the conclusion would have to be true; God is the light of the sun." Our guides explains.

"He changed his name to Akhenaten, living spirit if Aten. Pharaoh Akhenaten embarked on history's first attempt at monotheism.

"His artists created the yin and yang emotion, portraying physical feminine qualities in the pharaoh. It was the first time in history emotion was portrayed in pictures of the royal family interactions. He created art and beauty worshiping the one god, a universal spiritual presence. A new religion. Many of the common people had religious epiphanies and become increasingly drawn toward the new religion spreading throughout Egypt. Many hymns were beautiful statements to the doctrine of the One God. 'You are in my heart, Oh Lord.' The hymn type poems provide glimpses of the religious artistry in their literature, in the new temples, and in the completely new capital, Amarna, Egypt.

"King Tut ascended to the throne at nine when his father died. Tut listened to his fathers two closest confidents: Ay and Horemheb. Without his father, Tut was pulled by Ay toward the gradual return of the old gods and the restoration of the power of the Amun priests. The priests promoted hate crimes against the Aten's devotees. Tut intended to promote Aten worship throughout Egypt, but it would earn him the hatred of the country's corrupt and politically active priesthood.

"After Ay died, the new ruler was Horemheb. He eliminated all references to the monotheistic movement. He deleted the names of his immediate predecessors from all historical records. Horemheb desecrated Ay's burial tomb, erased royal cartouches in his tomb wall paintings and smashed his sarcophagus. He left Tut alone, because of Tut's blue bloodline.

"Pharaoh Horemheb, instigated a campaign of damnatio memoriae against all pharaohs associated with the Amarna religion. It is a Latin phrase meaning 'condemnation of memory.' A judgment declaring a person must not be remembered. It was a dishonor passed by the Roman Senate on traitors who discredit to the Roman Empire. It was now being used in Egypt by Horemheb to ban the religion of a single god. The intent was to erase the religion from history and bring back many gods to bankroll the treasuries of the priesthood.

"The Hebrews had a belief in one god. He made slaves of the people living in the land of Goshen. Hebrews did not worship Aten, but the Hebrew people knew about the one God from the stories about Joseph. Horemheb did not know Joseph. The pharaoh wanted many gods. He was called the Pharaoh of Oppression.

"For his own use, Horemheb enlarged Ay's mortuary temple Medinet Habu. Ramesses III increased and renamed it, the Mortuary Temple of Ramesses III. All Amarna Pharaohs were black balled from the Kings A lists and erased from history.

"Ramesses I, was next in line to be the king. Finally, Ramesses II said to Moses, take your 'One God' believing people out of here. 600,000 men got up and left."

"Thank you, we needed that, it is very helpful to have a summary of historical facts. I appreciate it very much." Moon Bear then says a silent blessing over the guide as we all shake our heads in appreciation.

**Pharaoh Tutankhamen
on a dangerous lion hunt...**

Kendall age 13

Mystical Karnak

A wonderful picnic lunch on the East bank of the majestic Nile in one of the most exciting, delightful and intriguing settings. The peaceful garden reflect the region's exotic atmosphere and Moorish style. We walk through the flowers and tropical plants and rest on the hotels lounge chairs. We are all exhausted. "I cannot see one more tomb," Sharon stresses, "I just cannot."

"Could you live here? I wonder if I could?" I utter thinking out loud. "There are 20 million people in Cairo."

"I do love where Alexandria lives in the Paris on the Nile. It is different on holiday, there is so much here stimulating me. Do you think there really are Emerald Tablets?" I question, wondering if it is a possibility.

"I would like that, we will only know if the tablets are found. They are the combined works of the Greek God Hermes and the Egyptian God Thoth. Secrets of the universe. I think it is interesting to have such a popular name in a country that worshiped the name for three thousand years." There is a sense of truth in stories that become myths. False stories are fables." Sharon reveals.

"I am going to call Todd and see if they want to join us at the temple. Hello, Todd, do you and Liz want to come play with us at the Karnak Temple? Fifteen minutes is lovely."

"He must be close." Sharon smiles relaxing a bit.

"The two towns melt together, he is probably taking a carriage. I am going to close my eyes and take a quick nap." I chuckle.

I feel a soft touch on my arm. Todd is standing over me, he pulls a chair close and does not say a word, just smiles at me.

"Where are the others?" I wonder.

"I left them at the Winter Palace with some of the group from our conferences, Elizabeth is chatting away about Amir's plane to Aswan. Are you doing okay?"

"Yes, the Tut tomb was everything and more."

Sharon came back, "Ready to walk around Karnak? Hello big boy. The three of us, interesting. Maybe we can lose Louise."

"Oh, I think she would always be with us. Let's get headsets, these will be great, if I start singing information, sing with me, we will all be on the same page."

"The Karnak Temple complex, la de dah, was built over a period of 1300 years. Displaying several of the finest examples of ancient Egyptian design, dum de dum and architecture, a walk down the Avenue of the Sphinxes." Todd is singing as he walks along.

"Now I know why we like him, he is just plain funny. I want to listen to the information. Todd, do not give me that look, I know I can read it in a book. Get a hair cut, Samson." Laughs Sharon.

The Great Hypostyle Hall is considered one of the world's great architectural achievements with 134 massive carved columns covering an area of 64,500 square feet.

Thutmose, means Thoth born, he was the third pharaoh of the 18th dynasty, "baby, let's do the dy nasty." Todd is singing loudly on purpose and moving his body to his own beat.

"We are paying no attention to you. If you do it again, I will take your headset away. You are a child, naughty attention still gets you attention," I try my best to say the words with a straight face while the other tourists are cracking up. "He is not funny, do not encourage him."

"Todd, the word enthusiasm come from the Greek word entheos. Theos is God. Be full of enthusiasm, be full of God. Children know that; ask them the next time you see a child with an enthusiastic personality, they know it is a God given gift." Sharon declares.

"Yes, Todd you have entheos, a pocket full of God."

As I admire the carvings at the tops of the strong columns, I think to myself, 'they are like the carvings I made on the blank urn when I was 21 years old, the same type of carvings.' I still have that big clay urn that I made in pottery class and I remember the feel of the wet clay in my hands, cutting the clay on a wire, spinning the wheel, watering the clay as it was forming the shape of the large urn, carving the figures and the hieroglyphics. I remember I had to use a special paint and paint each figure over and over until I got the colors just right. 'Maybe this is where I got all my creative energy for this lifetime, because I have done all forms of art that can be touched with the human hand. Thoth was also, the God of Art, that feels like an interesting fact.'

"I have an illustration of the urn as you start to read my chapter. Do you like it?"

"Our brains are now overloaded, let's play a game, with the same information." Todd is craving attention. "We do not need headsets."

"Sharon, how about a quiz, whoever wins gets whatever she wants. This could be dangerous, are you both game? Okay. What was the King Ahmose known for?"

"Louise?"

"He expelled the Hyksos from the north of Egypt."

"What else?"

"He defeated the Nubians that were in the South."

"Louise one, Sharon zero."

"Next, Tuthmoses lll. Louise you should get this he has your name."

"He waited a long time to become king, he had a victory at Megiddo, and Thebes became the wealthiest city in the world."

"Louise two, Sharon zero."

"Hatshepsut, what did she have to do unique?"

I whisper to Sharon, "Hatshepsut was a spiritual leader for 22 years, she changed her look, wore a beard, to look like a male ruler, that is all I know"

"Louise two, Sharon one."

"Amenhotep lll?"

"Louise?"

"He did not fight, he was smart, he married well, was a diplomat, and he had collected mass amounts of gold."

"Louise three, Sharon one."

"Akenhaten?"

Both girls together, "Father of Tut."

"What else?"

"Louise?"

"He changed religion from Amun to the Aten, the one God."

"Louise four, Come on Sharon?"

He whispers this one her way, "Tutankhamen?"

"Boy king."

"Louise four, Sharon two." He put his arm around Sharon, "Come on pretty one, how are we going to have fun if you do not try, get some passion. Who was called the great?"

"Not you, but Ramesses ll. Give me the money." Sharon laughs.

"Playing for money is illegal. What else do you want." Todd smiles using his clever creative charm.

"If Sharon wins, what would each of you contestants want?"

"I want to go back to the Soiftel Hotel where we met and have a sunset drink, looking over the breathtaking Nile."

"I will get us a carriage," As we climb inside Todd tells the driver to take us to the hotel. Todd is growing frustrated, he decides to keep talking to get his mind off his feelings. "One more question on our way back? Who can name the 7 wonders of the ancient world? The Pharaohs Ptolemy l and ll the built lighthouse in Alexandria, that was Cleopatras family."

"The Hanging Gardens of Babylon."

"Temple of Diana at Ephesus."

"Statue of Zeus at Olympia."

"Great Pyramid at Giza."

"Colossus of Rhodes."

"We do not know any more information. What is it you do for a living, brain testing?" Sharon laughs heartily at herself.

"The Mausoleum at Halicarnassus," he answers, "it is a hard one."

"Can you write it in hieroglyphics?" Sharon is on a roll laughing herself silly.

"OK, I will play your game. I will ask you something you could know. Tell me the first four lines in your Torah. In Hebrew. Also, a quick history, and Louise, you translate."

"Ha, I grew up in a Jewish neighborhood, Todd. You are on, go for it Sharon." I laugh trying to recall.

Sharon thinks for a minute, "in the Torah of Mosheh scrolls, the Hebrew reads, *Bereshit bara elohim et hashamayim ve'et ha'arets. Veha'arets hayetah tohu vavohu vechoshech al peney tehom veruach Elohim merachefet al peney hemayim. Vayomer Elohim yehi or vayehi or. Vayar Elohim et ha'or ki tov vayavdel Elohim beyn ha'or uveyn hachoshech.*"

I take a deep breath, and think to myself, 'I should know this without having to translate.' "In the beginning God created heaven and earth. The earth was without form and empty, with darkness on the face of the depths, but God's spirit moved on the water's surface. God said, 'There shall be light and light came into existence.' God saw the light was good, and God divided between the light and the darkness."

"Sharon, what is the history of Moses' name?" He asks.

"Mosheh, the one who was drawn out." Sharon says.

"What about the Coptic version?"

"Tell us, oh great learned one?" We giggle like school girls with a crush on our teacher. Yet, we are quite pleased with his caring to enlighten us.

"You girls are cute." He pauses to collect himself, "Josephus believed Egyptian etymology, the Coptic word 'mo,' water and 'uses,' to save, or deliver, meaning 'saved from the water.' Some suggest there was a connection to the name with the Egyptian 'ms,' as found in Ra-messes meaning 'born' or 'child.' Was he drawn from the water by Ramesses' daughter?" Todd laughs at his rhyme.

"It is funny how water and daughter can rhyme, yet the spelling is not even close." Sharon shakes her head. "We must be tired, you are getting goofy."

He pays the carriage driver and we enter the relaxing gardens of the grand hotel walking directly to the terrace overlooking the view of the tranquil Nile River. "Three large mineral waters, a plate of all your best appetizers and a menu please," he asks the waiter.

"We will miss you, Todd." We both say together. "We will really miss your humor and your kindness."

"Todd, can the carriage drop us girls off at the tour boat?"

"Yes, Louise, I know you want to say your good byes. You know I will miss you, being together each day in classes and meditations, all equal and supportive. This was the best time of my life. I will stop before we are all in tears."

What Decision Would You Make?

Amir is at the house when the carriage arrives. "Liz and Todd are leaving tomorrow, Louise," he says. "You are staying, yes?"

"I do not know what to do." I say. "I did not plan to stay. It is confusing for me and a bit fearful."

"I understand fears. Studies were done at my university showing about 7,000 different fears, we learn 6,998 new fears; fear of intimacy, fear of judgement, fear of the future. What an over whelming amount of fear society has put on man. Fear of being unloved, fear of being controlled, fear of being alone. Our tests show that certain companies benefit most from fear. Drug companies make fortunes, they have a pill for every fear and if you develop a side effect, they have a pill for that." He says trying to explain.

I begin to laugh. "We have amazing lives. I believe every fear is born from a feeling of being cut off from God. When people think God is upset with them, they develop guilt, but, there is a pill for that," I laugh more about that idea. "I know God is in this land, He is everywhere, yet, I feel safer at home, I feel a bit cut off from Him here when I hear the sirens calling people to prayer."

"I agree with you completely, we have complained about the pitch, it is as if they want to instill fear in the hearts of the nation." Amir is upset.

"I thought that the first time I heard the sirens, I cannot imagine Jesus having sirens." I feel a bit nervous from the sound. I feel uncomfortable.

"You are so correct. I cannot imagine Jesus wanting sirens. The Jesus of Egypt we knew enjoyed nature and peaceful sounds. The sound is frightful, we talk about the fact that there could be an underlying reason, besides making sure everybody hears the prayer call five times a day."

"What is that?" I ask feeling very unsure of today's events.

"Subliminal fear, control." Amir is disappointed.

"Whether we are sitting on the boat on the gentle Nile in the morning, listening to the lapping of the water or on the bluff at the Giza pyramids in late afternoon, as the sky turns orange behind the great pharaonic tombs, the sounds become the same. We can hear the 5 o'clock call to prayer rise from mosques in the Nile River Valley below until our ears becomes filled with an annoying drone. The loud calls are frustrating early in the morning when we want to sleep, plus the loudspeakers are unsightly.

He says, "Hundreds of Muezzins, criers, call the faithful to prayer five times a day. The call is issued from 4,000 Cairo mosques. The cacophony of the call to prayer is required daily of orthodox Sunni Muslims."

"It feels so wrong of me to say, but the sirens are dreadfully loud." I admit. I believe young Jesus of Egypt would have been upset with the sound, it is the opposite of church chimes.

Fear is a big business. Loud sounds affect a woman's emotions.

"Egypt has to examine it's soul. My dream is for the young generation to have a healthy brain, free of drugs. The creativity of the female brain has the capacity to send signals back and forth between the right and left hemispheres of the brain with superior speed. A person who is logical, analytical and objective, like myself, is considered left brained, able to visualize and solve both simple and complex problems. A person who is subjective, intuitive and creative is thought to be right brained. Women can flow through both sides of the brain with warped speed being able to both create and execute the ideas," Amir declares with pride.

"If we want an advanced society as we had in Ancient Egypt, we need to nurture the whole brain, the heart and soul and not suppress women. Female energy is the God flow of the most creative human form, mother.

Where would I be without her? I am here because of a woman, the goddess mother," he says with his artistic flare.

"Whenever women are suppressed there will be instability, if mama ain't happy, no country gonna be happy." I laugh.

Suppression leads to depression of creativity.

Will the new generation of Egypt love and respect the faces of the art form called woman? Thoth ruled the heart of Ra. Jesus is the heart of man, using the words of God who is love.

"I worry about you." I express with deep concern. "What is the government in this country going to do? Will there always be conflict, anger and low self esteem?"

"I worry about me, too. Yet, I am drawn to help the world in the best way I can, it just seems like an endless battle and it is frustrating."

"Talk to me about these frustrations." I ask him.

"I want people to stop causing themselves and their families harm. The difference between self image and self esteem, I want everyone to love what God gave them and not have low feeling about themselves, because it feeds the work I have to do. Self image is what you perceive others think of you, and self esteem is what you feel about yourself. When these are disconnected people become very reactive. I teach them to take a breath and observe the reaction to react. Anger destroys compassion. Drugs and alcohol are symptoms not the root. Always think, am I drinking this poison to kill the enemy? Will taking drugs get over the bitterness? The big problem is the fact that drugs are acidic chemicals and the drugs are destroying the kindness centers of the brain, causing paranoia and more fear. Because there are fortunes being made on fear, it really is huge business, and drug companies know this fact, drugs are sold to numb fear. Legal or illegal the goal is the same, deaden the pain, deaden the nervousness, deaden the fear.

Egypt is a land bustling with life, sound, visual beauty and excitement. It links two continents, stretching across the North eastern corner of Africa and the South western edge of Asia. Afghanistan is the largest opium and hashish producer in the world. Opium is an opiate, the worse drug to take because it destroys the neurotransmitters in the brain.

I pour him some wine. "Amir, I believe Valium is a legal opiate. That is why a prescription is needed. I asked my doctor for some once and he ordered it for me. When I picked it up and opened the container there was one tiny little pill. I laughed so hard. I was the one who always said drugs are bad for the brain and he made me stay true to my word. But, there is nothing wrong with taking drugs when there is an emergency. By the way, I thought our military was going to get rid of the opium growing in Afghanistan? I ask wondering why it is still a business.

"After 8 years of the US military and the Karzai Government, poppy production is at an all time high. The rumors are that Karzai and his criminal brother were the ones behind the production and marketing of the poppy crop, its current production exceeds world demand, creating vast stockpiles of the drug. At the center of this trade was the half brother of President Karzai. We heard Kazai called for 20 billion in foreign aid to help the farmers. Where do you think that money will end up? He runs the government from a penthouse in Dubai.

"You are like an innocent child, your eyes are like the heavens on a clear day, you stand for truth, you have courage, you are the light. The families in Afghanistan have lost that light, they just want to feed their children, as do the Africans in Sierra Leone, as do the parents in Columbia. Do you know more land is now used for opium in Afghanistan than for coca cultivation in Latin America? Do you know that Afghanistan has been Europe's main heroin supplier for more than 10 years?

"Know that we love you. God does not give us fear, but a spirit of power, self control and love. I feel a persons level of success directly depends on the number of people he serves, I want the world to dream big, serve unconditionally and have enormous faith. My heart is like yours and the Indian chief, I want a kind, loving world, keep your innocence it is truly part of your beauty, you love unconditionally. That is the way of God."

"Amir, would you like my thoughts." I ask quietly.
"Yes, I respect your opinion, please."

"If going to Afghanistan bothers you so much, stop going to Afghanistan. You have my permission to take care of yourself." I suggest, wondering if Amir is hooked on the adrenal rush and is now feeling adrenal fatigue.

"I appreciate your kind heart. I almost forgot. I have something for you."

Amir hands me a charcoal drawing of a boat we saw on the Nile, "It is beautiful, you added treasures and you made us young and slim. I am proud to receive such a refined work."

'You are so young in spirit, I made us young and slim to fit into the narrow boat." He laughs at his creativity. "I made us the age of when most people start their lives together."

"My wish for you, Amir, is to find a wonderful Coptic woman with children. Alexandria would love grandchildren. I see the way you look at kids, you just have so much to offer them. You travel so much, your spouse will not feel lonely. Also, I would love if you could use your artistic talents to open a creative art center to teach the young children to use their talents."

"You are a mind reader, mother has been saying that for years. We have a building that would be perfect for such activities. There is a woman I met who used to teach dance and she does have adorable children, her husband died last year."

"Amir, it would give you a focus for the creative side of your life, the teaching of artistic pursuits. You have the space, the knowledge, the talent, just think how excited Alexandria will be with all the children around her. I know she wants a purpose at this stage of her life. I can picture her now directing a play, she will probably even write an amazing part for herself. She will be the head mistress of her dreams." I declare with an enthusiasm for a new vision. You can teach the children to draw pictures of 'Jesus of Egypt.' You will be able to bring back the old bedouin stories and paint each story on the landing of your building." I suggest my thoughts.

"I can find some of the old bedouins that could tell of their father's wisdom. We could have story time with tales of old Egypt, of the days when Jesus of Egypt walked our earth. He would have been the same age as some of the students, just picture how their minds will be filled with wonderment to know they are the same age. I can see many paintings and crayon drawings of them with their new best friend playing in the waters of the Nile. Louise you are a genius. I will make you proud! I am so excited. I will tell mother after you leave, she will need cheering up when you are gone. When I say it was your idea, she will know for sure you two are of the same mind." Amir's spirit lifts as he speaks.

"Maybe Alexandria's Theater Troupe can weave a magical tale in which modern mortals encounter ancient gods. Give traditional music a contemporary twist, allow the youngest theatre goers to be inspired to explore their imaginations and create their own stories!" He laughs.

"I used imagination when I taught fourth grade. I taught everything through art. We drew a mural for the back wall of the room each month. We took huge rolls of paper, laid them on the floor and painted the mural. Each day when we entered the room, and looked at the landscape on the wall, it was like a window through which our imagination was being transported. We were in a new land with a different culture. We formed teams to record the questions of the day. The children became involved, with inquiries, curiosity and wonderment. My class ended up scoring highest in math and reading skills in the school because they wanted to be involved. We became part of the country we studied. We built houses for our villages on a table in front of the mural. We used balsa wood, coated it with putty and added bits of tiny gravel to look like stone work. We precut the windows and floors. The roofs were usually gray sand paper strips cut to look like slate shingles. My boys who thought they had no talent in art, soon learned they were master craftsmen building clever replicas, learning art comes in many forms." I say recalling my past teaching days.

"Your mother aches to be with you. Do you think this might bring you peace, also?" I ask with sincerity. "I understand a mothers heart."

"She did not want me volunteering in Afghanistan. It will make my mother happy in these days, and that in itself will bring me great peace. I do know people who did not spend time with their parents in their later years, and they, regret it." Amir responds pensively. "I do believe in collective consciousness and being able to attract that which I believe to be true for myself. I thought I came into your life to help you, to show you our ways, yet, I know it was the other way around. You brought your tenderness toward people into my life. Not just with children, you can walk into a room of strangers and make deep intimate friends. That is a gift. I appreciate knowing you." He says as he wipes his tears.

"You do not have to pressure yourself anymore. When God laid out a plan for your life, He lined up all the right people to open the right doors. He had your 'thank you' and 'yeses' planned out for you. Yes, you can overcome your obstacles. The question, Amir, is are you going to say yes to God's yes, to get into agreement with His promises?" I continue.

"I get the attention of the children when I tell them I know Steve Sakane, the concept creator of the Batmobile. Start the ignition in your brain, open yourself to the infinite possibilities the good Lord has available for you. Creativity comes in many forms."

"You are correct, many forms." Amir agrees.

"I will donate my new belly dancing outfit to your class. I know I will not use it, it will be just one more thing in my closet. I got caught up in the moment. The kids will love the beautiful fabric. It will be great for a play or just for playing. I will feel good knowing I gave the kids something to dream on." I sit watching and appreciating the magnificence of the ancient Nile, I speak of my home, of the smell of the salt water, the sounds of the waves lapping against the sand and the gentle squeaking of the boat docks moving and heaving with the rhythm of the water. I have seals swimming and basking on the docks as if they own the harbor. We both smile at the picture I am painting for him. I am so thankful for the beauty of living in a place where the teal colored sea rises up to kiss the blue heaven. As night falls my neighbors on the peninsula light their homes, from my distance, across the harbor, it looks like diamonds on a dark sky. As I speak I am getting homesick.

"Let's walk back, I am now excited to start a new adventure in my life. Your artistic encouragement will be my inspiration. I see the way kids love your spirit, maybe you can come back and be a guest speaker." He says.

"Amir, I would love it and I feel better about leaving now."

We walk to the old building, listening to the whistling of the birds, opening the door to the lush atrium courtyard, His paradise behind closed doors. Alexandria is waiting for us.

David smiles with his big grin, "You made the right decision, home is always where the heart is, when you cosy up in your own room you will feel excited to be back in your culture. Just know you will be the topic of conversation for years to come, and you know how stories go, you will not age, you will always be as we remember you today, and you will become a legend in this house, there will be great tales of the Indian chief and Moon Bear. My cherished one, what joy you brought us and no one can take away my memories."

The bell rings with the most interesting chimes, "Who could that be?" Alexandria presses the intercom button.

"Hello Alexandria," the exuberant voice on the outside was the sound of Sharon, "I want to say goodbye and remind Louise we have to be at the airport at four for our seven o'clock flight on Sunday morning. Our group is flying back to Cairo tomorrow afternoon. I am ready to leave, Alexandria I am so glad you are home."

"I am glad, also, my angel, come in for good bye kisses, I just adore the time I shared with you girls. Amon and I will be good friends now and he can tell me all about your adventures in America."

"Thank you so much, Louise for giving me your room on the boat, that was wonderful for me," Professor Amon hugs me so hard we start to laugh.

"The plane is available. I ran into these two yesterday. I wanted to be prepared, the pilot is on stand by," David tells the group.

"We can go together, how about you, mother?"

"I will stay here, the girls can stay at my home on the Island, they will love it," Alexandria states, "Louise will have to pick up her bag from the Mena House storage."

"We will fit; three men, two ladies and Sharon's big suitcase that equals the weight of the sixth person," Amir laughs, "let us leave here tomorrow after a good breakfast. You may change your mind, Mother and want to be with us rather than being here all alone."

"I will have Sacia send my suitcase to Cairo with the group, then there will be a seat for Alexandria on her own plane. You must come, please," Sharon says looking straight at her face.

It is exciting, feeling every emotion known to man, moving forward in a hurry is the best way, less thinking and more action. I am in my room packing and I set aside my turquoise Indian sari as a gift for Amir's mother. As I walk into the great room, Alexandria is standing there with a little gift box, "I want you to have this my precious child, it was my mother's ring and I know you will love the color."

I open the box, and there is the most ancient of stones, an antique turquoise ring raised with detailed golden scrolls of flowers, their golden leaves holding a large precious stone. "I do love it and will treasure it always."

"Amir, I left something for your mother on the armoire. Would you please bring it, it is not heavy," I chuckle.

Amir went into the bedroom and came back to us carrying the fabric. "Mother, this is what she was wearing when she walked into the lobby," and he hands his mother the silk sari.

"It is exquisite with the embellishments of tiny seed pearls and gold embroidery," I can not help but laugh, Alexandria says, "it matches your ring perfectly." We giggle at the exchange and congratulate each other on our most excellent taste.

"Now every time I take mother to the club, I know what she will be wearing as a shawl and I must say, it looks beautiful with her skin and dark hair. She will be the envy of all the ladies."

"My precious Louise," she declares as she flips the end of her new shawl over her shoulder, "it will look divine with the tiny golden pearls you bought me, son." In every country there is a special relationship between mothers and sons, mothers teach their boys to be the man they want them to be, the best father for their grandchildren, it is an inheritance of love.

The next day when the groups wakes, I have a buffet spread across the dining room table for all of us to enjoy.

"I love it," Alexandria proclaims, "now I must come to spend your last day with you at my home on the island. You are a delightful hostess."

"I have many years of entertaining under my belt. I do love helping you especially since you are appreciative." I say with great sincerity.

"We are very alike, you and I, generous and caring. It was fate that we met."

"Your flight is at 7 am, you need to check in at 4 for international flights, you need to leave Alexandria's house at 3:30, you have to get up at

2:30, you need to be in bed by 8. We need to be asleep by midnight or stay awake all night. You girls will sleep on the plane, Amir and I have work tomorrow," Amon the practical one has spoken.

We all laugh at his organizational skills.

"David will take us to mother's house, you are welcome to stay with us, Amon, you too Sharon. Then David, I need you to pick up Louise's big suit case at the Mena House. Louise, he will need your storage tag. Tomorrow we will be ready to load the limo at 3:15, David will have it outside ready to go to the international terminal. Sharon, I think it best if you stay with Louise tonight, we do not want to worry about you being late, it is just easier this way. We can walk to one of the open air ahwas, or coffee houses and have a bite to eat, we will enjoy mother's home, she lives on the island not to far from the opera house, great location.

"Thank you, Amir, I appreciate you." Amon says very thoughtfully. I will stay to walk around the island and have dinner, then I can catch a taxi home.

The five of us talk and laugh and have the most wonderful evening. We walk around the Zamalek Island, agreeing it is a glorious place to live, tree lined streets, French ex-patriots, Englishman and the very wealthy Egyptians. Amir and Alexandria are doing everything possible to make our time a calm healthy memory of the Egypt they know so well.

What a journey for a girl from America, a journey into the depths of the past.

I board the plane with Sharon and take my seat by the window, looking out at the runway and plane terminal. My mind flashes questions. Would I fly back to Egypt? It will not be the same. This is an experience beyond all others, to see what I have seen, to feel what I have felt, maybe I would rewind the emotions in my mind for all the days of my life, day dreaming about the hotel guests, walking back to the hotel from the Giza Pyramid, having tea, laughing, watching Amir write so proudly the recipe of King Tut's beer, trying to impress me with his cleverness. The beer parties at Professors Amon's tent with the Sphinx in the back ground. Meeting Amir's mother at the club, how lovely and grand her soul. Holding hands with the conference guests around the outside of the Giza Pyramid, the three hour ceremony inside the pyramid, the meditation inside King Tut's private chamber, and the special lunch at Alexandria's home.

Life is an amazing journey, I think about Chief Black Elks words. 'Being spiritually evolved can have great pain until we meet in heaven and feel supreme joy.'

My mind keeps repeating the images, the history, the majesty, the impressive wonders of this foreign land. The radiance of the full moon reflecting its magic on the waters of the Nile. The truck load of sitting camels that pulled beside our mini bus. Sharon's adventure riding in front of the pyramids, the stateliness of her graceful Arabian stallion. Thinking about my struggle with the ornery camel who was not pleased to take me for the famous camel ride through the Giza plateau. Holding on with all my strength when the camel got up, laughing about the structure of the amazing beast of burden. I am still giggling as I recall that most unusual evening. To think about kings and queens traveling in splendor, of the camel caravans on the desert sand under the orange sky. To stand on the plateau where some of the most famous people in the entire world have stood, is thought provoking. The grandeur of the moment, the feeling of awe enhances my imagination and takes me on the most enchanting magic carpet ride through the pharaoh's playground.

I see myself in my thoughts standing before the Luxor Temple with its opulent columns, the artistic magnitude to be copied by the great nations of Rome and Greece, the sky so blue and the clouds moving so slowly, the birds flying over head with ease and grace. So much magnificence. I lift my silk eye covering and decide to try to read my notes. Focusing on my adventures in Ancient Egypt, first drawn to the beautiful Blue Nile born in Ethiopia, where the river was considered holy, the Gihon River mentioned in the first chapter of the Bible, as the river flowing out of the Garden of Eden with its lush vegetation and magnificent waterfalls, so romantic were the pictures in my mind, I fall into my pages and deep into sleep.

In the beginning, men and women of Egypt were equal. Women were revered, the beautiful goddess culture was depicted on their murals and carved into the walls of the great temples. The fabulous faces of the women of Ancient Egypt. Who can forget the radiant face of Queen Nefertiti?

Such a contrast to many of the Egyptian women today, who choose to cover their faces because of Muhammad's central message of submission.

The Christian Bible refers to wisdom as a woman. Proverbs 3:13. Blessed is a man who finds wisdom, the man who gains understanding, for she is more profitable than silver and yields better returns than gold. She is more precious than rubies; nothing you desire can compare with her. Long life is in her right hand; in her left hand are riches and honor. Her ways are pleasant ways, and all her paths are peace."

Jesus does not suppress the female. The true personality of God is shown in one's culture, and the view of the people that serve their God. To me, my Jesus has a power of love, forgiveness, abundance and freedom.

Freedom is a sacred word.

Each step I take, like the stones laid tightly together in the Great Pyramid is another step closer to God; it is the goal of every great culture and civilization of the world, to get closer to God.

I love my relationship with my God, I love going to my churches and singing about Jesus. He is my Lord, my Savior, my Redeemer, my Salvation. That is just the way it is for me, I have felt that since I could talk and probably even before. I am not comfortable with loud siren type noises calling to prayer five times during my day; it just scares me, my relationship is private, I pray when I want to talk to God and I talk to Him often. I am thankful for my freedoms in America, to be able to do what we so take for granted.

I stand proud to have met my wonderful Egyptian friends and share the love of their homeland. I am so honored to have spent time in their company.

Love is what our life is all about; how much love we bring into each others lives, sometime for a day, sometimes it lasts an hour. My love for Egypt is special to me, how could I ever forget you once you have touched my soul.

Call to Prayer

Are we edging God out? Do we put something in His place as our object of worship? Do we replace the Lord with others as our major audience of self-worth? When we lose intimacy with God's unconditional love, we will fear intimacy with others, and when we rely on other sources for our security, we are edging God out of our lives. We allow our EGO, the false sense of self, to take over.

How important is God? He is the reason for all things. The time line of civilization was written because of the birth of our Lord. Before Christ is BC, then AD, Anno Domini, Latin for 'the year of the Lord,' and every year after is considered AD.

The angel said, "Do not be afraid. I bring you good news of great joy that will be for all people. Today in the town of David, a Savior had been born to you; he is Christ the Lord." Luke 2:10.

2,000 years ago we worshipped Christ; we saw Him as creator of our lives. Having a private relationship with the peace and love found only in God, you step into God's greater purpose for your life. No matter how difficult things may be right now, if you want to make your life meaningful; seize God's best for you with all your heart, mind and soul. You are only a prayer away. "Lord Jesus, I repent of my sins. I ask You to come into my heart. Today, I make you my Lord and Savior."

With this simple prayer, God will come into your heart and touch the core of your being. God, who created you in His image, will hear you. I encourage you to keep God first in your life. Call on Him often. Write three wonderful things He did for you today in a journal. You will sleep, knowing He blesses you.

God is going to pour out His favor,
and take you to places you've never
dreamed of. Ephesians 3:20.

JesusOfEgypt.com

LouiseToth.com